BETTING THE COMPANY

To Joe -
Thanks for making amazing bets every day to help our students + Marquette!

BETTING THE COMPANY

Complex Negotiation Strategies for Law and Business

Andrew Trask
Andrew DeGuire

OXFORD
UNIVERSITY PRESS

OXFORD
UNIVERSITY PRESS

Oxford University Press is a department of the University of Oxford. It furthers the University's objective of excellence in research, scholarship, and education by publishing worldwide.

Oxford New York
Auckland Cape Town Dar es Salaam Hong Kong Karachi Kuala Lumpur Madrid
Melbourne Mexico City Nairobi New Delhi Shanghai Taipei Toronto

With offices in
Argentina Austria Brazil Chile Czech Republic France Greece Guatemala Hungary
Italy Japan Poland Portugal Singapore South Korea Switzerland Thailand
Turkey Ukraine Vietnam

Published in the United States of America by
Oxford University Press
198 Madison Avenue, New York, NY 10016

Library of Congress Cataloging-in-Publication Data
Trask, Andrew, author.
Betting the company : complex negotiation strategies for law and business/Andrew Trask, Andrew DeGuire.
pages cm
Includes bibliographical references and index.
ISBN 978-0-19-984625-2 ((pbk.) : alk. paper)
1. Commercial law—United States. 2. Negotiation in business—United States.
I. DeGuire, Andrew, author. II. Title.
KF889.T73 2013
658.4'052—dc23 2012044824

Note to Readers
This publication is designed to provide accurate and authoritative information in regard to the subject matter covered. It is based upon sources believed to be accurate and reliable and is intended to be current as of the time it was written. It is sold with the understanding that the publisher is not engaged in rendering legal, accounting, or other professional services. If legal advice or other expert assistance is required, the services of a competent professional person should be sought. Also, to confirm that the information has not been affected or changed by recent developments, traditional legal research techniques should be used, including checking primary sources where appropriate.

(Based on the Declaration of Principles jointly adopted by a Committee of the American Bar Association and a Committee of Publishers and Associations.)

For Nikki, Eileen, & William and Kathleen & Alexandra

Contents

Acknowledgments

Writing this book has been a complex negotiation all its own. We could not have done it without a great deal of help. We would like to thank our families, Kathleen Lawton-Trask and Alexandra Trask, and Nikki Sohm DeGuire, and Eileen and William DeGuire, who put up with distracted husbands and dads for a long time. We would also like to thank Matt Gallaway, our editor at Oxford University Press, for invaluable help. And we would like to thank a host of other people, including Tom Spahn, Scott Cairns, Anders Grundberg, Joshua Zeitz, Tom Parkins, John Kennedy, Dave Myers, Mark Koczela, Mark Witt, and many others for their insights, comments, and stories throughout the process.

All errors, of course, are the responsibility of Andrew…No, the other Andrew.

1

Elements of Complex Negotiation

1.1 When Good Deals Go Bad

We begin with two stories of deals gone bad.

First, in 1982, James and Janet Baker founded a company in their West Newton, Massachusetts home.[1] Called Dragon Systems, the company sought to accomplish the holy grail of natural language computer speech recognition. Over the course of the next two decades, the couple built the company from one that offered only a small voice-recognition program to one that pioneered computer speech recognition. As a result, by 1999, Dragon Systems was valued at around $600 million.

At that point, various other companies took interest in Dragon Systems; good news for the Bakers, who needed an infusion of capital to keep working on their ultimate goal of natural language speech recognition. The small firm fielded offers from a number of sources, and actually engaged in talks with Ford Motor Company subsidiary Visteon.[2] That fall, Lernout & Hauspie Speech Products, N.V., a

1. *See* Loren Feldman, *Goldman Sachs & the $580 Million Black Hole*, N.Y. Times, July 14, 2012, http://www.nytimes.com/2012/07/15/business/goldman-sachs-and-a-sale-gone-horribly-awry.html (last viewed Oct. 6, 2012).

2. Baker v. Goldman Sachs & Co., 656 F. Supp. 2d 226, 229 (D. Mass. 2009).

Belgian speech-recognition company, approached Dragon Systems about a merger. The Bakers liked its initial approach and retained the investment-banking firm Goldman Sachs to advise them on the deal.

At first, Lernout & Hauspie offered to buy Dragon Systems with a mixture of cash and stock. But, citing another deal with Dictaphone, it eventually convinced the Bakers to take payment entirely in its stock instead.[3] Part of its argument for doing so was that it had a number of customers in Asia—including successful Korean companies like Samsung and LG Electronics—and was expecting them to fuel significant growth.[4] As a result, the Bakers expected that the stock component of the deal would be worth more than the cash component. Goldman's due diligence did not turn up any warning signs, so in June 2000, the Bakers consummated their merger with Lernout & Hauspie.

As it turns out, however, Lernout & Hauspie had been losing money for some time and had been looking for ways to cover up the losses. Between 1996 and 1999, it had fraudulently claimed approximately $60 million in income from its own research and development activities.[5] Moreover, while it told the Bakers that it had a number of Asian customers that were fueling its growth, several of those customers had never heard of the company, and several others had placed orders that were far smaller than what Lernout & Hauspie had represented.[6]

These are the kinds of issues that would usually be caught by due diligence, but the Goldman Sachs team had not been focused on the deal. While the four members of the team were no doubt qualified to

3. *Baker*, 656 F. Supp. 2d at 231.

4. Mark Maremont et al., *Lernout & Hauspie Surges in Korea, Raising Questions*, WALL ST. J., Aug. 8, 2000.

5. Complaint, *SEC v. Lernout & Hauspie Speech Prods N.V.*, Civ. Action No. 1:02CV01992, 9-15 (D.D.C. Oct. 10, 2002), *available at* http://www.sec.gov/litigation/complaints/comp17782.htm (last viewed Oct. 6, 2012).

6. Maremont et al., *supra* note 4.

handle a transaction like this, in the rarefied world of Goldman Sachs deals, this was a small-fee transaction. Nor was it entirely clear who was in charge of the team, or who was supposed to hire any forensic accountants. The Goldman team thought it was the Bakers' responsibility; the Bakers believed it was this kind of work that they had hired Goldman Sachs to do.[7]

Two months later, the *Wall Street Journal* reported about Lernout & Hauspie's fictitious Korean customers, a fact the reporters confirmed by picking up the phone and calling them.[8] And three months after that, in November 2000, Lernout & Hauspie filed for bankruptcy, reporting that at least $300 million had been either misreported or did not exist at all.[9] (Lernout and Hauspie each were each eventually convicted of fraud in Belgian court and sentenced to three years in prison.)[10]

Since the Bakers had received their payment entirely in stock, they lost everything once the bankruptcy was announced. Dragon Systems was put up for auction in bankruptcy, and both Visteon and ScanSoft bought portions of it.[11]

The final result of the transaction has been a billion dollar lawsuit the Bakers have filed against Goldman & Sachs that, as this book goes to press, is in the middle of trial.

Our second story begins in the early 2000s. Floridian Manuel Figueroa was one of many consumers who bought an Ionic Breeze ionizing air purifier from lifestyle retailer Sharper Image. As it turned out, there was a problem: there was no evidence the Ionic Breeze air

7. Feldman, *supra* note 1.

8. Maremont et al., *supra* note 4.

9. *Baker*, 656 F. Supp. 2d at 232.

10. John Martens, *Lernout, Hauspie Get Prison Sentences in Belgian Corporate-Fraud Case*, Reuters, Sept. 20, 2010, *available at* http://www.bloomberg.com/news/2010-09-20/lernout_Hauspie_get_prison_sentences_in_belgian_corporate_fraud_case.html (last viewed Oct. 6, 2012).

11. Feldman, *supra* note 1.

purifier actually purified any air. In 2002, *Consumer Reports* published an article reporting on the issue, prompting an unsuccessful libel lawsuit from Sharper Image.[12]

Shortly after the *Consumer Reports* article, several law firms filed class actions against Sharper Image, alleging that it had deceived its customers and owed them a refund. Mr. Figueroa served as a named plaintiff in one of the proposed class actions, *Figueroa v. Sharper Image Corporation*.[13] The *Figueroa* lawsuit was filed late in the rush, so Sharper Image's lawyers originally moved to stay the litigation, arguing that it could wait until the other cases were finished. But the court denied the motion, so the parties continued with discovery and briefing whether the case should proceed as a class action, although the *Figueroa* case was not one the of primary drivers of the litigation.

Right before the certification hearing in *Figueroa*, however, the parties informed the court that they had agreed to a comprehensive nationwide settlement. Sharper Image, suffering from weak sales, was close to bankruptcy and could not afford a protracted trial or massive damages. So it had struck up negotiations with the *Figueroa* lawyers. The proposed settlement provided:

- a $19 coupon for Sharper Image products,
- a chance to buy a new purifying attachment for $7, and
- a few, minor modifications to Sharper Image's advertising.[14]

It also contained an extremely broad release and a nondisparagement provision. The court—which, under federal law, had to approve any classwide settlement—expressed a few misgivings about the terms but set a date for a preliminary fairness hearing, which, remarkably,

12. Associated Press, *Consumer Reports Calls Air Purifier "Unhealthy,"* MSNBC, Apr. 5, 2005, *available at* http://www.msnbc.msn.com/id/7391185/#.UH-5hTm_Amk (last viewed Oct. 18, 2012).

13. 517 F. Supp. 2d 1292 (S.D. Fla. 2007).

14. *Figueroa*, 517 F. Supp. 2d at 1297.

drew several objectors. (Objectors usually appear at the final fairness hearing.) The court rejected this first agreement but preliminarily approved one that limited the release and dropped the nondisparagement provision. Once notice went out, objectors appeared in droves. Most notably, thirty-six state attorneys general—all notified pursuant to the Class Action Fairness Act—protested that the coupons did not provide real relief to the class.[15] In response, on the last day for objections, the parties filed an amended settlement that addressed some concerns, but kept the coupons. (This eleventh-hour amendment drew further objections.)

The parties then submitted a third agreement that made the coupons transferable and added a provision for *cy pres* relief (essentially, a payment to a third party that could benefit unidentified class members). But objectors still complained that the settlement was a "reverse auction"—where defense attorneys pick the most compliant plaintiffs' lawyers from competing class actions and settle on unduly favorable terms, precluding the other class actions. The court rejected the settlement. While it found no evidence of collusion, it agreed that Sharper Image had conducted a reverse auction:

> Sharper Image selected counsel confronted with a most precarious position, insisted upon amendments to the pleading to broaden the scope of this litigation to obtain a global peace, and then proceeded to . . . convince Class Counsel to accept highly undesirable terms to settle the case.[16]

As a result, the court ruled, the settlement was "not the product of informed, arms-length negotiations between effective Class Counsel and the Defendant."[17] The court was sending a clear message: settlements resulting from reverse auctions would not be tolerated. From a

15. *Id.* at 1301–02.

16. *Id.* at 1321.

17. *Id.* at 1323.

strategic standpoint, the lesson is broader: in class actions, trying too hard to settle on the cheap can get very expensive.

Sharper Image filed for bankruptcy in early 2008, a direct result of the market's reaction to the failure of the *Figueroa* settlement.[18]

In each of these two cases, the principals engaged in a negotiation in which they bet their company. And in each case they lost. Neither of these two cases involves stupid people. The Bakers were clearly brilliant: they had come up with a solution to a problem that had vexed the computer industry for years. Goldman Sachs is not known for hiring dumb people. Sharper Image was represented by Thelen Reid Brown Raysman & Steiner, a prominent law firm that hired lawyers from top law schools.[19] So how did these smart people wind up making deals that went so wrong?

The answer is that each of these people were engaged in complex negotiations, where it is next to impossible to keep all of the potential issues and pitfalls in one's head. These were not failures of intelligence. These were failures of process.

1.2 The Nature of Negotiation

Works discussing how to engage in negotiations date back at least as far as the Renaissance.[20] At first, they mostly comprised ad hoc advice to diplomats or others whose professions required them to

18. *Sharper Image, Lillian Vernon File for Bankruptcy*, Reuters, Feb. 20, 2008, *available at* http://www.cnbc.com/id/23252484/Sharper_Image_Lilian_Vernon_File_for_Bankruptcy (last viewed Oct. 6, 2012).

19. Thelen itself went bankrupt in 2009, the consequence of an unsuccessful law-firm merger. *85-year-old US Law Firm Thelen Files for Bankruptcy*, BIGLAW, *available at* http://biglaw.org/news/2392/85-year-old-us-law-firm-thelen-files-for-bankruptcy (last viewed Oct. 18, 2012).

20. *See, e.g.*, BALDESAR CASTIGLIONE, THE BOOK OF THE COURTIER (George Bill, trans.) (1967).

have some skill in negotiating agreements.[21] The formal study of negotiation as a separate discipline began during the Cold War, when several economists used game theory to model the steps that two otherwise implacable adversaries might take to reach peaceful coexistence.[22] These early attempts at negotiation theory began from the assumption that individual negotiators were purely rational, and mapped out how negotiations were likely to proceed under certain sets of circumstances.[23]

Another breakthrough in negotiation theory came with the development of the Harvard Negotiation Project, which sought to synthesize various insights from psychology and economics into practical advice for resolving disputes.[24] One of the most important results of the project was the theory of principled negotiation, best captured in *Getting to Yes*.[25]

Since that time, the study of negotiations has exploded into a multidisciplinary blend of ethics, economics, and psychology. In fact, there now appear to be as many theories of negotiation as there are individual negotiators.[26] Some of these theories have gained currency

21. *See id.*

22. *See* Deepak Malhotra & Max Bazerman, *Psychological Influence in Negotiation: An Introduction Long Overdue*, Harvard Bus. School Working Paper 08-058, 1 (2008) (providing general history of Cold War–era negotiation theory) (emphasis added).

23. *See generally* John Nash, *The Bargaining Problem*, 18 ECONOMETRICA 155 (1950); John Nash, *Two-Person Cooperative Games*, 21 ECONOMETRICA 128 (1953).

24. *See, e.g.*, ROGER FISHER ET AL., GETTING TO YES: NEGOTIATING AGREEMENT WITHOUT GIVING IN xviii (1991).

25. *Id.* Advocates of "principled negotiation" argue that negotiators should identify underlying values that both sides wish to serve and use those to create common ground. *Id.* 14. Doing so, they argue, changes negotiation from a personal clash of wills to a common exercise in problem solving. *Id.*

26. *See* Michael Moffit & Scott R. Peppet, *Action Science and Negotiation*, 87 MARQ. L. REV. 649, 650 (2004) ("Negotiators have no shortage of theories of action. In describing approaches to negotiation, one person may say that she 'always looks for common ground.' Another says that he 'tries to knock the other side off balance.' A third insists that she 'sticks to her guns,' and a fourth says that he 'tries to remain open to learning' throughout the conversation.").

by encoding fundamental insights about how to negotiate successfully. Others offer advice about when to negotiate and when not to.[27] And, of course, a number of other works have sprung up that critique each of these theories.[28] One drawback to this proliferation of theories is that many of them cover the same phenomena, just using different language.[29] Another drawback is that there is an increasing split between negotiation theory and practical negotiations.[30]

There are many, many books that discuss how to engage in negotiations, from the basics of haggling over price to the intricacies of dealing with difficult personalities or people whom one has reason to despise. The vast majority of literature on negotiations assumes, for simplicity's sake, that negotiations occur between two individuals, who often share a number of cultural assumptions and who seek to reach agreement on a limited number of issues over the course of a single bargaining session. While there are many negotiations that fit this model well, there are many more that do not. And the ways in which these other negotiations differ from the two-person model create a host of complications that can make arriving at a sound deal very difficult.

Most people have an intuitive understanding of what a negotiation is. But for the purposes of this book, it is helpful to establish

27. *See, e.g.*, ROBERT MNOOKIN, BARGAINING WITH THE DEVIL: WHEN TO NEGOTIATE, WHEN TO FIGHT 1 (2010) ("A disputant must decide: should I bargain with the Devil or resist?").

28. Moffit & Peppet, *Action Science and Negotiation*, *supra* note 26, at 650 ("One of the assumed tasks of the negotiation literature has been to critique various theories of action, sorting good advice from the less universally helpful."); Andrea Kupfer Schneider, *Shattering Negotiation Myths: Empirical Evidence on the Effectiveness of Negotiation Style*, 7 HARV. NEGOTIATION L. REV. 143, 145–46 (2002) ("For every text that advocates problem-solving behavior, another touts the advantages of sitting in bigger chairs than your opponents or the dangers of being too idealistic in negotiation.") (internal footnotes omitted).

29. Schneider, *supra* note 28, at 151 ("As the body of negotiation-related literature grows, we are beginning to experience label confusion.").

30. Malhotra & Bazerman, *supra* note 22 (noting disjunction between expectations of negotiation theorists and "real-world" negotiators).

a working definition. A negotiation is an interaction between two or more parties, with the purpose of effecting an exchange that will leave both parties better off than if no negotiation had taken place. (By definition, this means the negotiations we talk about here are all "good faith" negotiations. A "bad faith" negotiation is designed to only help one party by gaining some strategic advantage from appearing to negotiate.)

Most negotiations (if not all) involve a series of offers and responses. A single offer and response is not a negotiation, it is simply a bargain (offer, acceptance) or an unsuccessful exchange (offer, termination). So, in a negotiation, both sides are committed enough to the *idea* of an agreement to stick through a first round that does not immediately yield success.

Moreover, negotiations all involve an exchange of information. The parties lead each other to different areas of agreement by releasing information to each other. Some information, such as identifying a term as a "deal breaker" or revealing that another interested party has made a better offer, may tell a party what deals are not possible. Other information, like how badly one side needs the deal (think of the Bakers' cash flow problems) may tell the other party what value it can extract for the deal. And some information—such as Lernout & Hauspie's fictitious Korean customers—is misleading or outright false. (We call these bluffs and lies.)

In the ultimate simple negotiation, the two sides would tell each other their ideal terms and their walkaway point, and then they'd split the difference. But human beings do not work like that. They usually (but not always) try to get more for themselves. So they will hide some information, give out some, and use some to misdirect the counterparty to a deal more favorable to themselves.

Making negotiations even more interesting, despite their best efforts to hide their intentions, human beings constantly leak information. Phrasing, body language, even clothing can convey information to one's counterparty, either consciously or unconsciously. Sometimes even the act of *not* talking reveals too much.

For example, when Ross Johnson, CEO of RJR Nabisco, was considering a leveraged buyout of his own firm, he took great pains to make sure the information did not leak, because he did not want to alert buyout specialists like Kohlberg Kravis Roberts, whose competing bids might drive up the price of the company. Unfortunately, his very efforts at secrecy wound up tipping off Henry Kravis of KKR.

Drexel Burnham banker Jeff Beck had been pestering Johnson about working together for some time, and Johnson would humor him by listening to his pitches and then gently letting him down. But—perhaps because he was afraid he might inadvertently reveal something—once he pursued the buyout, Johnson stopped talking to Beck. The result?

> "I think it's time to do something about RJR," Beck said.
> "Why is that?" Kravis wondered.
> "For some reason Johnson's stopped taking my calls. He's having Jim Welch call me back. We ought to just have a meeting and make an offer."
> "You're probably right," Kravis said. "Get me the numbers and set something up."[31]

In this case, the very act of not talking told Johnson's rivals exactly what he did not want them to know. Moreover, in addition to leaking information, because we are human we often do not process the information we do receive accurately. We do not always know what is best for us, and our previous experiences will color how we look at things.

31. Bryan Burrough & John Helyar, Barbarians at the Gate: The Fall of RJR Nabisco 126 (2d ed. 2003).

1.3 The Problem of Complex Negotiations

This book is about the ways in which that "simple" negotiation can be distorted. One can plausibly argue that *any* negotiation—even a basic one-to-one exchange over a convenience store counter—has the potential to be complex. All negotiations require adapting discussion to at least one unique personality and at least one unique set of factual circumstances.[32] Moreover, because a negotiation is a strategic interaction between two parties, the actions of one party will inevitably affect the actions of the other party.[33]

But, as complex as they may appear to psychologists or economists, individual negotiations over a single issue in a short span of time tend to be small enough that a person can follow the entire exchange with little difficulty. By contrast, negotiations between organizations involve enough side issues and other factors that it becomes difficult to keep track of the entire transaction. That difficulty can turn to disaster should any further problems arise.

Returning to our two deals gone wrong, the Dragon Systems acquisition was already complex when it was "just" a stock-for-company acquisition; in fact it was complex enough that the Bakers retained Goldman Sachs to guide them through the process. Adding in Lernout & Hauspie's fraud was simply more than the Bakers and their advisers could process comfortably. Similarly, the class action settlement that lay at the heart of the *Figueroa* litigation already required the participation of a team of lawyers on each side and a federal judge; it grew

32. *See* David M. Tressler, *The Soldier and the Sheik: Lessons from Negotiating in Iraq*, 13 HARV. NEGOTIATION L. REV. 67, 76–77 (2008) (in interviews, soldiers all stressed importance of context for each negotiation in which they engaged).

33. MNOOKIN, *supra* note 27, at 33 ("Disputes are dynamic, not static. Your moves affect the other side's moves, and vice versa. If you were to draw a decision tree, it would be extremely complicated. Economists call this 'strategic interdependence.'").

well-nigh unmanageable once multiple private objectors and state attorneys general demanded their say as well.

Throughout this book, we use "complex negotiations" to mean negotiations with (or among) organizations.[34] Why? Because negotiations between organizations have a number of characteristics that may place them on the complex end of any spectrum. There are six characteristics of complex negotiations, each of which presents itself most visibly in negotiations between organizations.

- *Complex negotiations amplify the effect of nonrational judgments*. Individual negotiations involve nonrational components and strong personalities. For various reasons we will explain in greater depth, these nonrational judgments are more frequent (and more severe) in organizations than among individuals.
- *Complex negotiations also involve multiple parties*. Even if the negotiation is only one organization negotiating with another, the negotiation will likely be handled by teams, and those teams will represent constituents that must be mollified.
- *Complex negotiations involve multiple issues*. Negotiations over a single issue depend on the amount of bargaining power each party has. By contrast, negotiations over multiple issues provide greater opportunities for agreement (where concessions on one issue can be traded against gains on other issues) or deadlock (by providing additional areas for distrust or disagreement).
- *Complex negotiations take place over an extended period of time*. When negotiations take place over a course of months or

34. *See* Stephen E. Weiss, *Analysis of Complex Negotiations in International Business: The RBC Perspective*, 4 ORG. SCI. 269, 270 (1993) ("When organizations are the primary parties to a negotiation, proceedings are often, if not always, complex. This article focuses on these negotiations and uses the terms 'complex' and 'interorganizational' interchangeably.").

years, the parties develop relationships that affect the nature of the exchange.

- *Complex negotiations are heavily regulated.* They occur against a background of complex rules and laws. They may also occur against a background of organizational rules.
- *Complex negotiations are intercultural.* Each organization has its own culture. And negotiations that cross international boundaries may involve different national cultures as well.

Of course, many of these characteristics occur even in "simple" negotiations. It is possible for negotiations between individuals to involve nonrational components, third parties, multiple issues, or culture clashes. However, as explained in greater detail later in this book, because of the ways in which members of groups interact with each other, these issues are *more* likely to arise in the context of negotiations between organizations.

One central irony we will discuss throughout this book is that organizations are extremely helpful with complex issues: they allow us to throw more resources at a problem; they check individual personality quirks that might lead us astray; and they allow us to add expertise on new issues when necessary. But at the same time as they solve some challenges, organizations intensify others: organizations multiply the number of people who must be satisfied with the outcome; they lengthen the time required to consummate a deal, allowing new events to intervene; they can even amplify undesirable personality traits and entrench them as corporate culture.

In short, complex negotiations mean lots of moving parts, which in turn means lots of distractions and lots of chances to knock a negotiating team off its original plan. So one of the things this book is about is how to maintain strategic focus when events are exploding around you.

These problems are not insurmountable or no organizations would ever make deals with each other. But concluding good deals on a reliable basis requires both a solid understanding of the many issues that may arise and a reliable process for addressing them. That is what this book is designed to do.

* * *

In the first part of this book (chapters 2–7), we will examine just what makes these negotiations complex. We will examine in depth the various elements of a complex negotiation and specific strategies designed to address each of those elements. Part one is designed so that a reader can simply turn to the appropriate chapter to read up on an issue. Each chapter in part one describes the basic theoretical underpinnings of the issue as well as offering concrete practical suggestions that will help minimize the problems posed by that complexity.

Part two (chapters 8–10) is more ambitious. It offers a framework for conducting any kind of complex negotiation, whether it is a multi-sided business deal or the settlement of a class action in a multi-district litigation. It draws heavily on the research and the practical suggestions found in part one.

Between us, we have more than thirty years of experience conducting negotiations on behalf of large organizations, be they corporate acquisitions, joint ventures, or settlements of complex, multi-district litigation. While that experience includes spearheading certain negotiations, it also includes time spent as members of larger negotiating teams, and time spent sifting through the wreckage of failed negotiations. Because of fiduciary duties we each owe to our employers and clients (which in many cases include a duty to protect the attorney-client privilege), we cannot necessarily reveal the details of negotiations we have engaged in ourselves. As a result, we have relied heavily on examples of negotiated agreements in the public record. Where accounts comport with common sense or our own experience, we have used them. Where they may not, we have tried to identify what biases may have influenced those accounts.

As a result, throughout this book, we refer to various negotiations in the public record. Some of these—those which illustrate particular challenges—we will describe at the beginnings of chapters. Others, however, are well known, well documented, and span a range of different issues. These include the failed 2011 debt-ceiling negotiations (extensively reported at the time and the subject of Bob Woodward's 2012 book *The Price of Politics*), the infamous bidding war over RJR Nabisco (the subject of the business classic *Barbarians at the Gate*), and the 1919 Paris peace talks. When we have selected examples, we have tried to keep in mind a few principles. (1) The historical examples should be familiar to most of our audience, or there should be an easy way of getting hold of a popular account of the negotiation. (2) These examples should reflect our own experience in negotiation complex cases and business deals.

Who are we, and why should you listen to us about complex negotiations? After all, we are not university professors or famous negotiation consultants. We are, however, two men with more than thirty years of combined experience negotiating complex business deals and litigation settlements. We have spent that time learning from some of the best in the business. They have been on our side of the table as well as very capable counterparties. The contents of this book are essentially things that we wished somebody had told us decades earlier. Instead, we have had to learn them the hard way. We have seen it done well, tried it ourselves, struggled, and then tried it again until we figured out how and why it worked. What has become clear to us is that we may have been doing our jobs well individually. However, until we understood how all of the pieces of the complex negotiation needed to fit together, our efforts were always suboptimal. We have attempted to put together those pieces for you so that you can see not only the scope of the "what" that needs to happen in a complex negotiation but also the "why" and "when" those need to happen.

Andrew DeGuire has been involved in acquisitions and divestitures for more than seventeen years both as a management consultant and as vice president of strategy and acquisitions at a Fortune 100 manufacturing firm. He has been a part of and led teams responsible for over $4 billion in value. He has been engaged in more than

ils that have closed successfully and—just as important—
n two hundred that have not.

Andrew Trask has litigated class actions for fourteen years, a large part of which has involved negotiating settlements of complex litigation. In addition to negotiating a number of class action settlements himself, he has written extensively on the issues that face class action negotiators.[35] As a result, he now frequently consults on class action settlements even when he is not personally negotiating their resolution. And, when he has not litigated class actions, he has litigated complex contract, fraud, and antitrust cases, giving him an up-close look at deals that went wrong in various ways.

35. *See, e.g.*, Brian Anderson & Andrew Trask, The Class Action Playbook (2d ed. 2012).

2

Nonrational Judgments

Snapple is a popular brand, one that projects an image of both health (juice!) and fun (goofy ads!). Back in the 1990s, it must have seemed like the perfect acquisition for Quaker, the food company best known for oatmeal, but one that had also managed to increase sales for its one beverage brand—sports drink Gatorade—tenfold over ten years.[1]

Quaker certainly thought so. In 1993, it bought Snapple for $1.7 billion, beating out multinational beverage companies like Coca-Cola in the process. But only four years later, in 1997, it sold the Snapple

1. *See* John Deighton, *How a Juicy Brand Came Back to Life*, HARV. BUS. SCHOOL WORKING KNOWLEDGE, Feb. 4, 2002.

brand for a mere $300 million to Triarc Beverage, a loss of $1.4 billion, or more than 80 percent of the price it originally paid. Chief Executive Officer (CEO) William Smithburg left Quaker soon after, a direct consequence of the failed Snapple acquisition. And three years after it sold Snapple at a loss, Quaker was taken over by Pepsi.

So what went wrong? The after-the-fact analyses (and there have been many) have focused on the mismatch in corporate cultures (Snapple was loose and fun-loving, Quaker was staid and cautious), or on Quaker's inability to adapt to Snapple's unconventional distribution chain, which focused as much on local bodegas as it did national supermarkets.

But all of these analyses mention one common issue, Quaker was not just interested in a deal with Snapple, it was desperate for one. Quaker was aware that it was vulnerable to a takeover and viewed the deal with Snapple—which would diversify its beverage business and, if all went well, provide the same economies of scale Gatorade had—as "a matter of corporate survival."[2] That urgent need for a winning merger led Quaker to ignore a number of red flags in the transaction, including the unconventional distribution scheme and a number of substantial "integration costs" that drove up the price of the deal relative to the revenue it would generate.

Why focus in on Quaker's desperation to get a deal done? Because researchers have found that corporate mergers are a particularly dangerous area for businesses. According to one study by the consulting firm McKinsey & Co., only 12 percent of all corporate mergers generated enough revenue to justify entering into the deal in the first place.[3] This lack of return is not surprising, given economic logic: most takeover targets are publicly traded, meaning they already have an observable stock price. Taking over a public corporation means paying a premium over that price, which in turn means that the buyer

2. *See id.*

3. Matthias M. Bekier et al., *Why Mergers Fail*, 2001(4) McKinsey Q. 6, 8.

believes that the market has drastically undervalued the target.[4] It is extremely difficult to second-guess the market. Nonetheless, businesses still pursue mergers with great gusto. The issue is widespread enough that scholars have engaged in a twenty-five-year debate over whether the hubris of business executives is the best explanation of the rate at which corporations pursue mergers, with many of them answering "yes."[5] In other words, corporate acquisitions are rife with judgments that do not match up with what we consider economic rationality, and the Quaker-Snapple deal is a prime example.

This is the first reason that negotiations between organizations are complex: organizations are made up of human beings, and we humans are marvelously complex creatures. Much as we like to believe ourselves to be rational, most of us are subject to the same irrational urges and quasi-rational mental shortcuts, all of which distort a negotiation from the rational ideal that many negotiation theorists like to espouse.

Economists tend to refer to rational behavior as behavior that maximizes profits (sometimes also known as "optimizing" behavior).[6] In others words, when making a decision, a purely rational person would fire up a spreadsheet, calculate the costs and benefits of each option, and choose the option that provides the most benefit for the least cost. This is a definition that has largely been adopted by both businesspeople and lawyers. (Technically, economists recognize that people are human, not Vulcan, so they say that people largely

4. Richard Roll, *The Hubris Hypothesis of Corporate Takeovers*, 59 J. Business 197, 198 (1986).

5. *See, e.g.*, Roll, *supra* note 4, at 197; Mathew L. A. Hayward & Donald C. Hambrick, *Explaining the Premiums Paid for Large Acquisitions: Evidence of CEO Hubris*, 42 Admin. Sci. Q. 103 (1997); Pekka Hietala et al., *What Is the Price of Hubris? Using Takeover Battles to Infer Overpayments & Synergies*, NBER Working Paper 9264 (2002), *available at* http://www.nber.org/papers/w9264 (last viewed Oct. 9, 2012).

6. Herbert A. Simon, *The Behavioral Foundations of Economic Theory*, 59 J. Business 209, S210 (1986). Professor Simon refers to this as "substantive" rationality, because it makes the claim that there is a single standard for rationality that is the same for everyone.

act "*as if*" they are completely rational.) Cognitive psychologists, on the other hand, treat rationality as a *process*, where the goal is taken as a given, and the question is how best to reach that goal.[7] In other words, to psychologists, crazy people can still—within the context of their delusions—be "rational."[8]

If negotiations were solely about the exchange of information, they could be done by computer program. Nonrational judgments change the way we perceive the information we receive in a negotiation. We cannot avoid these effects; they are hardwired into the human brain.[9] These effects include emotional responses (either for or against) specific people or positions. They also include specific mental shortcuts (sometimes called heuristics) we use to process incoming information and decide which information is relevant or important.

These effects also mean that people are more receptive to certain kinds of information. In some cases, they are more receptive to certain ways of packaging information. One human characteristic that plays strongly into these phenomena is the tendency toward "strong reciprocity."[10] From an evolutionary standpoint, humans have developed the capacity to reciprocate treatment, treating others as those others have treated them.[11] This tendency allows people to make agreements with one another. (You hold to the agreement, I will as well.)[12]

7. *Id.* at 210.

8. *Id.*

9. *See* PETER POLITSER, NEUROECONOMICS: A GUIDE TO THE NEW SCIENCE OF MAKING CHOICES 72-116 (2008) (explaining neurological foundations for various decision-making heuristics).

10. PAUL SEABRIGHT, THE COMPANY OF STRANGERS: A NATURAL HISTORY OF ECONOMIC LIFE 80–85 (rev. ed. 2010).

11. *Id.* at 33–34.

12. For more on this mechanism, *see* chapter 5.

These nonrational judgments exist whether or not someone works in an organization. But working in an organization amplifies the effect of some of these shortcuts. As a result, it is worth being particularly careful in guarding against these effects. In order to examine these nonrational effects, we need to delve into several areas of psychology and behavioral economics. We will keep this discussion as free from needless jargon as possible; after all, we are more interested in how negotiators can use these concepts than in the concepts themselves.

2.1 Heuristics—When Our Mental Shortcuts Get Us into Trouble

"What Romantic terminology called genius or talent or inspiration is nothing other than finding the right road empirically, following one's nose, taking shortcuts."

—ITALO CALVINO

As we will discuss more in later chapters, holding information about multiple negotiating partners and multiple issues in one's head (let alone analyzing it with any sort of rigor) requires a lot of brainpower. As a result, humans have evolved a number of mental shortcuts (also known as *heuristics*) to assist them in complex situations. These heuristics are largely helpful; they allow for both rapid decision making and more effective group behavior, each of which was an adaptive response that allowed the species to survive in environments of scarcity and competition.[13] But, as we discuss below, they do not work in all circumstances. Some of

13. *See* GERD GIGERENZER, RATIONALITY FOR MORTALS: HOW PEOPLE COPE WITH UNCERTAINTY 20–64 (2008) (explaining evolutionary fitness of "fast and frugal heuristics"); SEABRIGHT, *supra* note 10, at 37–90 (providing evolutionary account of social instincts).

the shortcuts that work particularly well at protecting apes on the African savannah are nowhere near as effective at navigating the perils inside a corporate conference room.

Oddly, it turns out people cannot eliminate these biases just by learning about them. Once we know about these biases, most of us simply assume that the other side is subject to them, while we have rooted them out of our own decisions.[14] This means that it is important to develop processes (away from the table) and tactics (at the table) that will counteract the downsides of these biases.

Fortunately, at this point, there is a robust literature on how these shortcuts operate. The emerging discipline of behavioral economics has identified a number of phenomena that, while not strictly rational, have been verified in both the laboratory and the real world. Behavioral economics is much like classical economics: it is interested in how people behave given certain conditions. But unlike classical economics, it does not assume that human beings are rational. Instead, it uses field observation and laboratory experiments to observe how people actually behave in various situations.[15] Behavioral economics does not replace classical economics; it supplements it.

What we will do here is to describe a number of cognitive biases that come into play most often in negotiations. Then, at the end of the chapter, we will provide several tactics that, in our experience, have proven most effective at neutralizing the ill effects of these biases.

14. Linda Babcock & George Loewenstein, *Explaining Bargaining Impasse: The Role of Self-Serving Biases*, 11 J. ECON. PERSPECTIVES 109, 115 (1997) ("When they learned about bias, subjects apparently assumed that the other person would succumb to it, but did not think it applied to themselves.").

15. DAN ARIELY, THE UPSIDE OF IRRATIONALITY: THE UNEXPECTED BENEFITS OF DEFYING LOGIC AT WORK AND AT HOME 6 (2010) ("In this field, we don't assume that people are perfectly sensible, calculating machines. Instead, we observe how people actually behave, and quite often our observations lead us to the conclusion that human beings are irrational.").

2.1.1 Priming and Anchoring—Taking Cues from Context

"These aren't the droids you are looking for."
"These aren't the droids we are looking for."

—OBI WAN KENOBI AND STORMTROOPER,
Star Wars (20th Century Fox, 1977)

We human beings like to believe we make rational decisions based on good information, but in reality we are very suggestible. Psychologists have, through a number of experiments, demonstrated we are all susceptible to a phenomenon known as *priming*—the tendency of people to unknowingly assume various emotional states simply by exposure to words that reflect those states. As one experiment demonstrated:

> when people play a word game that contains terms "relevant to the elderly," like grey, old, wrinkle, and Florida, they walk more slowly after finishing the word game than people who played a word game with "age non-specific words" like birds, tree, and book. Unbeknownst to the players with the first set of words, they were primed to conjure the "elderly" stereotype. By unconsciously priming this stereotype, the players behaved more like their perception of the stereotype, that is, they walked more slowly.[16]

Social scientists have documented the effects of priming in a number of different situations over the past decade.

Priming can have significant effects on a negotiation. In 2004, several social scientists set out to test the effect of priming using

16. Carrie Sperling, *Priming Legal Negotiations through Written Demands*, 60 CATH. U. L. REV. 107, 131 (2010).

the Prisoner's Dilemma.[17] The Prisoner's Dilemma is a problem from game theory. It was first developed in the 1950s as a way of explaining why individuals might choose selfish paths that lead to worse outcomes than cooperation, even when they knew that cooperating would lead to better outcomes. In the Prisoner's Dilemma, the police arrest two criminals and place them in separate interrogation rooms. The district attorney has enough evidence to convict them each on a charge that would lead to a one-year sentence, but if she can get one of them to confess, she can convict the other on a ten-year charge. If both confess, they will each go to jail for six years. So each prisoner faces a choice: confess or stay quiet. The answer seems obvious: if both stay quiet, each serves only a year in jail. But sitting alone in an interrogation room, neither prisoner knows what the other will do. What each *does* know is this: if he stays quiet, he winds up in prison no matter what, and he could serve ten years if his partner confesses. If he talks he might do six years, or he might do none, and he knows the other prisoner is thinking the same way. The logic of this situation is inexorable: unless they figure out some pressure-proof agreement or some way to communicate, each prisoner will confess, sending them both to jail for six years.

The social scientists conducted a series of experiments using the Prisoner's Dilemma with both Stanford undergraduates and Israeli Defense Force pilots. But instead of calling the problem the Prisoner's Dilemma, they renamed it. For half of their test subjects, they called it "The Wall Street Game." With others, they called it "The Community Game."

What the researchers found was that the name of the game had a significant effect on players' strategies. When the Stanford students played, half of the Wall Street games resulted in mutual defections, while half of the Community games played resulted in mutual cooperation. The game was structured slightly differently

17. *See* Varda Liberman et al., *The Name of the Game: Predictive Power of Reputations versus Situational Labels in Determining Prisoner's Dilemma Game Moves*, 30 PERSONALITY & SOC. PSYCH. BULL. 1175 (2004).

for the Israeli pilots, but provided similar results. When the game was called the Bursa (Wall Street) game, sixteen of the twenty participants started out by defecting. When it was called the Kommuna (Community) game, eleven of the twenty participants started out by cooperating.

One further twist to the experiment provides two more insights. In each case, the experimenters chose their subjects by going to authority figures who knew the participants: for the Stanford students, they went to resident advisers; for the pilots, they went to flight instructors. In each case, the experimenters asked the authority figures to stack the deck by giving them the people they thought were most cooperative and those they thought were most competitive. But stacking the deck made no difference. In fact, a statistical analysis of the game results showed two things: (1) priming works even on people we think are predisposed to act in the opposite way, and (2) people tend to be very bad at predicting how competitive or cooperative someone will be based on personality alone.

Priming does not simply operate on one's tendency to cooperate. One subset of priming is an effect known as *anchoring*. From an economic standpoint, anchoring means that negotiated prices tend to cluster around the first price offered. (Hence the name; the first price acts as an "anchor.") The most important feature of anchoring is that the effect of the first anchor persists even after a party introduces new, more relevant anchors to the negotiation.[18] Behavioral experiments have shown that anchoring is common in negotiations and that it can occur in unexpected ways. For example, social scientists have been able to influence a person's estimate of the value of a house in Des Moines, Iowa, by showing her the median home price in faraway (and

18. Ariely, *supra* note 15, at 35 ("This means that although both groups had been equally exposed to the suggested 50 cents, as their focal anchoring response (to 'Hypothetically, would you listen to this sound again for 50 cents?'), the first anchor in this annoying sound character (which was 10 cents for some and 90 cents for others) predominated.").

far more expensive) Honolulu.[19] The anchor does not even have to be minimally relevant to the negotiation: researchers have influenced people's estimates of the number of African countries in the United Nations by spinning a wheel of fortune and reporting the number to which the arrow pointed.

Priming and anchoring pose one of the greatest challenges to negotiators because they get in under the negotiator's conscious thought. Merely being aware of these tendencies is not enough to dispel the problem, either. But that does not mean that there are no solutions to the problem of priming. At the end of this chapter, we will discuss several practical techniques that can guard against the ill effects of not only priming, but other heuristics as well.

2.1.2 Hyperbolic Discounting—Birds in Hands

"I'll gladly pay you Tuesday for a hamburger today."

—WIMPY,
Popeye

Classical economists assume that people discount future income (or future goods) by some rationally predictable discount rate. This means a person is likely to prefer money today to money tomorrow, but you can convince her to accept money tomorrow by giving her more then, so long as it is enough to offset the discount rate. (Or, as the old adage goes: "a bird in the hand is worth two in the bush.")

In fact, people tend to discount future benefits by much more than one might expect. As a result, people *really* prefer to collect gains now, and they *really* prefer to postpone losses until later. We are, far more than we may think, a species that demands immediate gratification.

19. *See* Dan Orr & Chris Guthrie, *Anchoring, Information, Expertise, & Negotiation: New Insights from Meta-Analysis*, 21 OHIO STATE J. DISPUTE RESOLUTION 597, 601 (2006) (summarizing research).

These preferences can have odd effects on negotiations. Among other things, they can influence each party's attitude toward timing and progress. If a negotiation is a projected "win-win," then both parties may be in the position of wanting to complete the deal as soon as possible. After all, why postpone the great feeling they will get from closing a successful deal? Similarly, in an adversarial—or "zero-sum"—negotiation, where one party will necessarily benefit at the expense of the other, the party most confident it has something to gain will want to push forward quickly. For example, during the negotiations over the RJR Nabisco buyout, takeover artist Henry Kravis was in a constant rush to move events along: "*Fast, fast, fast,* Kravis thought. *Everything had to move fast.*"[20] By contrast, the party that is negotiating to limit its losses (say, a defendant in litigation) will not feel the same urge to rush the deal to completion. Indeed, it may actually want to stall the negotiations in order to put off the inevitable day when it must pay out.

2.1.3 Loss Aversion

"I love winning... It's like, you know, better than losing!"

—EBBY CALVIN "NUKE" LALOUSH,
Bull Durham (Orion Pictures, 1988)

On average, people do not like losses. In fact, they will often pay to avoid them. (We call these payments insurance.) But what is interesting is that the average person treats identical risks differently depending on how each risk is framed. If a risk is framed as a chance of gaining something, it is more attractive. (Hence the appeal of lottery tickets.) But if a risk is framed as a chance of losing something, it is much less attractive. Moreover, the prospective loss appears to hurt worse than an equal prospective gain tantalizes. In fact, experiments have shown that most people will demand a 50 percent chance

20. Bryan Burrough & John Helyar, Barbarians at the Gate: The Fall of RJR Nabisco 207 (2003).

of gaining \$200 to \$300 to compensate for a 50 percent chance of losing only \$100.[21]

Loss aversion helps to explain several other phenomena that matter in negotiations. The first of these is the *status quo bias*, in which people evaluate new options in comparison to their current situation. As a result, potential disadvantages to a new option will loom much larger than potential advantages.[22] Consequently, many negotiators will believe that they have conceded more than their counterpart, because the potential losses hurt more than the potential gains help.[23]

Loss aversion also helps to explain another, related phenomenon known as "regret aversion," or the tendency to avoid making decisions that may turn out badly.[24] Regret aversion can lead to indecision or even an active rejection of objectively favorable deals.

2.1.4 Herding Behavior and Normality Bias—The Lemming Urge

"Failing conventionally is the route to go; as a group, lemmings may have a rotten image, but no individual lemming has ever received bad press."

—WARREN BUFFETT, "LETTER FROM THE CHAIRMAN," *Berkshire Hathaway Annual Report, 1984*

Herding behavior describes human beings' natural inclination to follow a group. Social scientists have performed experiments demonstrating that people interacting in groups tend to shift not just

21. Richard Birke & Craig R. Fox, *Psychological Principles in Civil Settlements*, 4 HARVARD NEGOTIATION L. REV. 1, 43 (1999).

22. *See, e.g.*, Daniel Kahneman, *Maps of Bounded Rationality: Psychology for Behavioral Economics*, 93 AM. ECON. REV. 1449, 1457–58 (2003).

23. Amos Tversky & Daniel Kahneman, *Rational Choice & the Framing of Decisions*, 59 J. BUSINESS S521, S262 (1986).

24. Geoffrey P. Miller & Gerald Rosenfeld, *Intellectual Hazard: How Conceptual Biases in Complex Organizations Contributed to the Crisis of 2008*, 33 HARVARD J. L. & PUB-

their behavior but their preferences to adapt to a group, whether or not someone in "authority" is at the head. For example, in 1936, social psychologist Muzafer Sherif conducted a series of experiments in which he showed groups of people in a dark room a pinpoint of light, then moved it and asked them to estimate how far it had traveled. He made two discoveries important to work on group conformity: people tended to conform to what they heard others guess, and even wildly divergent guesses would affect the overall consensus of the group. This dependence on the group persisted over time as well: Sherif began to gradually replace the members of the group, but the consensus on how far the light had traveled remained relatively constant.[25] In other words, if a person does not know much about a subject or a situation, she will take her cues from the group.

There is a cognitive bias that goes with herding behavior known as *normality bias*. In cases involving normality bias, people treat bad outcomes that follow abnormal circumstances as worse than bad outcomes that follow more "normal" circumstances.[26] When the average person looks at what behavior may have "caused" a bad result, she tends to give the benefit of the doubt to those engaged in more "conventional" or "routine" behavior and offers less sympathy to those trying something new or different.

Another bias associated with herding behavior is *authoritarian bias*, or the tendency to overvalue information that comes from "authoritative" sources.[27] In fact, most of us will defer to someone we perceive as an "expert" in her field.[28] Depending on the culture of

LIC POLICY 807, 818 (2010) ("Another form of asymmetry bias is regret aversion, the tendency to avoid making decisions that turn out badly.").

25. *See* Neal Kumar Katyal, *Conspiracy Theory*, 112 YALE L.J. 1307, 1309 (2003).

26. Robert A. Prentice & Jonathan J. Koehler, *A Normality Bias in Legal Decision Making*, 88 CORNELL L. REV. 583, 588 (2003).

27. *See* Miller & Rosenfeld, *supra* note 24, at 814–15.

28. Robert S. Adler & Elliot M. Silverstein, *When David Meets Goliath: Dealing with Power Differentials in Negotiations*, 5 HARV. NEGOTIATION L. REV. 1, 27 (2000)

a given organization, members may be particularly reluctant to challenge the decisions of authority members.

There are good reasons why human beings developed an authoritarian bias. In times of crisis—particularly in conflict—it helps when one person is clearly in charge and can give orders that will be followed. (In fact, most militaries spend an extraordinary amount of time and resources *inculcating* authoritarian bias into their members.)

Authoritarian bias has a clear downside as well. In team negotiations, it can stifle contributions from those who disagree with the team leader. Authoritarian bias can also lead to negotiators rejecting information that does not come from sources previously established as credible.

These behaviors make sense from an adaptive perspective. As we evolved, herding behavior helped us survive by getting us into groups that would protect us from predators or natural accidents. And organizations are—in a very real sense—the modern equivalent of the herd. For many individuals, career success (which brings with it the ability to feed one's family) depends on success within an organization. The organization provides status, salary, even (in the United States) healthcare. So it can take a great deal of willpower and personal risk to place one's own individual judgment over that of the herd.

But necessary as it may be to an individual's security, herding behavior can have a downside. It can discourage necessary course corrections from independent thinkers. And it can also encourage extreme viewpoints. Social scientists have performed experiments

("Those who are viewed as having mastered an area of knowledge can often influence a proceeding by expressing an opinion about a critical point in contention, often without justifying the basis of their opinion. For example, the ability of experts to sway juries has long been recognized, so much so that it has drawn increasing court scrutiny of expert testimony.").

that show that groups that deliberate tend to reach more polarized outcomes than individuals, as different people strive to establish their credibility within the herd by proving themselves a better fit with the herd's interests than others. Moreover, if the herd is moving in the wrong direction to begin with (if, say, it has poor leadership), it can be much harder to change its direction, even if one can muster the personal will to resist. A number of social scientists have attributed the widespread ethical lapses that doomed Enron and Arthur Andersen in the early 2000s, for example, to instances of herding behavior.[29]

2.2 Professional Biases—How Training Colors Our World

In addition to the various cognitive biases hardwired into the human brain, there are additional biases that come from professional training or experience that may be difficult to shed during a high-stakes, complex negotiation. Some of these can come from "professional ideology," a series of valued and norms inculcated by various professions. Thus, lawyers might be considered more status-conscious and risk-averse. Businesspeople might be considered more profit-oriented. (It is worth noting that these are simply trends; individual members of different professions will clearly not fit these generalizations. But those trends are still discernible.)

Professional biases can encompass a number of differences, but in complex negotiations one of the most important is in attitudes about risk.

29. *See, e.g.*, Stephen M. Renas & Richard J. Cebula, *Enron, Herding, & the Deterrent Effect of the Disclosure of Improprieties*, 64 Am. J. Econ. & Soc. 743 (2005); Joel S. Demsky, *Corporate Conflicts of Interest*, 17 J. Econ. Perspectives 51 (2003).

2.2.1 Businesspeople

2.2.1.1 Executives

"These walls are funny. First you hate 'em, then you get used to 'em. Enough time passes, you get so you depend on them. That's institutionalized."

—ELLIS BOYD "RED" REDDING,
The Shawshank Redemption (Castle Rock, 1994)

For our purposes, the most important characteristic of a business executive is that she is attached to an institution—the corporation for which she works—and, for the time that she is there, she identifies with its goals. As a result, most business executives are motivated by several different needs, but the two most common are the need for their company to make money (profit) and the need for the company to succeed well into the future (legacy). Each of these issues will help determine the executive's standing within the company, which, in turn, will satisfy any need she may have for money or prestige.

Overall, it is important to remember that business executives tend to be skilled at climbing and navigating an organizational hierarchy. (In fact, given the intensity of employment tournaments in large organizations, for some that may be their primary skill.) As a result, they often have a dual focus in negotiations. On the one hand, they clearly have a strong incentive to get the best deal possible for their firm. But, at the same time, they have a clear personal incentive to protect and enhance their position *within* the organization. So executives may at times face a conflict between self-interest and the interests of their firm, a classic example of what economists call an "agency problem."[30]

While organizations are not exclusively one type or another, these provide at least a basis for understanding their risk appetite. Executives

30. Troy A. Paredes, *Too Much Pay, Too Much Deference: Behavioral Corporate Finance, CEOs, & Corporate Governance*, 32 FLA. ST. U.L. REV. 673, 688–89 (2005)

are in business, which usually requires some acceptance of risk. But they are not typically as enthusiastic about risk as entrepreneurs.

2.2.1.2 *Entrepreneurs*

"Innovation is the specific tool of entrepreneurs, the means by which they exploit change as an opportunity for a different business or a different service."

—PETER F. DRUCKER

Even more than regular business executives, entrepreneurs—that is, people who start their own businesses—tend to be risk-*seeking*. Entrepreneurs do not have to be formally educated, though many are Bill Gates and Steve Jobs—two famously successful examples from one industry—each dropped out of college.[31] They are typically driven by a vision of what is possible and how it can change an industry or people's lives. Given the funding constraints that typically accompany starting and growing a business, they are typically very focused on bringing their vision to life and believe that it will have significant financial reward. They are regularly evaluating the mix of what will drive growth versus personal value. That focus is incredibly powerful.

However, that single-minded focus can pose a challenge in large-scale negotiations. Entrepreneurs' commitment to their vision and what they see as possible may keep them from seeing the benefits of engaging in negotiation and may be less sensitive to perceived losses as they see the world differently from others. In order to build any common ground that serves as the basis for negotiation, it is critical to understand the nature of their vision and personal goals and their sensitivity to different types of risks. These tie back to the types of attraction described earlier in the chapter.

31. Paul Schmitz, *Lessons from Famous College Dropouts*, CNN.com, Dec. 31, 2011, *available at* http://edition.cnn.com/2011/12/30/opinion/Schmitz-college/index.html (last viewed Oct. 18, 2012).

2.2.2 Lawyers

"Daddy's a litigator. Those are the scariest kind of lawyer.... And daddy's so good he gets $500 an hour to fight with people."

—CHER,

Clueless (Paramount, 1995)

Lawyers can make unusual negotiators. Unlike businesspeople trained to build relationships or take interesting risks, lawyers tend to be detail-oriented, risk-averse, adversarial, and highly educated. Businesspeople often tend to view lawyers as overly cautious, or even as outright naysayers. John Whitehead, the head of investment banking at Goldman Sachs in the 1980s, once called lawyers the "people who said you couldn't do something."[32] Decades later, another Goldman Sachs banker wrote: "On Wall Street, lawyers have been second-class citizens for decades... if you're a Wall Street deal lawyer, you're a well-paid functionary."[33] This aversion to lawyers in negotiations is longstanding: President Woodrow Wilson famously declared that he had no intention of allowing any lawyers to draft the peace treaty at the end of World War I.[34]

Part of this reluctance stems from lawyers' reputations for being adversarial, sometimes needlessly so.[35] This reputation may stem from exposure to litigators, who spend much of their time on actual disputes. Transactional lawyers tend to be more deal- and solution-oriented.

32. BRETT COLE, M&A TITANS: THE PIONEERS WHO SHAPED WALL STREET'S MERGER AND ACQUISITIONS INDUSTRY 32 (2008).

33. Evan Newmark, *Mean Street: The Mysteries of the Miserable Wall Street Lawyer*, http://blogs.wsj.com/deals/2011/01/18/mean-street-the-mysteries-of-the-miserable-wall-street-lawyer/ (last viewed May 2, 2012).

34. MARGARET MACMILLAN, PARIS 1919: SIX MONTHS THAT CHANGED THE WORLD, Kindle location 3068 (2003).

35. *See* Robert H. Mnookin & Lewis Kornhauser, *Bargaining in the Shadow of the Law: The Case of Divorce*, 88 YALE L.J. 950, 986 (1979) ("lawyers may be more likely

There is no question that, as a group, lawyers tend to be more client-oriented and risk-averse. Being a lawyer, of course, requires not just a bachelor's degree but—at least in the United States—an advanced degree as well. Lawyers are also certified by a governing professional body, a hurdle businesspeople rarely have to vault. The education required to gain these credentials further inculcates particular approaches and ways of thinking. That extensive legal education does not guarantee training in negotiation techniques—at least not in the classroom.[36]

The reputation for adversarial practice also has some foundation in truth. Whether or not a given law school includes any negotiation training, all law schools focus on analytic training that allows lawyers to identify various solutions and compare them against different standards for fairness. This is of particular use in adversarial agreements, where the best alternative to negotiating an agreement may be a jury trial, and where, as a result, the parties may frame any agreement in terms of legal remedies (such as "injunctive relief" or "damages for breaching a contract").[37]

2.3 Personality and Emotion—Nobody Is Spock

"How do you translate a business strategy into an emotion?"

—ARTHUR,

Inception (Warner Bros., 2010)

Negotiations, even complicated negotiations that take place over long periods of time, prompt emotional responses. The single

than lay people to adopt negotiating strategies involving threats and the strategic misrepresentation of their clients' true preferences in the hope of reaching a more favorable settlement for the client").

36. Alex J. Hurder, *The Lawyer's Dilemma: To Be or Not to Be a Problem-Solving Negotiator*, 14 Clinical L. Rev. 253, 254 (2007).

37. *Id.* at 253, 263–64 (internal footnote omitted).

most common one is fear: *Will I screw this up*? French Prime Minister Georges Clemenceau reportedly had no trouble with abuse in negotiations, but would lay awake at nights if he thought he had made a fool of himself.[38] Many people find it difficult to discuss the role of emotion in negotiation, because emotions usually push discussion out of the rational, quantifiable areas of discussion and into the realm of subjective personal experience.[39] Moreover, because emotions are personal and subjective, attributing emotions to groups can seem strange. Generally, we do not think of organizations as having personality or emotion.[40] In reality, if an organization has an emotional disposition, it likely reflects the emotions of its managers.[41]

Nonetheless, emotions and personality traits have had measurable effects on complicated negotiations. In particular, behavioral experiments have shown that attempts to achieve an "unfair" outcome may provoke animosity or a desire to punish,[42] and that that this tendency is more pronounced in groups.[43] Similarly, rhetoricians have long recognized that naked appeals to emotion (or *pathos*) can be extraordinarily effective at persuading people.[44]

38. MACMILLAN, *supra* note 34, at Kindle location 5429.

39. *See, e.g.*, Jon Elster, *Emotions & Economic Theory*, 36 J. ECON. LIT. 47, 47 (1998) (discussing lack of overlap between economists and psychologists on one hand, and "emotion theorists" on the other).

40. Nonetheless, some scholars have taken a stab at measuring whether organizations can display emotional states. *See* William J. Dixon, *Measuring Interstate Affect*, 27 AM. J. POL. SCI. 828 (1983).

41. *Id.* at 828, 831.

42. HERBERT GINTIS, THE BOUNDS OF REASON: GAME THEORY & THE UNIFICATION OF THE BEHAVIORAL SCIENCES 64 (2009) ("punishing norm violators is very common but not universal, and . . . individuals are prone to be more harsh in punishing those who hurt them personally").

43. *Id.* at 77 ("even a single hint that there may be a basis for inter-group competition induces individuals to exhibit insider loyalty and outsider hostility").

44. *See Aristotle*, RHETORIC 8 (W. Rhys Roberts, trans. 2010).

And display of emotion in negotiation can also invoke an emotional state in one's counterpart.[45] As a result, negotiators will want to be aware of both the emotions their counterparts are advertising, as well as their own emotional states.

So what do we mean by "emotions" in this context? Emotions are associated with "action tendencies"—jargon for urges: guilt, for example, comes with an urge to atone; anger with an urge to hurt.[46] As economist Paul Seabright has persuasively argued, our emotions are an elegant (and possibly entirely rational) adaptation to the environment early humans faced for much of the evolution of the species.[47] And historic and business accounts of important negotiations are rife with descriptions of the parties' emotional reactions to various tactics and events.

Moreover, as legal scholar Eric Posner has pointed out, people do not necessarily act irrationally when they are emotional; instead—while they continue to act rationally, they assume new goals, preferences, and beliefs.[48] As Professor Posner explains, emotional people do not necessarily act reflexively; instead, they either over- or underestimate probabilities based on their emotional state.[49]

This understanding of emotion means that tactics based on manipulating emotional states can be an effective, though risky, strategy. And, in negotiations between organizations, certain kinds of emotions—like anxiety—may be more likely to occur. (After all, a negotiator within an organization will feel some anxiety about representing the other members of her organization.)

45. *See, e.g.*, Arif Nazar Butt et al., *The Effect of Self-Emotion, Counterpart Emotion, and Counterpart Behavior on Negotiator Behavior: A Comparison of Individual-Level & Dyad-Level Dynamics*, 26 J. ORG. BEHAVIOR 681, 685 (2005).

46. Elster, *supra* note 39, at 51.

47. SEABRIGHT, *supra* note 10, at 41.

48. *See* Eric A. Posner, *Law and the Emotions*, John M. Olin Law & Economics Working Paper No. 103 (2d Series), 5 (2000).

49. *Id.* at 4–5.

It may rely on part, however, on the nature of complex negotiations. Complex negotiations may also attract outsized personalities because the deals (or the lawsuits) are so big that working on them requires a degree of obsessiveness (call it workaholism). As corporate lawyer Martin Lipton (one of the founders of the famous Wachtell Lipton law firm) said in an interview about the large mergers on which he worked, mergers-and-acquisitions lawyers are

> obsessive, compulsive people... People who come here and are not so compulsive and obsessive and dedicated to doing it don't stay that long. You've got to love doing this. You can't do it otherwise. It doesn't work.[50]

Just as they can encourage extreme emotional states, negotiations between organizations are particularly susceptible to extreme personalities. There is a Darwinian logic behind this phenomenon. To rise to a level where one represents an organization in negotiations (meaning that one has likely become management), a person must often survive the equivalent of a "tournament" at the workplace, where promotion to each rung on the corporate ladder winnows out candidates who lack the ambition, the skill, or even just the plain old luck to advance.[51] As a result, those at the top of an organization are often those with the personality (including the willingness to take large risks) necessary to survive multiple elimination rounds of a tournament.

50. COLE, *supra* note 32, at 61.

51. Paredes, *supra* note 30, at 673, 684–85; Donald C. Langevoort, *The Behavioral Economics of Mergers and Acquisitions*, Georgetown Business, Economics & Regulatory Law Research Paper No. 10–17, http://ssrn.com/abstract=1692777, at 10 (Oct. 2010).

2.3.1 Personal Attraction—Don't Fall in Love with the Deal

"Don't fall in love with the deal."

—ANONYMOUS

It is no secret to most people that we prefer to work with those we like.[52] This exhibits itself in a number of ways. Studies have consistently shown that physically attractive people have an easier time getting jobs and are paid more on average than their plainer peers.[53] Similarly, studies have also shown that companies prefer CEOs that are considered "charismatic."[54]

But personal attraction also matters in negotiation. An important component of this is the concept of rapport. Rapport is the ability of two people to work together. Fostering rapport can foster trust. And the more trust between the parties, the shorter the final contract needs to be.

Similarly, personal attraction may also rely on previous relationships. We tend to trust those people with whom we have worked before.[55] That kind of relationship can be particularly helpful when negotiating.[56]

52. Chris Guthrie, *Principles of Influence in Negotiation*, 87 MARQUETTE L. REV. 829, 831 (2004) ("individuals prefer to comply with requests made by those they know and like").

53. CATHERINE HAKIM, EROTIC CAPITAL: THE POWER OF ATTRACTION IN THE BOARDROOM & THE BEDROOM 170 (2011); *see also* Guthrie, *supra* note 52, at 831.

54. *See* Rakesh Khurana, *The Curse of the Superstar CEO*, HARV. BUS. REV. 3, 4 (Sept. 2002) (detailing rise of charisma as factor in lateral CEO selection).

55. Guthrie, *supra* note 52, at 831.

56. ROGER FISHER ET AL., GETTING TO YES: NEGOTIATING AGREEMENT WITHOUT GIVING IN 19 (1991) ("The process of working out an agreement may produce a psychological commitment to a mutually satisfactory outcome. A working relationship where trust, understanding, respect, and friendship are built up over time can make each new negotiation smoother and more efficient. And people's desire to feel good

And, to the extent that being around people may put one in a state of sexual arousal, it may affect willingness to agree to options one might not otherwise consider.[57] Economist Daniel Ariely performed an experiment in which he asked college-age males to evaluate whether they would engage in behavior they found personally or ethically distasteful if it would enhance their chances of having sex.[58] He asked again when the men were in a state of sexual arousal.[59] In an aroused state, the men were far more likely to agree to actions they had previously declined.[60] This conclusion is hardly shocking: salespeople have long "softened up" potential buyers or clients in part by relying on "erotic capital."[61]

Of course, physical attraction is no guarantee of a good agreement. For an interesting natural experiment, take the case of Queen Marie, who ruled Romania from 1914 to 1927. In 1919, as the primary Western powers were determining the fate of post–World War I Europe, Romania, like many other countries, was lobbying for control over as many territories as possible. As part of its campaign, Romania sent its queen, formerly the Princess of Edinburgh, to reinforce its diplomatic corps. Queen Marie was a celebrated beauty (the French paper *Le Matin* took special note of "the glitter of her golden hair, the clarity of her pink and white complexion, the glow in her imperious yet soft eyes...") She was also famously in sexual demand,

about themselves, and their concern for what others will think of them, can often make them more sensitive to another negotiator's interests.").

57. GINTIS, *supra* note 42, at 2 (noting sexual deprivation can change preference ordering).

58. ARIELY, *supra* note 15, at 124–25.

59. *Id.* at 125. To accomplish the experiment, Ariely used a laptop both times, and the second time had the men masturbate while they answered questions. *Id.* 126.

60. *Id.* at 127 ("Across the board, they revealed in their unaroused state that they themselves did not know what they were like once aroused. Prevention, protection, conservatism, and morality disappeared completely from the radar screen. They were simply unable to predict the degree to which passion would change them.").

61. HAKIM, *supra* note 53, at 178.

entertaining a number of then-prominent lovers. And she flirted successfully with British Prime Minister David Lloyd George and Clemenceau. (She shocked President Wilson when she began a meeting talking of "love.") Romania's great charm offensive had little effect on its diplomatic goals, however. As historian Margaret MacMillan noted, Queen Marie "might have been better advised to spend more time on the subordinates of the great men." When the Romanian commission met, it ceded most of the territory Queen Marie had sought to Hungary and Yugoslavia.[62]

Attraction goes well beyond the physical. And it is these other forms of attraction that provide the most opportunities to influence negotiations. There are several different types of attraction that can be present that alter a decision or prioritization process.

2.3.1.1 *Charisma*

"I think you can probably get away with bad material if you've got charisma."

—RICKY GERVAIS,
Interview with CNN (2005)

The first of these is the attraction to charismatic business leaders. Some leaders have charismatic personalities that make them more persuasive and genuinely interesting. People just want to work with or for them. In fact, a number of modern corporations recruit their executives for just these qualities.[63] A number of the most celebrated business leaders of the last few decades have managed to get their subordinates engaged in deals because of the attraction to their vision. Jack Welch (former chairman of General Electric) and John Chambers (chairman at Cisco) each engaged in a dizzying number of acquisitions

62. MACMILLAN, *supra* note 34, 133–35. Her Romanian "subordinates" however, performed admirably, gaining a number of lower profile but important concessions.

63. *See, e.g.*, Khurana, *supra* note 54, at 2, 4 (noting "the widespread quasi-religious belief in the power of religious leaders").

in their industries, allowing their companies to rise to the top of their markets; a part of the attraction of doing a deal with GE or Cisco was the attraction of being on the same team with these men.

Business leaders might also offer a singular business vision that allows for the same pull. Charisma does not guarantee successful negotiating, however. Two more executives famed for their vision and their charisma were Enron Chairman Kenneth Lay and his protégé, CEO Jeffrey Skilling. Throughout the 1990s, their aggressive moves and acquisitions fueled the growth and reach of their company into new sectors and offerings. Partly because of their reputations, Enron was able to attract many of the most talented minds in business.[64] But all of the vision in the world, and all of the talent it attracted, was not enough to overcome mismatches in skill and experience.

While some executives have personalities that are compelling and charismatic, others just have reputations as being "nice," "reasonable," or otherwise easy to work with. Executives like A. G. Lafley (former CEO of Procter & Gamble) or Eric Schmidt (former CEO of Google) have been regarded by both their employees and business partners as "people you want to do business with." Board members at Procter & Gamble, for example, have referred to Lafley as someone "who wears well."[65] Eric Schmidt's "nice-guy" image was so prevalent that some speculated it may have served as one reason Google's board eventually replaced him as CEO.[66] While both lawyers and business negotiators tend to undersell niceness, there is no denying that it can provide a strategic edge in consummating certain agreements. Clearly, both

64. Malcolm Gladwell, *The Talent Myth: Are Smart People Overrated?*, NEW YORKER, July 22, 2002, at 28.

65. Alex Markels, *Turning the Tide at P&G*, U.S. NEWS & WORLD REPORT, Oct. 22, 2006, *available at* http://www.usnews.com/usnews/news/articles/061022/30lafley_print.htm (last viewed Sept. 10, 2012).

66. *See, e.g.*, Farhad Manjoo, *Erich Schmidt Is the Nicest Guy in Tech: Is that Why Google Replaced Him with Larry Page?*, SLATE, Apr. 13, 2010, *available at* http://www.slate.com/articles/technology/technology/2010/04/eric_schmidt_is_the_nicest_guy_in_tech.html (last viewed Oct. 18, 2012).

Lafley and Schmidt accomplished a number of significant business deals (including key strategic acquisitions) during their times at P&G and Google.

The importance of reasonability as an attractor is sometimes more visible when it is not present. During the debt-ceiling negotiations in 2011, for example, congressional negotiators refused to work with Jack Lew because they found his practice of lecturing his counterparts without conceding any substantive points himself "exasperating." The complaints about Lew grew so vociferous that the White House eventually replaced him with Bill Daley, with whom negotiators got on better.[67]

Similarly, in the post–World War I peace negotiations in Paris, the Americans, English, and French often met to negotiate among themselves. During these sessions, the Americans and English often had an easier time reaching agreement. Some of this ease can be attributed to common strategic interests or even common language, but some also came from the fact that American President Woodrow Wilson and British Prime Minister David Lloyd George made efforts to develop a personal relationship outside the formal negotiations, often visiting or dining with each other. French Prime Minister Georges Clemenceau, by contrast, did not much like Wilson or Lloyd George. (He found Wilson too priggish and Lloyd George too devious, leading him to famously complain that he felt himself trapped between "Jesus Christ on the one hand, and Napoleon Bonaparte on the other."[68]) Consequently, Clemenceau kept to himself and found it more difficult to reach agreement on points important to him.[69]

Finally, people may become attracted to the goal a negotiation serves. In technology deals, negotiators often are attracted to what they consider the world-changing aspects of the deal. Cisco, for

67. Matt Bai, *Obama vs. Boehner: Who Killed the Debt Deal?*, N.Y. TIMES MAGAZINE, Mar. 28, 2012.

68. MACMILLAN, *supra* note 34, at Kindle location 876.

69. *Id.* at location 863.

example, often touts its desire to "unleash the power of the network." That unknown but powerful and creative spirit provides clear attraction to people on both sides of the deal because there is perceived great power that can be tapped through a successful result to the negotiation.

Another example involves negotiations where the ultimate agreement promises to change people's lives for the better. For example, pharmaceutical and biotechnology deals often focus on joint efforts to combat some disease or accelerate the production of some necessary medication. The markets still value these agreements in monetary terms, and there is certainly no question that biotechnology and pharmaceuticals are two extremely profitable industries. But because the results of these transactions can have a very real physical impact on people's lives, negotiators may feel additional motivation to make the deal work. Pharmaceutical giant Merck acquired stem-cell storage company SmartCells in 2010, for example, in part because it saw a way to accelerate the search for a cure for diabetes:

> "At SmartCells, we have made important progress in rapidly advancing from early concept towards clinical development," said Todd C. Zion, Ph.D., president, co-founder and chief executive officer. "This acquisition positions our novel technology for success in the hands of a leading pharmaceutical company with proven expertise and exceptional resources to deliver breakthrough diabetes products to patients."[70]

This phenomenon applies to litigation as well. For example, the class actions seeking to recover money from Swiss banks that had been left during World War II was a personal mission for many of the attorneys, particularly Michael Hausfeld. While the focus of the case was about money (compensation for victims' families), there were

70. *See* http://www.mercknewsroom.com/press-release/corporate-news/merck-acquire-smartcells-inc (last viewed December 29, 2012).

many elements that were motivating participants to "do the right thing."[71] Indeed, many class action lawyers try to replicate this sense of mission when they recruit plaintiffs for their lawsuits; experience has taught them that the promise of doing good provides more incentive to stay in difficult litigation than the promise of modest financial gain from an individual settlement.[72]

A significant downside to attraction to the negotiation process is that it may lead to poor judgments about the overall agreement. Participants can become emotionally attached to a particular deal, a phenomenon often called "falling in love with the deal." As a result, they do whatever they can to make the negotiation successful not necessarily because of its merits but because of some attraction in the negotiation.

2.3.1.2 Trust

"I trust everyone. I just don't trust the devil inside them."

—TROY KENNEDY-MARTIN,
The Italian Job (Paramount Pictures 2003)

Technically, it is difficult to characterize trust as an emotion. But it is an important, quasi-rational component of any negotiation.[73] Trust often arises when parties feel positive emotions towards one another.[74] Trust can stem from a number of sources. A long-standing

71. For more on the Holocaust litigation, *see* JANE SHAPIRO, INSIDE A CLASS ACTION: THE HOLOCAUST AND THE SWISS BANKS (2003); Morris A. Ratner, *The Settlement of Nazi-Era Litigation through the Executive and Judicial Branches*, 20 BERKELEY J. INT'L L. 212 (2002).

72. *See* Stephen Meili, *Collective Justice or Personal Gain? An Empirical Analysis of Class Action Lawyers and Named Plaintiffs*, 44 AKRON L. REV. 67, 72–73 (2011).

73. Adler & Silverstein, *supra* note 28, at 82–83 ("Trust is essential for effective negotiation in all settings, even those involving elements of competition and aggression.").

74. *Id.*

working relationship is often an excellent source of trust.[75] A party can also have someone else vouch for her.[76]

Trust also makes negotiations smoother;[77] after all, if one can trust the other party when she says something, one does not have to spend resources to verify her information. In other words, trust can help to reduce the costs of vigilance or diligence. The more trust that exists between the parties, the more likely it is that they will focus on solutions that can benefit both sides; less trust means the parties will be more concerned with dividing up what limited resources they perceive to be there.[78]

Trust is more complicated once one looks at it from an organizational perspective, however. First, on an organizational level, trust does not work if it focuses only on an initial connection between two people. It has to last even after the original parties are no longer in the room. It has to work even when subordinates are meeting with each other and asking the difficult—but necessary—questions required to perform due diligence on the deal. Building this kind of trust between groups—as opposed to between individuals—is significantly more complicated.

75. For more on working relationships over time, *see* § 5.5. *See also* FISHER ET AL., *supra* note 56, at 157 ("Build a working relationship. Knowing the other side personally really does help. It is much easier to attribute diabolical intentions to an unknown abstraction called the 'other side' than to someone you know personally.").

76. SEABRIGHT, *supra* note 10, at 252 ("Dysfunctional though your neighborhood may seem, if you move away you lose the few ties that protect you from the worst; you no longer have others to vouch for you, you become an anonymous drifter in a world where identity is everything.").

77. FISHER ET AL., *supra* note 56, at 19 ("The process of working out an agreement may produce a psychological commitment to a mutually satisfactory outcome. A working relationship where trust, understanding, respect, and friendship are built up over time can make each new negotiation smoother and more efficient. And people's desire to feel good about themselves, and their concern for what others will think of them, can often make them more sensitive to another negotiator's interests.").

78. P. V. (Sundar) Blakrishnan et al., *Toward a Theory of Agenda-Setting in Negotiations*, 19 J. CONSUMER RESEARCH 637, 647 (1993) ("In negotiation contexts, both social psychologists and consumer researchers have found that low levels of trust

In cooperative negotiations (such as the typical business deal), building trust is often a vital early part of the negotiation. It helps the negotiation to be successful. It takes risk out of the outcome as both sides understand not just what is written in an agreement but how it will be implemented. There are many pieces of information that can come out during a negotiation if there is trust that have nothing to do with what goes into the contract, but will need to be dealt with in some fashion. If there is not trust, then it is far less likely that the parties will share that information.

Negotiators employ several different methods to help build trust. First, they will often work to connect the negotiating teams beforehand. While there is a strong temptation to jump directly into discussing terms of an agreement, doing so can miss an important opportunity to build connections. Instead, experienced business negotiators will have each side provide a brief overview of their business and major goals. This ensures that the key players on each side have established a common set of knowledge about each other, regardless of what other intelligence they may have gathered. They may also arrange a visit to the other side's operations to meet the extended team. Finally, and most important, they will arrange for the teams to share dinner, ideally in a nonformal setting. Unlike a formal dinner in a high-class restaurant, the informal setting introduces a limited degree of spontaneity and flexibility, providing a place where members can learn more about each other as people in addition to the business discussions. These more personal connections can help to build trust over the long term.

There may be one drawback to building trust in an adversarial negotiation. At least, that is what a recent set of experiments conducted by several business professors suggests. The researchers found that negotiators who developed a rapport with their counterparts were more likely to compromise their clients' interests. This is not necessarily all that surprising. Depending on the client, the lawyers may have longer-term relationships with each other. And a

are associated with distributive behavior, while high levels of trust are associated with integrative behavior.") (internal citations omitted).

lawyer may justify compromising his client's interest in all kinds of ways, such as telling himself that the long-term relationship with opposing counsel will benefit future clients, or that the compromise is the only way to get the client at least some of what she wants. The researchers also found that negotiators who develop rapport were more likely to deceive each other. While the conclusion seems counterintuitive, it turns out negotiators will often hide or downplay bad news in order to maintain the rapport that they have.[79]

As a result, in more adversarial negotiations, it becomes more important to maintain a cordial distance from the other side.

2.3.2 Personal Animosity—"That F@$%ing Guy"

"From the deepest desires often comes the deadliest hate."

—SOCRATES

Negotiations between organizations must also overcome the problem of personal animosities. Stories abound in the business press of how particular grudges have prevented (or derailed) extremely lucrative business relationships. Organizations are not immune from this problem: Robert Mnookin details how IBM and Fujitsu spent years locked in a legal war fueled partly by mistrust and a long-held grudge,[80] and how the San Francisco Symphony Orchestra was mired for years in a fruitless conflict between its performers' union and board of directors.[81]

Negotiations between organizations also can fall prey to personal animosities.[82] In fact, several high-profile implosions of deals

79. *See* Sandy D. Jap et al., *The Dark Side of Rapport: Agent Misbehavior Face-to-Face and Online*, Working Paper 2011, *available at* http://ssrn.com abstract=1789782.

80. ROBERT MNOOKIN, BARGAINING WITH THE DEVIL: WHEN TO NEGOTIATE, WHEN TO FIGHT 139–76 (2010).

81. *Id.* at 177–208.

82. Personal animosities are hardly confined to negotiations between organizations. *Id.* at 1 ("By 'bargain' I mean attempt to make a deal—try to resolve the conflict

occurred, at least in part, because of the individual personalities involved.[83] Given the tendency of groups to adopt more extreme positions after deliberation, organizations may be more susceptible to entrenched animosities.[84]

From an evolutionary perspective, these grudges make sense. When dealing with strangers, humans developed the ability to punish those who treated them badly, even if doing so required time and resources better spent elsewhere. Doing so enabled a system in which negotiation was possible.

But what worked for hominids on the savannah is less effective in corporate boardrooms. Negotiators who hold on to resentments tend to find them blowing up at the wrong times. And the business literature is filled with stories of deals that failed because individuals could not see past their resentments to work together.

2.3.2.1 Anger

"We have an old saying in Delta House: don't get mad, get even."

—DANIEL SIMPSON DAY "D-DAY,"

Animal House

Most businesspeople think of anger as something to avoid in negotiation. Depending on the context, displaying anger may be considered unprofessional in the course of a negotiation. Moreover,

through negotiation—rather than fighting it out. By 'Devil,' I mean an enemy who has intentionally harmed you in the past or appears willing to harm you in the future. Someone you don't trust. An adversary whose behavior you may even see as evil.").

83. *See, e.g.*, JAMES STEWART, DISNEYWAR 480 (2006) (then Pixar CEO Steve Jobs blames collapse of negotiations with Disney on inability to work with then Disney CEO Michael Eisner); BRUCE BUENO DE MESQUITA, THE PREDICTIONEER'S GAME 70 (2009) (ascribing breakdown in merger negotiations between two pharmaceutical companies to personal animosity between CEOs).

84. MNOOKIN, *supra* note 80, at 106 ("Both sides viewed negotiation as a sign of 'weakness and betrayal.' Both sides had declared that they would not 'come to the

anger may blind a negotiator to the benefits of certain deals. An angry negotiator may also be more concerned with exacting revenge (or forcing a concession) than with taking actions that would benefit the final deal. And an angry negotiator may be more likely to anger his counterparts, which is also more likely to doom any prospective deal.[85]

Nonetheless, anger may also confer certain benefits in negotiation. Some people believe that anger can help them focus. And some studies have shown that angry negotiators may be better at extracting concessions from their counterparts.[86] This may be because anger signals that the negotiator is less likely to be reasonable in exchanging concessions, leaving his counterpart with a clear choice: negotiate or walk away.[87] (In that case, it would make sense that those counterparts who stay with a given negotiation would offer larger concessions.)

This suggests, of course, that some negotiators might consider displays of anger to be an effective negotiating tactic. Others might just be angry people. Joseph Daly[88] studied the effects of anger during

table until the other made significant concessions.' This is a classic problem in prolonged conflicts. Adversaries establish preconditions to negotiation that require the other side to sacrifice most of its bargaining power before talks can even begin. Naturally, neither side agrees to this and the conflict simply persists.").

85. Posner, *supra* note 48, at 26.

86. Gerben A. Van Kleef et al., *The Interpersonal Effects of Emotions in Negotiations: A Motivated Information Processing Approach*, 87 J. PERSONALITY & SOC. PSYCH. 510, 511 (2004) ("participants with an angry opponent placed lower demands and made larger concessions than did participants with a nonemotional opponent").

87. *Id.* at 511 ("Negotiators used their opponent's emotions to infer the location of his or her limits and subsequently used this information to make a counteroffer. In other words, negotiators who were confronted with an angry opponent estimated the opponent's limit to be high, and to avoid costly impasse, they placed low demands and made large concessions").

88. Joseph P. Daly, *The Effects of Anger on Negotiations over Mergers and Acquisition*, NEGOTIATION JOURNAL 31 (Jan. 1991).

acquisition negotiations, interviewing both company sides as well as lawyers and investment bankers to understand the causes and effects of anger on negotiations. He documented sixteen behaviors reported as triggering anger. These ranged anywhere from misrepresentation to insulting the other party to lacking commitment to achieving an agreement to showing excessive concern for unimportant details. Even when material sums of money should have overridden a rational individual's emotions, the appearance of anger led to inhibiting the angered negotiator's ability to find mutually agreeable solutions. Additionally, the goal changed from profit maximization toward punishing or retaliating against the offending party.

Sometimes, however, anger is not strategic. Sometimes it is just anger. Anger may come from the fact that one party feels it has been unjustly treated. In select cases, parties may have a particular condition identified as *face threat sensitivity*.[89] Face threat sensitivity is a sensitivity to how the bargain reflects on the individual doing the negotiating.[90] Threats to face can affect whether a negotiator takes a cooperative or competitive approach to a bargain.[91]

A person's sensitivity to face threats depends in part on her role in the negotiation.[92] And face threat sensitivity appears to be greatest when one is negotiating in front of an audience or reporting back

89. *See generally* Judith B. White et al., *Face Threat Sensitivity in Negotiation: Roadblock to Agreement and Joint Gain*, 94 ORG. BEHAVIOR & HUMAN DECISION PROCESSES 102 (2004).

90. *Id.* at 102, 103 ("Face includes the value to a person of his or her public image, reputation, and status vis-à-vis other people in an interaction. A person's face, then, is the social value of who and what they hold themselves out to be.").

91. *Id.* at 102 ("When a person's face is threatened in a negotiation, it can tip the balance of his/her behavior away from cooperation toward competition, resulting in fewer agreements and/or less cooperative agreements.").

92. *Id.* at 102 ("We find that a negotiator's face threat sensitivity affects the negotiation process and outcomes when his or her face includes the resources being negotiated, a factor that varies with role.").

to constituents.[93] (Both of these situations are more likely to occur when one is negotiating on behalf of an organization.)[94]

Negotiating may also affect a party's (or an organization's) reputation. In situations where a party has been accused of bad conduct, it may signal some degree of guilt or remorse. In situations where a party has been the target of hostile behavior, it may signal weakness.[95]

2.3.3 Overconfidence—Everyone's Above Average

"Overconfidence blurs out the risk. Inferiority magnifies it."

—TOBA BETA,
Betelgeuse Incident

When CEOs of corporations rise from within a firm, they usually exhibit the characteristics of successful tournament players, which may include "a bias toward overconfidence, risk-taking, and ethical plasticity."[96] Similarly, CEOs hired from outside a firm are often

93. *Id.* at 104 ("Negotiators who are accountable to constituents show increased competitiveness, although gender of the constituent may moderate this effect. Negotiators who are told that they appeared weak before an audience of their peers become even more competitive in later rounds of negotiation; they take the opportunity to retaliate against their opponent, even though it costs them in absolute tangible rewards. High-profile CEOs who believe the whole world is watching them may become more competitive and less cooperative in business negotiations.") (internal citations omitted).

94. FISHER ET AL., *supra* note 56, at 30 ("In dealing with negotiators who represent their organizations, it is easy to treat them as mere mouthpieces without emotions. It is important to remember that they too, like you, have personal feelings, fears, hopes, and dreams. Their careers may be at stake.").

95. Robert Mnookin, *When Not to Negotiate: A Negotiation Imperialist Reflects on Appropriate Limits*, 74 U. COLO. L. REV. 1077, 1087 (2003).

96. Donald C. Langevoort, *Overcoming Resistance to Diversity in the Executive Suite: Grease, Grit, and the Corporate Promotion Tournament*, 61 WASH & LEE L. REV. 1615, 1631–32 (2004); *see also* Daniel C. Feldman & Barton A. Weitz, *From the Invisible Hand to the Gladhand: Understanding a Careerist Orientation to Work*, 30 HUMAN RESOURCE MGMT. 237, 251 (1991) (study of business-school graduates indicated correlation between promotions at work and self-absorption).

selected, at least in part, because of their personal charisma.[97] And with the increasing focus on "Superstar CEOs" has come a growing literature documenting the problem of "CEO overconfidence," a phenomenon that can skew investments and affect negotiation strategies.[98]

Some CEOs (or executives on their way to that position) may go so far as to exhibit clinical narcissism. The DSM-IV (the best diagnostic tool for psychiatric professionals) defines "narcissistic personality disorder" as "[a] pervasive pattern of grandiosity (in fantasy or behavior), need for admiration, and lack of empathy . . . "[99] As a number of observers have commented, narcissism may actually help CEO candidates to rise in an organization.[100] And, in most organizations, the upper echelons are often populated with CEO candidates. Narcissism also has its dark side. Because narcissistic leaders can be incredibly difficult to work for, they can place a huge drain on an organization's resources.[101]

97. Khurana, *supra* note 54 at 3, 4 (detailing rise of charisma as factor in lateral CEO selection). Paredes, *supra* note 30, at 675–76 ("It is not new to suggest that business executives, particularly CEOs, suffer from overconfidence—often referred to more pejoratively as executive 'ego,' 'hubris,' or 'arrogance.' In fact, it is reasonable to believe that people in powerful and influential positions with track records of success—qualities that typify CEOs, especially of large public companies—might particularly be overconfident and prone to believe that they are in control.").

98. Antonio E. Bernardo & Ivo Welch, 2001, *On the Evolution of Overconfidence and Entrepreneurs*, 10 Journal of Economics and Management Strategy 301 (2001); Hayward & Hambrick, *supra* note 5, at 103; Pekka Hietala, et al., *What Is the Price of Hubris? Using Takeover Battles to Infer Overpayments and Synergies*, 32 Fin. Mgmt. 1 (2003); Ulrike Malmendier & Geoffrey A. Tate, 2005, *CEO Overconfidence and Corporate Investment*, 60 J. Fin. 2661; Roll, *supra* note 4, at 197.

99. DSM-IV, 301.81.

100. James W. Barnard, *Narcissism, Over-Optimism, Fear, Anger, and Depression: The Interior Lives of Corporate Leaders*, 77 U. Cin. L. Rev. 405, 410 (2008) ("The existence of narcissism at this level is no coincidence: successful managers typically exhibit narcissistic personality traits throughout their business careers. Stated another way, narcissism conscientiously deployed often begets success.").

101. Barnard, *supra* note 100, at 410 (2008) ("No matter what their strengths, productive narcissists are incredibly difficult to work for. They don't learn easily from

Even if CEOs (or other high-ranking corporate officials) merely have strong but healthy egos, many of these same effects still exist. Among others, *personal investment* in particular negotiation issues may have an effect on the negotiation. In other words, a negotiator (or her chief constituent) may come to identify the resolution of a particular issue with the maintenance of her self-esteem.[102] (As negotiation godfather Roger Fisher has identified, this may also result from positional—as opposed to principled—bargaining strategies: bargaining over a position may result in a negotiator locking herself into that position.)[103]

Negotiations between organizations feature quasi-rational components more frequently than one-on-one negotiations. Why? First, the social pressures within organizations tend to magnify cognitive errors.[104] In fact, the simple act of deliberating within a group can lead

others. They are oversensitive to any kind of criticism, which they take personally. They bully subordinates and dominate meetings. They don't want to hear about anyone else's feelings. They are distrustful and paranoid. They can become grandiose, especially when they start to succeed. Perhaps their most frustrating quality is that they almost never listen to anyone.").

102. Blakrishnan et al., *supra* note 78, at 647 ("Therefore, in terms of negotiation issues, ego involvement may be defined as a bargainer's perception of a close association between certain issues and his or her self-esteem. The concept of ego involvement may be particularly relevant in the context of intergroup consumption decisions and interorganizational buying and selling where an individual member has championed a specific part of a plan or purchase decision. Under these circumstances, these individuals feel personally responsible for these issues when they are negotiated, and the success or failure of the negotiations with respect to these issues is perceived by them to reflect directly on their self-esteem.").

103. FISHER ET AL., *supra* note 56, at 4 ("When negotiators bargain over positions, they tend to lock themselves into those positions.").

104. Cass R. Sunstein, *Deliberative Trouble? Why Groups Go to Extremes*, 110 YALE L.J. 71, 85 (2000) ("Group polarization is among the most robust patterns found in deliberating bodies, and it has been found in many diverse tasks.") (internal footnotes omitted).

its members to commit certain cognitive errors.[105] And for certain groups that value consensus (such as corporate boards), "groupthink" poses a particular risk.[106]

2.3.3.1 *Practical Implications*

So if these nonrational judgments are all in our heads, how do we counter them? How do we make sure they are not unduly influencing our judgments when we sit down across the table from another party?

The most effective way to prevent these shortcuts from unduly influencing negotiations is to have what some scholars have called a good "outside strategy." An outside strategy is any strategy that gets the negotiator out of her own head, since that is where the anchoring effect is happening.[107]

Consult third parties. The single most important benefit from consulting third parties is not the expertise that they might offer. Instead, it is the fact that they can provide a more objective perspective when the parties themselves may be subject to various cognitive errors or other biases.

Have someone in the room one step removed from the negotiations. Bring in a team member who is familiar with the overall goals and issues but not engaged in the day-to-day discussions. Make his or her job to observe the other side and test team assumptions on key issues.

105. *Id.* at 71, 114 (suggesting strategies to avoid homogeneity of thinking in groups).

106. Stephen M. Bainbridge, *Why a Board? Group Decisionmaking in Corporate Governance*, 55 VAND. L. REV. 1, 32 (2002) ("Highly cohesive groups with strong civility and cooperation norms value consensus more than they do a realistic appraisal of alternatives. In such groups, groupthink is an adaptive response to the stresses generated by challenges to group solidarity.") (internal footnote omitted).

107. *See* Orr & Guthrie, *supra* note 19, at 626.

Do an early test of the other side's position. It is often worthwhile to float a few hypothetical questions or positions to the other side on potential scenarios for how the negotiation will play out. The goal is to uncover if there are any "iron rules" or financial red lines that must be met. If you are clearly far apart, it is better to save both sides time and resources rather than embark on a negotiation that has a very low likelihood of succeeding.

Do your homework. For various negotiations, framing and priming can have a huge effect on the final resolution of the negotiation. To the extent that a party makes an attempt to determine the value of a deal *before* engaging the other side, they will be less influenced by anchoring or other framing effects, because they will already have a frame in place. (For more on effective methods of preparing for a negotiation, see chapter 8.)

Make personal connections where possible. Often the mere act of dealing with a rival feels like too much of a compromise. Particularly in adversarial negotiations, dignifying a complaint with a response can feel like encouraging extortionate behavior. How does one make it past this initial reluctance to negotiate? Harvard Law Professor (and co-founder of the school's Program on Negotiation) Robert Mnookin offers the example of Nelson Mandela, who was able to secure compromises from an all-white South African government by making (and then maintaining) personal connections with individual Afrikaner leaders. Once they had a personal connection to Mandela (as well as a sense of mutual respect), they could, as one described it, "make concessions and yet maintain one's self-respect."[108]

Similarly, the friendly relations between President Wilson and Prime Minister Lloyd George in Paris were based on a conscious effort to build a personal connection between the two men. As Lloyd George

108. MNOOKIN, *supra* note 80, at 133.

explained it, the routine of dining together had immediate political benefits for the negotiation process: "If you meet for social purposes you can raise a point. If you find you are progressing satisfactorily, you can proceed, otherwise you can drop it."[109] In other words, the personal relationship allowed for a low-cost, low-risk way to broach difficult issues.

Build trust early with substantive, mutually beneficial proposals. Trust takes time to earn, and it can be difficult to recover from a deficit of trust. Negotiators who build trust and set a tone of respect from the beginning tend to have a wider range of tools available throughout the course of the negotiation. Those who go negative early tend to significantly limit their options and may in fact create obstacles to completing a negotiation successfully.

Proposing a "win-win" in a negotiation has become a cliché. But experienced business negotiators are aware that making substantive, mutually beneficial proposals can help to build trust. A substantive proposal that addresses major issues and terms sends a signal to one's counterparty that the party is interested in actual progress and leading the process versus reacting to the situation. Moreover, by offering a proposal that focuses in part on the counterpart's goals, a party can show that it listening and is willing to work in good faith. If the proposal comes across as completely one-sided, then there will not be a negotiation because the other side will perceive there is nothing in it for them.

Provide context and data around your proposals (instead of just terms) to show you have listened to their issues and are trying to bridge the challenges. One of the most common mistakes is that a single document is left to do all of the talking. Because there are multiple interconnected issues, it is virtually impossible to have a set of papers convey the different trade-offs and constraints that were taken into account when formulating the proposal. With the context, the

109. MacMillan, *supra* note 34, at Kindle location 864.

other side has the opportunity to counter more intelligently through understanding the reasoning.

Include next steps, even relatively simple ones, to show that you are trying to move the overall process, not just win the negotiation. This both helps the other side see a path and does not require them to figure out where to go next. That may seem strange, but the nature of negotiation is that we are trying to create something that does not already exist. As a result, it is not common that both sides will have comfort and knowledge on how to get from A to Z. Laying out the steps provides a prospective pathway that both sides can walk together.

Use the sources of attraction to your advantage. Few people are motivated only by money. To the extent that negotiators understand the nonmonetary attractions of a deal for different players, they can set the agenda and flow for discussions. Addressing the different constituents' key issues in the right order will allow you to draw in the key players to get the negotiation moving and sustain momentum. Make sure you map these out in advance. While it won't play out exactly as you design, you will have at least thought through the major issues and their interactions with the teams involved and so give you a head start of where you want to steer things during live discussions.

2.4 Conclusion

We all have our way of seeing the world. It has been built up over time, training, and experience. The challenge in any negotiation is that no two people's way of seeing the world is the same. We can look at the same data and draw different conclusions. There is no one right answer. However, part of the art in getting from the negotiation to an agreement is understanding how to deal with these nonrational behaviors and funnel them toward a common end.

Managing two sets of nonrational judgments through a thorny business or legal issue is complicated enough. The challenges multiply when negotiators must face two or more parties across the table, or multiple issues that are interconnected. Dealing with these problems—multiple parties and multiple issues—will serve as the focus for chapters 3 and 4.

3

Multiparty Negotiations

Back in 2005, a Dubai-based company known as DP World bought the London-based Peninsular & Oriental Steam Navigation Company, sometimes called "P&O," for $6.8 billion. It was an unremarkable deal, except that P&O owned the rights to operate six ports in the United States: Baltimore, Miami, New Jersey, New Orleans, New York, and Philadelphia.

Before the ink was dry on the deal, a number of American politicians—including governors Robert Ehrlich (D-Maryland) and John Corzine (D-New Jersey), Senator Chuck Schumer (D-New York), and House Homeland Security Committee Chairman Pete King (R-New York)—had launched noisy protests of the deal; Senator Schumer and Representative King had even promised to introduce legislation that would block the deal before its completion. The fact that the agreement had passed scrutiny by the Committee on Foreign Investment in the United States (CFIUS) did not mollify the politicians. The problem, they claimed, was allowing a firm that was essentially part of a foreign government to own something as strategically vital as American ports.[1] The protests were effective; before a month had passed, DP World had announced it would divest itself of the six ports.[2]

At first, the controversy looked like an unusual outbreak of American xenophobia. Curiously, though, a few months later, Dubai International Capital bought Doncasters Group, an American precision manufacturer that made parts for the U.S. military, and Congress barely paid attention.[3] What changed?

What changed was that Dubai International Capital's deal did not jeopardize the interests of a small Florida steamship company called Eller & Company. Eller & Company was involved in several joint ventures with P&O and was worried about the effect of the buyout. (Ironically, it learned of the deal because DP World, doing its due diligence, had begun early discussion with CFIUS to clear the way for any transaction.) Eller & Company hired a semiretired lobbyist named Joe Muldoon, who began knocking on the doors of various congressional representatives whose constituents might be affected by the deal. He found a willing ear in Chuck Schumer, and the rest, unfortunately for DP World, was history.[4]

In other words, the Dubai ports controversy was not so much a spontaneous outpouring of American nativism as it was the result of a lobbying effort by a disgruntled third party that did not like the deal that was about to be consummated. DP World learned an expensive lesson from its foray into American port administration: it only takes a small objector to derail a very large deal.

1. *America's Ports & Dubai: Trouble on the Waterfront*, THE ECONOMIST, Feb. 23, 2006, *available at* http://www.economist.com/node/5551176/ (last viewed Oct. 10, 2012).

2. *Dubai Seeks to Calm the Storm over Ports*, THE ECONOMIST, Mar. 10, 2006, *available at* http://www.economist.com/node/5620236 (last viewed Oct. 10, 2012).

3. *Buying American Firms: Uncle Sam Says Yes*, THE ECONOMIST, May 4, 2006, *available at* http://www.economist.com/node/6891387 (last viewed Oct. 10, 2012).

4. Peter Overby, *Lobbyist's Last-Minute Bid Set Off Ports Controversy*, NPR, Mar. 8, 2006, *available at* http://www.npr.org/templates/story/story.php?storyId=5252263 (last viewed Oct. 6, 2012).

As the Dubai ports controversy illustrates, negotiations between organizations have strong potential to grow into multilateral negotiations. When large organizations (like corporations) negotiate, they frequently draw the attention of third parties, some foreseeable, some not. In merger negotiations, for example, third parties may be competitors. The same effect occurs when a corporation settles high-stakes tort litigation—in that case, the competition comes from other potential plaintiffs (or sometimes a government agency) rather than other corporations. For example, many public companies may prefer to settle allegations of wrongdoing with a government agency rather than negotiate with plaintiffs' counsel who will extract additional funds for attorneys' fees. In fact, in 2012, several publishing companies pursued just this strategy after they were sued in an antitrust class action accusing them of conspiring to set prices on e-books; rather than negotiate with the firm that filed the complaint, they turned to state attorneys general to cut a deal.[5]

Third parties may also be part of the deal themselves. The 1919 Paris peace negotiations that ended World War I, for example, included many discussions simply among the French, British, and Americans, who believed it important to reach agreement among themselves before engaging the various other parties to the negotiation.[6]

But, in addition to these possibilities, organizations are, by themselves, collections of people. And while some managers might love it if their organizations were monolithic, different individuals in an organization may have different views on how a deal should be conducted, or on which concessions are bearable and which are dealbreakers. Aligning one's own colleagues can be its own challenge. For example, during the negotiations over the raising of the debt limit in 2011,

5. Andrew J. Trask, *Recent Investigations into E-book Price Fixing Illustrate the Growing Acceptance of Government Investigations by Companies Looking to Thwart Follow on Class Actions*, 12(2) E-COMMERCE L. REP. J. 18 (2012).

6. *See generally* MARGARET MACMILLAN, PARIS 1919: SIX MONTHS THAT CHANGED THE WORLD, Kindle (2007).

the parties were not simply the Democrats and the Republicans, but the White House, House Democrats, the Senate Democrats, Speaker of the House John Boehner, and Majority Leader Eric Cantor (who spoke for a large contingent of "Tea Party" Republican representatives).[7] Similarly, many proposed business acquisitions require not just reaching agreement with the other side but also convincing a skeptical board of directors that the deal is in the company's best interest. In 2000, Coca-Cola CEO Douglas Daft tried to buy the popular sports drink brand Gatorade; despite strong reasons to pursue the transaction, his board vetoed the proposal. The opposition to the deal was led by the formidable investor Warren Buffet.[8]

Any transaction large enough will have lots of people negotiating with each other, even if they are ostensibly on the same side. Any executive or any lawyer who has sat on a conference call with co-counsel knows that getting everyone onto the same page can be a negotiation in itself.

In each of these cases, two problems emerge. First, each party must keep track of more information. Second, each party faces an increased risk that there is no agreement that will satisfy everyone who considers herself to have a voice. In those circumstances, the question often becomes which groups one can afford to leave dissatisfied while still preserving a workable agreement.

3.1 Multilateral Negotiations—More People, More Problems

To the extent that negotiations are about the exchange of information, there is no question that adding parties to a negotiation complicates the exchange. First, and most important, the parties have

7. *See generally* BOB WOODWARD, THE PRICE OF POLITICS (2012).

8. *Coke & Quaker Oats: Buffeted*, THE ECONOMIST, Nov. 23, 2000, *available at* http://www.economist.com/node/434161/ (last viewed Oct. 9, 2012).

to make sure the right information gets to the right people. Where there are multiple parties, however, there are several audiences for information that is released, and those audiences will interpret that information in different ways. Shareholders, for example, may have an entirely different view of a corporate acquisition than the firm's management. Similarly, in a class action settlement (like the *Figueroa* litigation discussed in chapter1), the members of the class may have very different opinions of the ultimate settlement terms than their attorneys.

In addition, negotiations involving multiple parties are more complicated to keep track of than binary (one-on-one) negotiations.[9] During the debt-ceiling negotiations in Washington, for example, negotiations among the various politicians got confusing enough that there were at least two (and possibly three) parallel negotiations going on at the same time—between Senate Democrats and Republicans, between President Barack Obama and Speaker John Boehner, and among the bipartisan "Gang of Six"—each involving parties who were not necessarily informed about the other tracks.[10] For game theorists (who often provide important insights into negotiation strategy), modeling a two-party negotiation on its own, while hardly simple, is at least possible. But modeling a multiparty negotiation is exponentially more complex. As political scientist Bruce Bueno de Mesquita has explained:

> All in all, taking all the layers of information being traded back and forth among just these five decision makers, there are 120 possible exchanges or imagined exchanges (that is, 5 factorial, or 5x4x3x2= 120) to know about. Keeping track of

9. *See* James K. Sebenius, *Negotiation Arithmetic: Adding and Subtracting Issues and Parties*, 37 INT'L ORG. 281, 306 (1983) ("It is almost axiomatic that the more parties (and issues), the higher the costs, the longer the time, and the greater the informational requirements for a negotiated settlement.").

10. *See generally* WOODWARD, *supra* note 7.

those 120 possible offers and counteroffers that might be on the table is essential in sorting out what is best to do at any moment in a negotiation.[11]

It is not just the numbers that make a multiparty negotiation complex. Multiparty negotiations are also less stable than two-party negotiations. In other words, in a two-party transaction, as long as both parties understand the concept of rationality, some point of agreement ("equilibrium" in game-theory terms) should be possible.[12] However, as numerous economists have learned, the same is not possible in multiparty negotiations.[13] Adding parties to a negotiation increases the likelihood of a holdout—a participant who sees more to gain from refusing to agree than from reaching a compromise.[14] It also involves a more complicated game, in which bargaining in coalitions is possible.[15] And once bargaining in coalitions becomes

11. BRUCE BUENO DE MESQUITA, THE PREDICTIONEER'S GAME 52 (2009); *see also* Robert H. Mnookin, *Strategic Barriers to Dispute Resolution: A Comparison of Bilateral and Multilateral Negotiations*, 8 HARV. NEGOTIATION L. REV. 1, 2 (2003) ("The axiomatic approach of game theoretical work on 'n-person games' is mathematically daunting, has restricted descriptive power, and makes no claims at offering powerful prescriptive advice for negotiators.") (internal footnotes omitted).

12. Game theorists refer to this as a "Nash equilibrium," where no party can employ a strategy that would improve her position. *See* HERBERT GINTIS, THE BOUNDS OF REASON: GAME THEORY & THE UNIFICATION OF THE BEHAVIORAL SCIENCES 35 (2009).

13. GINTIS, *supra* note 12, at 149 (unlike in two-player game, in three-player game, "mutual knowledge of rationality and beliefs is not sufficient to ensure that a Nash equilibrium will be played").

14. *See, e.g.*, Paola Conconi & Carlo Perroni, *Issue Linkage and Issue Tie-in in Multilateral Negotiations*, 57 J. INT'L ECON. 423, *11 (2002) ("There is a further complication, arising from the non-superadditive structure of the game: when a subset of players form an agreement, it is possible that the payoffs they can obtain are less than the payoffs that are feasible in the absence of the agreement; thus, the fallback position may involve higher payoffs than are possible in the presence of the agreement itself. It is true that, if this is the case, then the corresponding agreement structure could never be stable according to our definition.").

15. Jeffrey T. Polzer et al., *Interest Alignment and Coalitions in Multiparty Negotiation*, 41 ACADEMY OF MGMT. J. 42, 42 (1998) ("Multiparty negotiations are complex social

possible, the number of possible outcomes becomes too complicated for human beings to map out in advance.

While not all parties have the same level of decision-making power or influence, the reality is that most groups have a cultural need to get team members "onboard" with the direction at least so they do not disrupt the flow of negotiations between the overall organizations. Rarely is all decision making deferred to a single individual. As a result, aligning an internal team to have a consistent and coherent position before discussing with the other side is critical. It only gets more complicated when outside parties are brought in to the mix.

Adding parties also adds more opportunities for private information, where certain parties are privy to information no one else knows. This asymmetry in the information available to parties can be valuable in conferring advantage to one side or the other. It also can serve as a distraction, since there is a tendency at the beginning of negotiations to treat all information as equally important. As a result, when there are multiple parties, managing the flow of information will affect how the negotiation proceeds.

3.1.1 Auctions—What's Your Bet on the Future?

Auctions are exciting. They have captured the popular imagination enough that, when discussing the sale of a company, many immediately picture the hordes of corporate executives, fund managers, investment bankers, and lawyers that populated the leveraged buyout of RJR Nabisco in *Barbarians at the Gate*.

Most negotiators, however, prefer to avoid auctions—which we will define as escalating bids from competing parties—if at all possible. While there is no question that they are good for sellers (or for

interactions because of both the multiple sets of preferences that must be considered in fashioning agreements and the interpersonal dynamics that grow increasingly complicated as more people interact. An especially important source of complexity in multiparty negotiations, and one that is the focus of this article, is the inherent potential for coalition membership to influence the negotiated outcomes.").

corporate defendants in litigation), they create a host of complications for all parties concerned.

The most obvious complication for the buyer is that the auction will drive up the price of the target. Buyers also tend to avoid auctions because they understand them encourage nonrational judgments, which may lead to a buyer spending more on a deal than it is worth on paper, solely to win the auction. (This phenomenon is sometimes called the "winner's curse.")[16]

There are two prevailing reasons that a company might choose an auction. The first is that it believes that an auction will fetch the highest possible price for its shareholders. The second is that the value of the company depends on what a prospective buyer believes about its future growth prospects and its associated market, which means different buyers may reach significantly different valuations. Under those circumstances, an auction is an excellent way of sorting among offers from various corporate suitors. These reasons also work in reverse in settling high-stakes litigation, where corporate defendants may conduct *reverse auctions* to settle a lawsuit for the lowest acceptable price, or to get an idea of how different plaintiffs' firms value the litigation.

Are these reasons sound? Auctions may not yield as much price benefit as sellers think. Business professors Audra L. Boone and J. Harold Mulherin examined a sample of 400 takeovers from the 1990s that represented over $1 trillion in deal value. Half of the targets were auctioned among multiple bidders, the other half engaged in negotiations with a single buyer. Contrary to what one might assume, Boone and Mulherin found no difference in the premium that went to shareholders; auctions appeared to provide the same value as a negotiated transaction.[17] This does not mean that auctions never provide more

16. *See, e.g.*, Patrick Bajarl & Ali Hortaçsu, *Economic Insights from Internet Auctions*, 42 J. ECON. LIT. 457, 465 (2004).

17. *See* Audra L. Boone & J. Harold Mulherin, *How Are Firms Sold?*, 62 J. FIN. 847 (2007).

value than a negotiated agreement, but it does mean that sellers need to understand which method is a better fit with their specific circumstances.

Auctions also tend to be effective when there are uncertainties about how much a company (or a lawsuit) is worth. Parties tend to prefer negotiation when there is roughly equal market information and when the firm's performance is relatively consistent. Under those circumstances, a body of data exists that does not require many assumptions or guesses, allowing both sides to engage in a straightforward discussion about value. Assuming that the two parties have familiarity with each other and some base level of trust on genuine interest from both sides, a buyer and seller would be willing to invest in this discussion because it has an equal likelihood of success and sharing of pain on both sides.

Auctions also come with significant drawbacks, even for the seller. In an auction, a bid can cost each of the participants anywhere from hundreds of thousands to millions of dollars just to participate, even if there is a low likelihood of success (though likelihood increases as other bidders are eliminated or drop out).

Sellers tend to prefer this route when there is no clear outlook for the future. These kinds of sellers typically fall into two camps. One camp contains companies with a new technology or capability that has yet to penetrate a market (in some cases, because the market is not yet defined). As a result, it becomes difficult to value the company or the technology; valuation can depend on any number of factors, including the speed of adoption, the profitability of the technology, or the ability of competitors to keep pace with the change. For example, in 2012, Dell wound up in a bidding war to acquire Quest Software. The initial bid for the company, made by a venture capital firm, was $23 per share, or roughly $1.94 billion. Dell's final bid was $28 per share, a total offer of roughly $2.36 billion.[18] Dell's willingness raise

18. Victoria Stilwell & Drew Fitz Gerald, *Dell Wins Bidding War for Quest*, WALL ST. J., July 2, 2012.

its bid—several times in fact—was based on its belief of what the companies could earn once combined.

In the other camp are companies that are struggling or have experienced some material change in their performance. While the industry may be stable and competitive, the company's changed circumstances may make it harder to value. At that point, an auction may help the company determine its final value and also may help offset some of the negative perceptions buyers may have.

In both cases, the purpose of an auction is to allow the seller to uncover those different beliefs about future prospects and identify the buyer who is willing to offer the best terms. The auction process gives each of the bidders access to the same amount of information about the company for sale and then allows each of them to make up their mind on what it is worth to them.

The cost to the seller in the case of an auction is that it may disrupt the value in the existing business. Once employees and customers become aware that the company is for sale, they tend to reevaluate their relationship with the company. Even in a private auction that is not played out on the cover of the *Financial Times* or *Wall Street Journal*, the activities related to a sale can quickly become apparent to people not engaged in the sale process. Information leaks during the process can kill the deal, make it take longer, or reduce its value. We will discuss more of these impacts in chapter 4.

3.1.2 Necessary Third Parties—You Can't Avoid the Tollbooths

"We got to go in and visit the penguin."

—ELWOOD BLUES,

The Blues Brothers (Universal Pictures, 1980)

Sometimes, dealing with a third party in a negotiation is simply unavoidable. Often, in order to complete a negotiation, the parties must get approval from some third party. That approval may be legally required. (For example, U.S. law requires either the Department of Justice's Antitrust Division or the Federal Trade Commission to approve all proposed mergers.)[19] Or, it may simply be necessary as a practical matter. (For example, it is very difficult to buy a large company without financing, either from a bank or from outside investors.)

In these cases, while the third party is not necessarily opposed to consummating a deal, its interests will differ radically from the buyer's or seller's. In a corporate acquisition, for example, a government will be interested in whether the transaction complies with existing laws and rules regarding competition or share concentration, is current with tax obligations, or confers larger social benefits like worker safety or environmental compliance. A bank will be interested in whether the company will return a sufficient profit to support the financing provided.

The kind of third party involved may affect the transaction in various ways. Both banks and government agencies will require paperwork related to the deal. Banks mostly will want financial records and projected revenue and profit models. Government agencies will want paperwork related to the impact on their jurisdiction. The Department of Justice or the Federal Trade Commission will want competitive analyses. The Environmental Protection Agency will require analyses of environmental impact. The Federal Communications Commission will require analyses showing the effect of the deal on media markets.

The kind of third party involved also will affect the speed at which the transaction proceeds. All told, regulatory agencies tend to move more slowly than banks.[20] Companies that need cash (or need to

19. For more on U.S. antitrust law, *see* chapter 6.

20. This would tend to make sense: the bank wishes to make money, and time is of the essence. The government is interested in minimizing public risk; deliberation is more important in that case.

get rid of it) will be in more of a hurry than companies experiencing stable, predictable growth.

Third parties may influence the tactics that negotiators use. For example, if a government third party is involved, a negotiator may have to exercise care in what information it discloses, lest it invite investigation. Similarly, if a party is negotiating with multiple parties who have similar interests (such as multiple mass-tort plaintiffs or multiple distributors), it may find the concessions it makes to one party will affect the concessions it makes to other parties.[21] In the 1919 Paris peace negotiations, for example, British Prime Minister David Lloyd George struggled with whether to acknowledge Poland's claim to the then-German city of Danzig (Gdansk to the Poles); while he recognized the merits of Poland's claim, giving the Poles Danzig might require him to concede Italy's claim to the disputed city of Fiume.[22]

Finally, in some cases, a mediator may be a necessary third party to negotiations. When relations have deteriorated enough that a mediator is necessary, the parties are likely to view the mediator as a separate party with a distinct interest: getting an agreement, any agreement.[23]

3.1.3 Spoilers—The People from Left Field

Spoilers are third parties who have an affirmative interest in blocking or otherwise disrupting the proposed transaction. Sometimes, like the private equity firm KKR in *Barbarians at the Gate* or professional

21. This can also occur in seriatim negotiations, where deals will build on analogous previous deals. *See* Ben Depoorter, *Law in the Shadow of Bargaining: The Feedback Effect of Civil Settlements*, 95 Cornell L. Rev. 957, 960 (2010).

22. MacMillan, *supra* note 6, at Kindle location 4335.

23. Robert Mnookin, Bargaining with the Devil: When to Negotiate & When to Fight 238 (2010).

class action objectors, they are motivated purely by profit.[24] Recognizing that the deal is very important to the participants, spoilers will threaten to derail the ultimate deal (be it a merger or a litigation settlement) unless they are paid to go away.

Sometimes, spoilers act from other motives. Competitors may have an interest in maintaining the current competitive landscape. (Alliances or mergers can be tremendously destabilizing for others in the market.) Sometimes, spoilers may have ideological objections to the proposed transaction. (Political interest groups may not like the environmental effects of a merger; others may not like the policy implications.)

How do spoilers intervene in negotiations? In a transaction like a proposed acquisition, all a competitor must do is offer a competing bid to the seller. The competing bid will end in one of two results: the competitor acquires the company, or an auction ensues, forcing the buyer to pay more than the initially bargained amount. In more regulated transactions, spoilers may appeal to the appropriate governmental body. Competitors to a merging corporation in the United States may seek relief from the Federal Trade Commission or the Department of Justice's Antitrust Division. Objectors in complex litigation may seek to intervene with the appropriate court.[25] Increasingly, spoilers may file litigation of their own. For example, a number of plaintiffs' firms file securities class actions to extract payments from merging corporations.[26]

Spoilers also may intervene by seeking to influence one of the existing parties. Leaving aside the classic competing bid, spoilers may seek to influence shareholders through a proxy battle (that is, seeking

24. *See generally* BRYAN BURROUGH & JOHN HELYAR, BARBARIANS AT THE GATE: THE FALL OF RJR NABISCO (2003); ANDERSON & TRASK, THE CLASS ACTION PLAYBOOK § 8.3.5.

25. *See supra* note 24, at § 8.3.5.

26. *Id.* § 3.1.1 at 63–64 (describing merger class actions); *see also* Robert B. Thompson & Randall S. Thomas, *The New Look of Shareholder Litigation: Acquisition-Oriented Class Actions*, 57 VAND. L. REV. 133, 135 (2004).

control of one party's board of directors) or a derivative suit (a lawsuit brought on shareholder's behalf). Sometimes, in adversarial negotiations, one of the parties will invite in a spoiler. When this occurs in a hostile takeover, the third party may be called a "white knight." This is also becoming an increasingly popular option for class action defendants. When a company faces a class action brought by one firm, it may choose to negotiate with a second firm bringing a competing lawsuit, on the condition that the firm reduce its fee and class demands. (This process is called a "reverse auction.")[27] Alternatively, the defendant may choose to negotiate a settlement with a government agency in order to reduce the amount paid in attorney fees.[28]

3.2 Team Negotiations—I Love My Team/I Hate My Team

"Meetings: None of us is as dumb as all of us."

—DESPAIR.COM

Setting aside true multilateral negotiations, negotiations between organizations also require frequent discussions among multiple parties on each side.[29] Most classical negotiation texts focus on negotiation as a one-on-one exercise, with a single negotiator representing each side.[30] But increasingly, in both complex litigation and

27. Figueroa v. Sharper Image Corp., 517 F. Supp. 2d 1292 (S.D. Fla. 2007).

28. *See, e.g.*, Trask, *supra* note 5, at 18.

29. *See* THOMAS C. SCHELLING, THE STRATEGY OF CONFLICT 28–29 (1980) (discussing strategic complexities involved in negotiating treaties with U.S. executive branch when Congress not in session).

30. *See, e.g.* ROGER FISHER ET AL., GETTING TO YES: NEGOTIATING AGREEMENT WITHOUT GIVING IN 30 (1991); *see also* Nir Halevy, *Team Negotiation: Social, Epistemic, Economic, and Psychological Consequences of Subgroup Conflict*, 34 PERSONAL & SOC.

in complex deal making, there is a team, not an individual, doing the negotiations.[31]

There are solid reasons for favoring negotiating teams. Adding team members adds expertise, increases access to various pieces of information, and allows the team to address more complex tasks than an individual could.[32] As it turns out, diversity is a powerful processing tool, allowing larger numbers of people to solve problems more efficiently in practice than most would believe theoretically possible.[33] This works best when team members actually have diverse backgrounds or areas of expertise; otherwise one may end up with a collection of individuals who do not share work or information.[34]

Negotiating in teams may also check certain cognitive biases that stem from limited information. Having an expert on industry prices, for example, can help inoculate a team against anchoring effects, because the expert's knowledge of pricing can serve as an alternative anchor.[35] Similarly, if one team member is well versed in differences in national or corporate culture, that can reduce the potential for miscommunications between negotiators.

PSYCHOLOGICAL BULLETIN 1687, 1687 (2008) ("Social-psychology models often treat negotiating teams as unitary players, thereby ignoring the possibility of conflicting interests within negotiating teams.").

31. Halevy, *supra* note 30, at 1687 ("Negotiating teams are pervasive in business, politics, international relations, and other domains."); David Sally & Kathleen O'Connor, *Team Negotiations*, 87 MARQ. L. REV. 883, 884 (2004) ("Rather than send a solo negotiator to the table, decision makers may opt to pull together a team to hammer out the terms of a deal.").

32. Sally & O'Connor, *supra* note 31, at 887 ("[W]ith the addition of each new member of the negotiating team, the collective network of colleagues and acquaintances around the team grows. The larger the network, the better the access the team has to information that can help it in its negotiation.").

33. *See* JEFF HOWE, CROWDSOURCING: WHY THE POWER OF THE CROWD IS DRIVING THE FUTURE OF BUSINESS, Kindle location 1764 (2008).

34. Jessica R. Mesmer-Magnus & Leslie A. DeChurch, *Information Sharing and Team Performance: A Meta-Analysis*, 94 J. OF APPLIED PSYCHOLOGY 535, 543 (2009).

35. *See* chapter 2.

Negotiating in teams also spreads out the taxing cognitive demands of negotiation.[36] Making decisions takes energy. This is one reason that busy people may exhibit certain quirks, like eating the same sandwich every day for lunch, or rotating through only a few wardrobe choices. Similarly, knowing that there are other team members who share responsibility for a negotiation's outcome can reduce the stress any individual negotiator experiences. To the extent stress can induce errors in judgment, avoiding it will promote better outcomes.

Negotiating in teams also allows for certain tactics that are not available to solo negotiators: for example, it is extremely difficult for a single individual to engage in back-channel fact-finding.

The benefit from negotiation in teams is greater access to wider knowledge.[37] A well-selected team will know more things about the deal and the organization, because it will draw on experts from different areas within the organization. (Done well, this is also one way to fight against authoritarian bias. If team members are recognized experts in different areas, they may be less likely to defer to a single source.)

However, team negotiations also bring certain drawbacks. Some of these are logistical. Teams may face problems simply coordinating schedules. But more important, teams may face problems coordinating information.[38] The problem is that the team's knowledge is scattered among individuals. And, as anyone who has ever worked in a large organization will tell you, gathering knowledge from individuals presents a logistical challenge. Simply gathering the right people

36. Sally & O'Connor, *supra* note 31, at 884.

37. Mesmer-Magnus & DeChurch, *supra* note 34, at 535 ("A primary advantage of using small groups and teams in these situations is to expand the pool of available information, thereby enabling groups to reach higher quality solutions than could be reached by any one individual. Still, superior solutions to complex decision tasks require members to effectively integrate unique, relevant, and often diverse informational sets.").

38. Kristin Behfar et al., *The Team Negotiation Challenge: Defining and Managing the Internal Challenges of Negotiating Teams*, Working Paper at 9 (available at http://ssrn.com/abstract=1298512) ("A common challenge in this meta-category revolved

in a single room can take multiple communications and a noticeable investment of time. (There are techniques that can be used to mitigate this problem; they often go by the term "knowledge management.") Moreover, it is not always clear what information is necessary from each team member to get a negotiation done.

But even when interorganizational negotiations do not attract third-party competitors, they can still be characterized as multiparty negotiations. Different people in an organization each care about different issues.[39] This is true even on the team level. Because teams are composed of multiple individuals, they also face the same problems as one finds in other multilateral negotiations. Namely, different team members may have different agendas. To begin with, the lead negotiator may have different goals than the stated team goals, ranging from improving personal standing to pursuing an individual idea of the best possible outcome.[40]

Often team members are also accountable to different internal constituents with different expectations from the negotiation (deal developers may report to the head of corporate development while lawyers report to the general counsel).[41] Where a team may include outside consultants or counsel, some members may be motivated

around getting the right information to the table in time for adequate planning for the negotiation.").

39. *See* SCHELLING, *supra* note 29, at 29 (noting that agents in negotiations have independent set of incentives); Stephen E. Weiss, *Analysis of Complex Negotiations in International Business*, 4 ORG. SCI. 269, 269 (1993) (negotiations over telecommunications equipment "tend to involve 'a large number of parts that interact in a nonsimple way': many individual actors, several sets of issues within overall agenda, various arenas of activity, and numerous other factors.") (internal citation omitted).

40. Robert D. Putnam, *Diplomacy & Domestic Politics: The Logic of Two-Level Games*, 42 INT'L ORG. 427, 457 (1988).

41. Halevy, *supra* note 30, at 1687 ("Competition within negotiating teams results from the fact that while all team members have a common interest in achieving the goals set by their organization as a whole, different team members are also committed to the unique interests of different constituencies (subgroups) within the organization.").

by separate incentives, such as professional reputation or fee structure.[42] Finally, because negotiation teams involve multiple people, using them increases the chances of derailing a negotiation because of old-fashioned interpersonal conflict.[43] (We discussed these issues in greater depth in chapter 2.)

Nor can negotiating teams allow either principled or personality-based conflicts to fester. Teams that struggle with internal conflict tend to extract less value from negotiations and the long-term implementation of any agreement.[44] They also can suffer other consequences organizations would prefer to avoid.[45]

3.3 Negotiations with Organizational Constituents—Behind the Table

Most organizations have some form of constituency to which negotiators must report. Lawyers should recognize this issue immediately: after all, no matter how experienced a lawyer is at negotiating,

42. Burrough & Helyar, *supra* note 24, at 484 ("'Listen, Ross, they have their own reasons for doing this other than just buying the company,' he explained. He mentioned the $200 million in upfront fees Shearson would reap from a successful deal. He talked about the unmatched franchise benefits it would reap from having completed history's largest LBO. Johnson's problem was that he insisted on thinking in terms of the real world, real money, real investments. In effect, Goldstone said, this wasn't the real world. This was Wall Street.").

43. *See, e.g.*, Kristin Behfar et al., *The Team Negotiation Challenge: Defining and Managing the Internal Challenges of Negotiating Teams*, Working Paper 12 (available at http://ssrn.com/abstract=1298512).

44. Halevy, *supra* note 30, at 1694 ("The results of this experiment show that subgroup conflict has a detrimental effect on economic outcomes in team negotiation. Specifically, subgroup conflict decreased the teams' ability to implement mutually beneficial trade-offs (i.e., employ logrolling) vis-à-vis the other team, thus causing both parties to leave value on the bargaining table.").

45. *Id.* at 1696 ("Subgroup conflict had significant negative effects on group identification (social consequences) and internal consensus, and an enhancing effect on informational complexity (epistemic consequences).").

she must always report back to her client. But lawyers are not the only negotiators who find themselves answerable to constituents. Corporations, for example, have boards of directors.

More often, negotiations between only two organizations are, in a very real sense, multiparty negotiations. In that case, the additional parties are not third parties but interests within each organization. For example, once a solo negotiator reaches an agreement on behalf of an organization, she often must have that agreement ratified by her constituents, either by executives or the board of directors.[46] This need for ratification has an immediate effect on both parties in the current negotiation, turning any attempt at agreement into a "two-level game," where the negotiator must simultaneously concede enough across the table to keep discussion possible, while standing firm enough on certain issues to satisfy her constituents.[47] These difficulties are not limited to corporate acquisitions; they can occur in trade negotiations, labor negotiations,[48] and peace negotiations.[49] Nor is a negotiator constrained only by her own constituents; her counterpart has constituents as well.

As a result, parties will often pay attention to how one's constituents act, when those actions are easily observable. During the 1919

46. *See, e.g.*, Stephen M. Bainbridge, *Why a Board? Group Decisionmaking in Corporate Governance*, 55 VAND. L. REV. 33 (2002). For more on the legal background to ratifying deals with boards, *see* chapter 6.

47. Putnam, *supra* note 40, at 427, 434 ("The politics of many international negotiations can usefully be conceived as a two-level game. At the national level, domestic groups pursue their interests by pressuring the government to adopt favorable policies, and politicians seek power by constructing coalitions among those groups. At the international level, national governments seek to maximize their own ability to satisfy domestic pressures, while minimizing the adverse consequences of foreign developments."); *see also* MNOOKIN, *supra* note 23, at 133 ("The first tension is between what is going on *across the table* with your adversary and what is happening *behind the table* among your constituents.") (emphasis in original).

48. Charles J. Hunt, Jr., *Mediator Tactics: Strategies and Behaviors Utilized in Labor-Management Negotiations*, 6 APPALACHIAN J. L. 263, 267 (2007).

49. MNOOKIN, *supra* note 23, at 107 (Nelson Mandela "faced other pitfalls behind the table. What authority did he have to make such a monumentous decision on

Paris peace negotiations, for example, the nation of Hungary often found itself at a disadvantage because the Hungarian government had demonstrated its instability by announcing sensational but unenforceable policies like the prohibition of alcohol and mandatory baths for all children.[50] Observers of the regime knew it was unpopular and growing more so with each new "reform," making it difficult to trust it could follow through on any commitments it made. (It could not; ultimately neighboring Romania and Czechoslovakia both invaded, forcing further territorial concessions.)[51]

Often, a party must first engage in an internal negotiation with its constituents before it can turn to negotiating with its outside counterparty. As negotiation consultants David Lax and James Sibelius describe it, this is part of a larger "negotiation campaign" that a party must engage in with all possible counterparties. The negotiation campaign comprises a sequence of negotiations—some internal, some external—that ideally will bring about the desired big deal. Among the various fronts that a negotiator might have to navigate are the "internal front" that includes her clients or superiors; the "regulatory front" that includes appropriate governing authorities; and the "litigation front" that includes lawyers who might wish to interfere with a deal or sue a company for alleged wrongdoing.[52]

As political scientist Robert Putnam, one of the first scholars to formally address this problem, observed:

> The political complexities for the players in this two-level game are staggering. Any key player at the international table who is dissatisfied with the outcome may upset the

behalf of the ANC? None. The ANC was run collectively; no single leader could make decisions by fiat.").

50. MacMillan, *supra* note 6, at Kindle location 5275.

51. *Id.* at Kindle location 5313.

52. *See* David A. Lax & James K. Sebenius, *From Single Deals to Negotiation Campaigns*, Harv. Bus. School Working Paper No. 12-046 (Dec. 17, 2011), *available at* http://ssrn.com/abstract=1974610 (last viewed Oct. 10, 2012).

> game board, and conversely, any leader who fails to satisfy his fellow players at the domestic table risks being evicted from his seat. On occasion, however, clever players will spot a move on one board that will trigger realignments on other boards, enabling them to achieve otherwise unattainable objectives.[53]

In other words, negotiations that involve constituencies (like those on behalf of organizations) present both problems and opportunities that are not present in negotiations between individuals. These problems and opportunities will vary in part depending on who the constituents are.

3.3.1 Board of Directors

Every corporation has a board of directors. The board's primary function is to supervise management and ensure it is acting in the best interests of its shareholders.[54] Boards are typically composed of businesspeople themselves, either currently employed or retired.[55] In the case of closely held corporations, board members may even be family members.[56] Some boards also choose to have members who have special expertise. Leading academics knowledgeable about areas of technical importance to the company or former politicians

53. Putnam, *supra* note 40, at 434.

54. Bainbridge, *supra* note 46, at 33.

55. *See, e.g.*, Gantler v. Stephens, 965 A.2d 695, 699 (Del. 2009) (board of Trans Union comprised corporate officers of company, president of local heating and air-condition company, and principal of local law firm); Lyondell Chem. v. Ryan, 970 A.2d 235, 237 (Del. 2009) ("Lyondell's other ten directors were independent and many were, or had been, CEOs of other large, publicly-traded companies.").

56. *See, e.g.*, *In re* U.S. Sugar Corp. Litig., 669 F. Supp. 2d 1301, 1307–308 (S.D. Fla. 2009) ("U.S. Sugar is a privately held corporation founded by Charles Stewart Mott and it is largely controlled by his descendants. Defendant William S. White, the Chair of the Board of Directors, married one of Mott's granddaughters.").

and civil servants with experience in government procurement or regulatory practices are examples of this expertise. These board members are subject to the same cognitive limitations that we discussed in chapter 2.[57]

Corporate boards of directors are more likely to be risk averse than other components of an organization. There are several reasons for this. First, the board owes a legal duty of care to the corporation and shareholders.[58] But the board also faces a possibility of liability that may dampen its appetite for risk.[59] Corporations will carry directors and officers insurance (D&O insurance) in the event of liability for decisions made on behalf of the corporation that sparks a shareholder lawsuit.

Board decisions may involve even more parties. For example, many boards retain third-party consultants to advise on major decisions; in part because consultants can be useful, in part because third-party advisers may help reduce legal liability.[60] These consultants may be providing input on a range of issues, potentially including the fairness of a value of an acquisition, the likely impact of a lawsuit, or the compensation of company officers. Of course, additional advisers will bring their own agendas and priorities.[61]

57. James W. Barnard, *Narcissism, Over-Optimism, Fear, Anger, and Depression: The Interior Lives of Corporate Leaders*, 77 U. CIN. L. REV. 405, 405 (2008) ("More specifically, corporate directors are not merely economic actors; they are complex, multifaceted, imperfect human beings. They are also highly successful, competitive, and proud individuals. As such, they may enjoy a sense of infallibility and entitlement, and suffer from an inability to recognize their own failings. This confluence of characteristics can lead to dysfunctional boards.").

58. For more on the legal regime that regulates the actions a board may take, *see* chapter 6.

59. Bainbridge, *supra* note 46, at 42.

60. Charles M. Elson, *The Duty of Care, Compensation, and Stock Ownership*, 62 U. CIN. L. REV. 649, 683 (1995) (noting growth in use of third-party consultants once courts ruled use of consultants helped board qualify as "informed" under business judgment rule). For more on the business judgment rule, *see* chapter 6.

61. *Id.* at 684–85.

3.3.2 Lawyer-Client Relationship

Lawyers rarely negotiate on their own behalf (aside from taking their assignments). Instead, they represent clients, which means that any negotiation with lawyers becomes a multiparty negotiation very quickly. There are some limited exceptions to this general tendency. In some cases, lawyers may have full authority to negotiate without consulting their clients about the final arrangement. In others, they may have authorization to negotiate to a certain monetary amount. In most complex negotiations, however, lawyers will have to consult their clients at critical points.

The lawyer-client relationship carries with it certain duties. Among those are a duty of loyalty, a duty of care (enforceable by, among other things, malpractice laws), a duty to keep communications with the client confidential, and a duty to communicate offers to the client during settlement negotiations. Some of these duties are legally enforceable (meaning the client may sue if the lawyer does not meet them). Some of them are matters of professional responsibility (the lawyer will be disciplined by her bar association if she does not meet them). Lawyers also have a duty of candor, meaning they are not supposed to lie, even during negotiations. While different courts have interpreted this duty in different ways, most lawyers retain the ability to at least bluff.[62]

3.3.3 Shareholders

Finally, in some corporations, individual shareholders or shareholder blocs may have both distinct interests and the power to protect them, even at the expense of other internal factions.[63] For example, institutional investors or hedge funds may have

62. For more on these various legal duties, *see* chapter 6.

63. Paul Rose, *Common Agency & the Public Corporation*, 63 VAND. L. REV. 1355, 1359 (2010).

distinct opinions about a firm's overall strategy, the structure of the company's portfolio, or the performance of the management team. These shareholders or groups will use various means to achieve their ends, including formal corporate governance tools like resolutions at the annual shareholders' meeting or submitting an alternate slate of candidates for the board of directors. Less formally, though no less powerful, these blocs can use the media to bring public pressure on the management team to make the desired changes. Finally, shareholders may threaten to take over the company themselves. Billionaire Kirk Kerkorian, for example, tried to influence Chrysler's corporate strategy by participating in a leveraged buyout of the company.[64]

Finally, shareholders may try to influence corporate policy by engaging in either shareholder derivative suits or class actions. Shareholder-driven class actions tend to be lawyer-driven because most shareholders find them counterproductive: they mostly relocate money from the company to the shareholders while paying a 33 percent "lawyer tax" along the way.[65] Derivative suits, by contrast, are actions on behalf of the corporation against officers, directors, or third parties.[66] Consequently, shareholders may use derivative suits to force the corporation to pursue policies the officers or directors may not want.

3.3.4 The Other Side's Constituents

A negotiator must also be concerned with her counterpart's constituents. This may seem counterintuitive at first: her counterpart must answer to those constituents, not her. But to the extent those

64. Bill Vlasic & Bradley A. Stertz, Taken for a Ride: How Daimler-Benz Drove Off with Chrysler 2 (2009).

65. *See, e.g.*, Lynn Bai et al., *Lying and Getting Caught: An Empirical Study of the Effect of Securities Class Action Settlements on Targeted Firms*, 158 U. Pa. L. Rev. 1877 (2010) (describing "circularity problem" to securities class actions).

66. *Ross v. Bernhard*, 396 U.S. 531, 534 (1970).

constituents wield a veto over any agreement—or even just the ability to make an agreement more difficult to reach—they have significant leverage over the negotiation. If her counterpart's constituents are willing to accept a range of possible outcomes, then she has the leverage to bargain for a better deal.[67] Conversely, if the counterpart's constituents are not disposed to agree to many possible results, then the counterpart has more leverage.[68]

In addition, an awareness of these constituents' wants or needs may allow a negotiator to shape a deal that will be ratified by both sides. And, in certain situations, it may also allow a negotiator to go "over the head" of a particularly difficult counterpart.

At the end of the day, both sides need to "sell" the result of the negotiation to their side. This includes both the formal approvals as well as the broader group of stakeholders. If the negotiation result is so deeply unpopular with these constituents that it makes implementation of the agreement either unworkable or significantly less valuable, then the negotiation yielded little.

3.4 Practical Applications

Keep the number of parties down where possible. Since negotiations become more complicated the more parties there are, the simplest advice is to just keep a given negotiation to the minimum number of people. This advice is simple, but not easy. Sometimes third parties are necessary (other times they just show up uninvited). Sometimes constituents demand representation at the table. And often a deal is just too large for a single individual to keep it all in his head. Nonetheless, to the extent that one can limit the number of people sitting across the table, it is generally a good idea.

67. Putnam, *supra* note 40, at 440.

68. *Id.* at 440.

One method of keeping the number down is to make the negotiation personal. To the extent that a negotiator can forge personal connections with the negotiators on the other side (or with third parties), she can often reduce the extent to which the negotiation feels like a multiparty one. A negotiator can often accomplish this by creating trust across the table, or by creating some alternate method of communicating, like back-channels.[69]

Another method is to group parties when possible. Corporate defendants in mass-tort lawsuits have developed settlement matrices, where certain material facts (such as the injury suffered or the distance from an environmental hazard) will determine the settlement offer. Business negotiations that deal with multiple parties will often include a "most favored nations" clause to assure their counterparts they are receiving a good deal. The most favored nation clause also confers a benefit on the granting party: it has fewer terms to track in its various negotiations.

Use sound knowledge management. The largest drawback to using a negotiating team is keeping everyone on the same page. The various participants in the 2011 debt negotiations, for example, had so many parallel tracks with so many different negotiators, that it was often difficult for even the principals to keep track of who had agreed to what.[70] Organizations that have speedy and reliable methods of sharing knowledge with their own people are better equipped to take advantage of the benefits of a team without falling prey to the problems.

Get buy-in before showing up. To the extent that a negotiator may prove unable to limit the number of people at the table, she still may be able to ensure that they at least speak with one voice. Hence, early discussions with one's own side can be critically important to making sure that everyone is on the same page. Many corporations that repeatedly engage in complex negotiations may have prearranged

69. For more on these various techniques, *see* chapters 2 and 10.

70. *See, e.g.*, WOODWARD, *supra* note 7, Kindle location 3734.

procedures that they use to encourage buy-in from the right people.[71] Moreover, it may be worthwhile to have methods of ensuring buy-in at the negotiation itself from various team members.

Pay attention to the team during the negotiation. Good teams make for good negotiations. Bad teams make for bumpy ones. So what makes for a good negotiating team? Ideally, it includes people with diverse information, people who can represent different interests within an organization, and people who work well together. That, of course, is an ideal that is not always achievable. That said, there are ways to make sure that a negotiation team maximizes its strengths and minimizes its weaknesses.[72]

Figure out the decision rule. When there are multiple parties in a negotiation, figuring out how to make decisions can be crucial. On one end, parties can strive for unanimity, which tends to make agreements very stable, but very rare. Since any individual can veto a unanimous decision, the incentive for less influential negotiators to play holdout can be very strong. One of us (Trask) once defended a complex fraud lawsuit involving eighty-five individual plaintiffs, who had all decided that despite their varying circumstances, they would only accept a settlement that treated them all equally. The client (who was not responsible for the fraud) could not settle the case for the absolute maximum damages times eighty-five people, but the plaintiffs with the worst injuries would veto any deal that offered less. While the case eventually did settle, it took extra months of painful and costly litigation, and the plaintiffs' eventually abandoning their "all-for-one" rule.

At the other end of the spectrum is simple majority rule, which allows for faster agreements but can create agreements with substantial dissatisfied minorities. In the middle area are a number of other ways to arrive at a final decision, from other rules (supermajority, ratification by a steering committee) to fuzzier concepts like consensus.

71. For more on these procedures, *see* chapters 8 and 10.

72. For more, *see* chapters 8 and 10.

Consensus, which negotiating scholar Robert Mnookin defines as "when everyone agrees they can live with whatever is proposed, after every effort has been made to meet the interests of the parties,"[73] is particularly valuable because it tends to be the default in many multiparty negotiations. Moreover, striving for consensus on a given side can reduce some of the problems that arise from majority rules and create a greater sense of trust in the negotiators who actually sit at the table. Unfortunately, consensus is extremely difficult to reach, especially if the parties are polarized in any way.

The sooner the parties can work out how to arrive at final decisions, the smoother the negotiation should progress. If parties have difficulty reaching some kind of rule, however rough, that provides important information all by itself.

Reinforce the value of cooperation to your own side. In complex negotiations, particularly ones that begin from an adversarial stance, both parties must deal with disgruntled (and possibly polarized) constituents back home. And, as Robert Mnookin points out, no matter how skilled the negotiator is, if her constituents do not understand the importance of compromise, there will be no agreement. His suggestion? Continually reinforce the benefits of any compromise with your constituents. As he reported after mediating a particularly difficult labor dispute:

> I have a much deeper understanding of how difficult it is to change the negotiation culture of an organization. It requires not simply initial "buy-in" but constant reinforcement.... Without this reinforcement, their natural fears—the negative traps—may reappear.[74]

This continual reinforcement can be as simple as providing regular updates via e-mail or conference call.

73. Mnookin, *supra* note 23, at 201.

74. *Id.* at 208.

3.5 Conclusion

Complex negotiations are complex largely because they invariably involve many different parties with many different agendas. As mathematicians have demonstrated, the more people involved in a negotiation, the more challenging it is to reach a common agreement. But that does not mean that common agreements are not possible. Relying on negotiation teams, figuring out the decision rules for negotiations, and finding methods for keeping all parties informed of the progress of the agreement can help to corral side discussions or parallel negotiations. And having clear goals and good alternatives can help deter third parties whose primary goal is to spoil a deal or turn it into a competitive auction.

One issue that we have alluded to, but not discussed yet, is that additional parties will frequently bring with them additional issues to be negotiated, adding another layer of complexity. In the next chapter, we will explore the further complications that occur when a negotiation requires choices among multiple options or decisions on multiple issues.

4

Multiple Decisions

Perhaps no lawsuits have posed a greater threat to the workings of the American justice system than asbestos claims. The history of asbestos litigation, as one set of judges described it, was

> a tale of danger known in the 1930s, exposure inflicted upon millions of Americans in the 1940s and 1950s, injuries that began to take their toll in the 1960s, and a flood of lawsuits beginning in the 1970s.[1]

For decades, asbestos was used as a fireproofing material and was considered safe to be used in offices and homes. After it was discovered that asbestos significantly heightened the risk of contracting mesothelioma, the courts were swamped with cases. The cases were—by themselves—complicated, involving investigations into

1. Amchem Prods. Inc. v. Windsor, 521 U.S. 591, 598 (1997) (quoting REPORT OF THE JUDICIAL CONFERENCE AD HOC COMMITTEE ON ASBESTOS LITIGATION 2–3 (Mar. 1991).).

where exposure occurred, inquiries into plaintiffs' medical histories, and legal questions about how to recover money from bankrupt or long-defunct firms. The flood of lawsuits posed a logistical challenge to the U.S. court system, a financial disaster for the defendant companies, and a lucrative opportunity to anyone who could figure out how to resolve all of the claims in a single process.

Several groups of lawyers tried. One set of plaintiffs' attorneys tried to resolve all asbestos cases that had been transferred to multidistrict litigation in the Eastern District of Pennsylvania. (Multidistrict litigation is a judicial tool for coordinating multiple cases that arise involving the same subject matter, even if they are filed in different federal jurisdictions.) The lawyers were able to resolve many of the claims that had already been filed (what are often called "inventory claims" because they resided in a law firm's inventory of claims).

This negotiation was ambitious in scope: it sought to resolve not only all cases that had already been transferred to the Eastern District, but all future asbestos-related lawsuits as well. As a result, the lawyers sought to resolve various kinds of claims, including:

- claims on behalf of people who had been exposed to asbestos and had died;
- claims on behalf of people who had been exposed to asbestos and were suffering from mesothelioma or other illnesses;
- claims on behalf of people who had been exposed but had not yet exhibited any adverse symptoms;
- claims on behalf of any relatives of those who had died from asbestos exposure.

The end result of these negotiations was a class action settlement. It was a bold idea at the time because until then there had been no class action lawsuit. Instead, the parties put together a complaint, an answer, and a 100-page stipulation of settlement that described how the parties would administer the various claims and included a compensation schedule for those claimants who met defined exposure and medical criteria. The schedule covered various medical conditions, including mesothelioma, lung cancer, other cancers like colorectal or stomach cancer, and various "non-malignant conditions" like asbestosis (chest pain and shortness of breath attributable to asbestos fibers) and bilateral pleural thickening (scarring or calcification of the lining of the lungs). It also contained a procedure for dealing with "exceptional" medical cases.[2]

As impressive as the settlement stipulation was, when the parties presented it for final approval, it drew a number of objections.[3] Objectors criticized the distribution of awards, the levels of compensation for certain conditions, the lack of compensation for other conditions, the lack of any damages for medical monitoring (a legal cause of action in some states that provides the cost of going to the doctor to monitor a possible medical problem), and even the way in which the agreement accounted for inflation.[4] They also raised questions about whether the plaintiffs' attorneys faced conflicts of interest in negotiating the new settlement.[5]

The trial court approved the settlement over these objections, but the objectors appealed. Eventually, the case made its way to the U.S. Supreme Court. Both the Third Circuit Court of Appeals and the Supreme Court vacated the settlement. They had a number of reasons for doing so, but the primary reason was that the proposed settlement was the most "sprawling" it had seen, meaning that—in class action parlance—individual issues in each claim would predominate over issues that were common to the entire class.[6] Most important,

2. Amchem, 521 U.S. at 603.

3. For more on the approval process for class action settlements, *see* chapter 6.

4. Amchem 521 U.S. at 606.

5. *Id.* at 608.

6. *Id.* at 591, 624.

the differing issues raised by the settlement created conflicts within the class itself. As the Court wrote:

> In significant respects, the interests of those within the single class are not aligned. Most saliently, for the currently injured, the critical goal is generous immediate payments. That goal tugs against the interest of exposure-only plaintiffs in ensuring an ample, inflation-protected fund for the future.[7]

The settlement scuttled, the litigants went back to fighting out the cases in court. To this day, many courts preside over dockets filled with asbestos lawsuits.[8]

In the years since the Supreme Court's opinion, the case, *Amchem Products, Inc. v. Windsor*, has become one of the definitive opinions in class action litigation. Its influence extends far beyond class action settlements; defendants cite it regularly to oppose class actions that they wish to defeat in court. The reason the opinion has proved so popular with defense counsel in these cases is that it highlights the difficulties with trying to address too many issues in a single agreement. At some point, doing so neglects very real side issues that will cause later complications.

Complex negotiations do not just involve multiple partners competing over a single issue. (If they did, they would just be auctions.) Instead, most complex negotiations involve multiple decisions as well as multiple parties. This chapter will discuss two distinct but related issues: deciding among multiple options and deciding among multiple issues. In expanding a negotiation to multiple issues, an organization

7. *Id.* at 626. Technically, this language refers to the "adequacy of representation" requirement of Rule 23, but for our purposes, the adequacy problems clearly arose from the diversity of issues in the settlement.

8. *See, e.g.*, Mark Behrens et al., *Asbestos "Magnet" Courts Alter Procedures: More Changes on the Horizon*, 27(8) MEALY'S LITIG. REPORT 1 (May 16, 2012) (discussing procedures for asbestos dockets in Philadelphia, Pennsylvania, Madison County, Illinois, San Francisco Superior Court, California).

takes on strategic problems that do not exist when two parties haggle over the price of a used car.[9]

Multiple issues can sometimes make negotiations easier, allowing agreement on low-hanging fruit while saving more difficult issues for later.[10] But more often, they are a complicating factor in the negotiation. Much of the complexity in multi-issue negotiations stems from the fact that parties may value issues differently. (In analytic terms, certain issues have greater *salience* for certain parties.)[11] While these additional issues may offer some opportunity for agreement (one party may concede on its second most important issue to gain ground on its most important one), they also add a significant risk of confusing parties and offer more places for a contentious negotiation to break down.

These complexities are compounded in multilateral negotiations, where each additional party (or even just each additional team member) brings its own issues to the table.[12] Just as adding parties exponentially complicates any attempt to understand all of the various potential alliances at work, adding issues complicates that same inquiry along a different dimension.[13]

9. THOMAS SCHELLING, THE STRATEGY OF CONFLICT 30 (1960) (discussing strategic challenges posed by intersecting negotiations and by continuous negotiations about multiple issues over time).

10. *See, e.g.*, ROGER FISHER ET AL., GETTING TO YES: NEGOTIATING AGREEMENT WITHOUT GIVING IN 70 (1991) (recommending negotiators "'fractionate' your problem into smaller and perhaps more manageable units").

11. BRUCE BUENO DE MESQUITA, THE PREDICTIONEER'S GAME, Kindle location 1203 (2009).

12. *See, e.g.*, Paola Conconi & Carlo Perroni, *Issue Linkage and Issue Tie-in in Multilateral Negotiations*, 57 J. INT'L ECON. 423, *8 (2002) ("The concept of Stable Agreement Structure appears to be a natural extension of similar equilibrium concepts that have been described for games of coalition formation; as is the case for these analogous solution concepts, existence of an equilibrium may in general be problematic. In practice, the concept of Stable Agreement Structure may also be difficult to operationalize owing to the large number of potential objections and counterobjections that are involved.").

13. DE MESQUITA, *supra* note 11, Kindle location 1297.

Adding multiple issues (or multiple options) changes the mix of information available to negotiators. Instead of looking for a fixed point (the best price for the car), now the negotiators are looking for the best package of features. (The price for the car plus the length of the warranty.) In fact, this is how many car dealers negotiate in real life: they do not push on the price, they push on additional features that add to their profit margins. The problem is, it takes time (and usually other resources as well) to identify the best package, far more than it does to just identify the best price on something. Since many options will not be fungible, the "best package" for a given negotiation will vary from party to party.

4.1 Multiple Options

Everyone says they like having options. More options means more freedom. More options also means more routes to agreement, assuming that more than one package of options is within the zone of agreement.

4.1.1 More Options, More Problems

Options also have distinct drawbacks: because options are choices, choosing one option often means forgoing others. As a result, having too many options may paralyze negotiators or force them into making bad decisions. Introducing multiple options may change the way in which negotiators think about a deal in yet another way. Behaviorists in almost every discipline have documented a phenomenon called "decision regret": when there are multiple options on the table, choosing one means rejecting others; and rejecting options—any options—carries with it a cost of its own.[14] In other words,

14. *See* Chris Guthrie, *Panacea or Pandora's Box?: The Cost of Options in Negotiation*, 88 Iowa L. Rev. 601, 635 (2003).

the mere presence of options creates a cost.[15] (This is related to the problem of *loss aversion* as discussed in chapter 2. In fact, avoiding hard decisions in order to avoid forgoing some options is sometimes referred to as *regret aversion*.)

Decision regret. What is decision regret? "For every yes there must be a no. To decide one thing always means to relinquish something else. As one therapist commented to an indecisive patient, 'Decisions are very expensive, they cost you everything else.' Renunciation invariably accompanies decision. One must relinquish options, often options that will never come again."[16] In other words, decision regret is an extreme form of buyer's remorse. The more options there are in a negotiation, the more likely the negotiator will be dissatisfied with her decision, because she will be looking back at those options she decided against with rose-colored glasses.

Option devaluation. Basically, the more options one offers, the less attractive any option will seem. As Professor Chris Guthrie puts it, "Because the process of comparison brings to mind the relative advantages and disadvantages of the options under consideration, and because each option's disadvantages are likely to loom larger than its advantages, loss aversion implies that comparisons will decrease the attractiveness of every option under consideration."[17]

Context dependence. Context dependence is a more generalized form of a person's first cost, context dependence means that negotiators do not evaluate options in a vacuum; instead, they compare them against the other options they face. (See how that includes the first "option cost"?) As Professor Guthrie writes, "Psychologists have discovered, however, that people's assessments of initially considered options are often systematically influenced by the emergence of an additional, irrelevant option. People 'make context-based inferences about the worth of alternatives whether or not the context provides

15. *See id.* at 605.

16. *See id.* at 601.

17. *See id.*

a valid basis for such inferences.'"[18] This effect means that once there are multiple options on the table, it becomes easier to manipulate your counterpart's decisions by introducing options that—while not strictly relevant—will sway them toward options more favorable to you, either by making them seem more attractive by contrast, or by making them seem like a reasonable compromise.

Noncompensatory decision making. This is a way of saying that, when confronted with lots of options, people do not act like rational maximizers. As Professor Guthrie writes: "When several options are available, negotiators may make decisions based not on an evaluation of all available information (compensatory decision making), but rather on the basis of a simplified decision-making process (non-compensatory decision making)."[19] (We discussed a number of these effects in chapter 2.) It's worth noting that Guthrie may be underestimating their effects. Noncompensatory decision making occurs frequently, not just when one is confronted with multiple options.

When confronted with multiple options in a negotiation, it is worth consulting a neutral, relatively objective third party. The third party may not be more "rational" than other human beings, but the third party won't be as invested in the specific decision, and that should provide the detached double-check the negotiator needs.

4.1.2 Filtering

Inventing new options may also signal information about one's intentions. Every action a person takes leaves information behind, and negotiating is primarily achieved by selectively revealing information to the other side. If a party introduces new options into a negotiation, it may signal that one deal is more important than it had let on; or that the deal is about something different than its

18. *See id.*

19. *See id.*

counterpart thought.[20] (Game theorists refer to this as "private information.") Sometimes that extra information can help both sides. (It may help negotiators who are looking to "create value," for example.) Other times, however, it may compromise the party's strategic goals. If, for example, it becomes clear that a party wants a deal for the access to a market rather than the cash it will generate, the counterparty will have the leverage to raise or lower the overall price of the deal.

4.1.3 Information Leaks

A 2009 study[21] by Intralinks and the Cass Business School suggests that fewer than half (49 percent) of all leaked deals complete, compared with 72 percent of nonleaked transactions. Additionally, the premium paid by the winner in a leaked deal appears to be on average 13 percent lower than in nonleaked deals. This runs counter to the belief by some sellers that a premature announcement will attract more bidders and thus drive up pricing. Finally, the study also indicates that while the average time taken for a nonleaked deal to complete stands at sixty-two days, this increases by forty-three days (or 70 percent) if the transaction is announced prematurely.

The main challenge related to a leak is that it significantly increases pressure on the seller to complete the deal to preserve the value of his underlying business, and it creates more concern and potential delay on behalf of the buyer as she wants to make sure that the deal will be able to deliver the expected benefits. As a result, the more information that leaks out prior to an agreement to employees, customers, competitors, and the public in general, the more issues that both

20. Jim R. Oliver, *Artificial Agents Learn Policies for Multi-Issue Negotiations*, 1 INT'L J. ELECTRONIC COMMERCE 49, 49–50 (1997) ("In negotiation, each side has private information; neither typically knows the other's utility function. In fact, both sides often have an incentive to misrepresent their preferences.").

21. Intralinks, M&A Leaks—Issues of Information Control, August 2009, http://www.intralinks.com.

the seller and buyer must decide and manage its potential or actual impact.

4.2 Multiple Issues

"How many of them really know what they want, though? I mean, a lot of them think they have to know, right? But inside they don't really know, so... I don't know, but I know that I don't know."

—LLOYD DOBLER,
Say Anything

In addition to multiple options, parties may also face the problem of multiple issues. Where options just present a choice (one from column A and one from column B), issues present distinct points of contention in the negotiation. Unlike with options, where choosing one necessarily means *not* choosing the others, resolving one issue in a negotiation usually leaves the other issues unresolved.

Multiple issues can create a problem in negotiations. To the extent that negotiations require signaling one's intention to one's counterparty, and to the extent that any action one takes can convey information to the other side, adding issues into the negotiation creates opportunities for ambiguity when one side or the other acts.[22] (This is likely to be more important in adversarial negotiations than it is in cooperative negotiations.)

Multiple issues may also create "silent alliances" on the other side. Since multiple issues may divide members of a negotiating team (where one team member cares more about issue X, while another cares more about issue Y), it makes sense that the effect would

22. *See* George Bunn & Rodger A. Payne, *Tit-for-Tat and the Negotiation of Nuclear Arms Control*, 9 ARMS CONTROL TODAY 207, 215 (1988) ("the breadth of the international agenda assures ambiguity in superpower arms control bargaining... These vast agendas increase the likelihood that one state or the other will take actions that the opponent will find offensive, and as a result, clarity in negotiating forums would be difficult to achieve").

occur on the other side as well.[23] As a result, if a negotiation team has reached a rough consensus on its own priorities, it may find that multiple-issue negotiations are easier to resolve than single-issue negotiations might be.

4.2.1 Contingent Issues—Do Not Pass Go

Contingent issues are issues that must be resolved before the parties can address any other issues. For example, in class action settlements, the plaintiff may only be willing to settle on a classwide basis, while the defendant may only be willing to settle on an individual basis. Until that fundamental question gets resolved, other issues (like attorneys' fees) must wait. In fact, the outcome of those other negotiations will depend heavily on the resolution of the debate over whether the settlement is classwide.

One of the difficulties with contingent issues is that if the primary issue is a particularly contentious one, the parties may face a strong temptation to put off discussing it until later in the negotiation. In some cases, this tactic may prove effective; concessions on other issues may build goodwill between the parties. In others, the reasoning may at least be sound. But in many cases, putting off a core but contentious issue may endanger the entire negotiation, in no small part because it may reopen negotiation on other issues.

Contingent issues can be difficult to identify, because almost anything can prove a dealbreaker, or the undoing of what looked like a good agreement. The merger of Live Nation, the largest concert promoter, and Ticketmaster, the largest ticket-selling service, had not one but two sets of contingent issues. The various negotiations and approvals significantly lengthened the completion of the deal, which was announced in February 2009 but did not close until January 2010, eleven months later.

23. Robert D. Putnam, *Diplomacy & Domestic Politics: The Logic of Two-Level Games*, 42 INT'L ORG. 427, 444 (1988).

The first set of contingent issues involved the antitrust authorities. To prevent market concentration, the U.S. Department of Justice (DOJ) required Ticketmaster to license its primary ticketing software to a competitor, sell off one ticketing unit, and agree not to retaliate against venue owners who used a competing ticket service.[24] (The DOJ continues to monitor compliance with this consent decree.) Reaching these conditions required a preliminary set of negotiations between Ticketmaster and the DOJ.

Once Ticketmaster had cleared that hurdle, it had to resolve another issues: who would be in charge of the merged entity? The structure of the deal was a "merger of equals"—providing ownership of the company to the combined pool of Live Nation and Ticketmaster shareholders. As a result, before the two companies could agree to terms, they had to agree with the management structure of the combined entity. This negotiation was complicated by the oversized personalities on both sides of the deal including Barry Diller, John Malone, Irving Azoff, Michael Rupino, and Ari Emmanuel. To conclude the deal, they were able to reach agreement, with Barry Diller becoming chairman of the combined entity. However, this agreement proved short-lived as Diller resigned as chairman only eight months later[25] and completely from the board after a year.

The battle for Asia Pacific Breweries provides another recent example of contingent issues. Brewer Heineken was engaged in a joint venture with Asia Pacific Breweries, maker of Tiger Beer. Heineken was enamored enough of Tiger Beer that it decided to wrest full control from Fraser & Neave, the Singaporean conglomerate that held the majority stake in the brand. Heineken saw an opportunity when Thai billionaire Charoen Sirivadhanabhakdi began increasing his minority

24. Jeremy Pelofsky & Yinka Adegoke, *Live Nation, Ticketmaster Merge; Agree to U.S. Terms*, REUTERS, Jan. 25, 2010.

25. Tim Arango, *Diller Resigns as Chairman of Live Nation*, N.Y. TIMES, Sept. 29, 2010.

stake in Fraser & Neave and launched its bid for control then. While it appeared at first that Charoen was interested in the conglomerate's beer holdings, his primary target was actually its property assets.[26] As a result, Heineken and Charoen had to reach agreement first on the sale of the breweries. (Charoen had built up a 33 percent stake in Fraser & Neave, making him a critical shareholder for Heineken to satisfy.) Once the Heineken deal was concluded, Charoen could then focus on his bid for the overall Fraser & Neave conglomerate. The key for Heineken was understanding Charoen's overall goal rather than the bidding war for the breweries specifically.

4.2.2 Linking Issues—Leverage

In contrast to contingent issues, issue linkage is the deliberate linking of otherwise unrelated issues.[27] Issue linkage receives the most study from scholars of international relations, particularly trade and arms negotiations. In the international context, parties may use issue linkage to make sure that states (which often have strong incentives to go their own way on issues of collective importance) negotiate, by linking an issue they might not agree on (global environmental standards) with an issue they are eager to secure agreement on (bilateral trade).[28]

In its most general form, issue linkage looks a lot like the "creating value" that so many modern negotiators have gleaned from the book *Getting to Yes*. (In other cases, it might look more like blackmail

26. *Fraser & Neave Holders Approve Heineken's APB Bid*, Market Watch—Wall St. J., Sept. 28, 2012.

27. *See* Robert D. Tollison & Thomas D. Willett, *An Economic Theory of Mutually Advantageous Issue Linkages in International Negotiations*, 33 Int'l Org. 425, 437 (1979) ("by linking the two negotiations so that high benefits go to A in one area and high benefits go to B in the other, there may be a possibility to secure agreement in both negotiations in a way that brings benefits to both countries and brings the outcome much closer to the aggregate efficiency or potential welfare frontier").

28. *See* James K. Sebenius, *Negotiation Arithmetic: Adding and Subtracting Issues and Parties*, 37 Int'l Org. 281 (1983); Tollison & Willett, *supra* note 27, at 425.

or coercion, such as when a powerful party links something its counterparty needs—U.S. troops in Germany—to something it does not want to concede on—German financial policies.)[29] But it is a more specific concept than that. Unlike "creating value," issue linkage does not have to result from taking a step back and determining what principles each side is seeking to uphold. Instead, it can sometimes be the more naked introduction of an incentive to make an agreement on an unrelated issue.

Another useful way of looking at issue linkage is that if negotiation on each issue is a single negotiation "game," then the overall set of issues to be negotiated is a "supergame."[30] In the "supergame," one can trade off wins in one game against concessions in another game. Issue linkage can be used as either a carrot or a stick, depending on the circumstances.[31] Indeed, assuming there are enough issues in play, linkage should be a viable tactic for reaching *some* kind of agreement.[32]

Where a linked issue would benefit the side making the concession, we can call it a *side payment* (a slightly nicer term than the economist's "bribe").[33] "If you agree to X, I can also offer you Y." Where a linked issue would harm a side not making a concession, we can call it a *threat*. "Unless you agree to X, there is no way you will we Y."

29. *See* Tollison & Willett, *supra* note 27, at 425 (providing example of Cold War linkage between U.S. troop assistance to West Germany and change to West German fiscal policy).

30. *See* Sebenius, *supra* note 28, at 285.

31. *See* Tollison & Willett, *supra* note 27, at 425.

32. James D. Morrow, *Signaling Difficulties with Linkage in Crisis Bargaining*, 36 INT'L STUDIES Q. 153, 153 (1992) ("Given sufficient issues where the parties have divergent positions and different saliences, it should always be possible to construct a trade across issues that would satisfy both sides.").

33. *See* Tollison & Willett, *supra* note 27, at 435.

Negotiators may naturally gravitate toward linking issues somehow, even if it just involves agreeing on some general principle or formula for addressing the remaining issues.[34]

Linking issues can help turn issues into options, by packaging a set of discrete issues together into an option. In other words, it reduces the number of choices that the parties will have to make.

Linking issues can also help overcome issues with troublesome constituents. If some subset (call it a faction) of constituents cares deeply about one issue, the negotiators may link concessions on that issue to one that might—considered on its own—be more troublesome.[35] But, in cases like this, the linked issue must be of real value to the counterparty; otherwise the offering of a concession may look more like a token than a real offer.[36] (Tokens offers, of course, have the additional disadvantage of signaling an intention to exploit rather than compromise.)

Offering a linked issue may also signal that the offeror lacks resolve (or a viable alternative) should the negotiation fall through.[37] In these cases, negotiating parties may face a strange paradox: the offer to link issues appears more credible the *less* the offeree is interested in the proposal.[38]

In some cases (such as, paradoxically, already-complex multilateral negotiations), multiple issues can make agreement more likely by allowing parties to trade concessions on one issue with one party for reciprocity in a different subset of negotiations.[39] Trading concessions

34. Bunn & Payne, *supra* note 22, at 211 (reporting "formula/details approach dominant in international negotiations").

35. Putnam, *supra* note 23, at 427, 446–47.

36. Morrow, *supra* note 32, at 153.

37. *Id.* 167.

38. *Id.*

39. Conconi & Perroni, *supra* note 12, at *2 ("In some cases negotiation tie-in can facilitate multilateral cooperation by limiting the set of the feasible objections to joint cooperation arrangements.").

like this does not guarantee agreement: even in these cases, issue linkage can sometimes impede cooperation by forcing commitments that hold up a different subset of the negotiation.[40]

Linking issues may also be an effective tactic for bringing additional parties to the table, when doing so is necessary. A may need something from C to complete a bargain with B. C may have no interest in the deal between A and B. But if A or B throws in a concession that helps C, then C may be more prepared to deal.[41]

Linking issues is most effective when there will be more than one negotiation over a longer span of time. At that point, the parties have the option of trading a concession now for some kind of concession later. (Informally, this happens frequently in negotiations. One party will make an unsolicited concession in order to build goodwill with the other party. That's not just because the first party is a nice person—there's usually a hope for some future payoff.)

One difficulty with linking issues is that doing so may take the focus off of the substance of the issues to be negotiated and place it more onto the relative bargaining power of the parties.[42] After all, by linking unrelated issues, one sends the signal that the specific merits of a given point are not as important as the concession itself.

A second problem is that linking the wrong issues can actually destroy any possibility of agreement. If parties are close to an agreement and add in a sufficiently divisive issue, then no parties may agree

40. *Id.* at *2 ("in other cases, rather than inducing parties to trade across issues, a tie-in restriction can actually constitute an obstacle to multilateral cooperation, as it removes certain counterobjections that could be put forward, out of equilibrium, in order to support issue trading in equilibrium").

41. *See* Sebenius, *supra* note 28, at 298 (discussing addition of issues to negotiation to secure agreement from as many countries as possible on law governing seabeds).

42. *See id.* at 281 (quoting Roger Fisher, "Fractionating Conflict," *in* INTERNATIONAL CONFLICT AND BEHAVIORAL SCIENCE: THE CRAIGVILLE PAPERS 98 (Fisher, ed. 1964)).

to the final agreement.[43] In some cases, this result may come about because of either ignorance or overconfidence. But it is worth noting that, in certain circumstances, this may be a deliberate strategy.

In legislation, for example, a senator interested in preventing a popular law from passing may insert a "poison pill" amendment—an amendment on a divisive issue that must be voted on at the same time as the more popular legislation. The intent in these circumstances is that the unpopularity of the amendment (which is a method of linking the issue to the bill) will reduce the number of votes overall. For example, when congressional Democrats sought to pass health care reform through a budget reconciliation process requiring a simple majority (which they had), congressional Republicans threatened to amend the bill with politically sensitive proposals that would threaten some members' reelection.[44]

This kind of linkage also works without a desire to kill a bill. Then it's just referred to as a "non-germane" amendment. To provide a more recent example, in April 2012, the U.S. Senate set aside several days to debate possible reforms to the U.S. Post Office. At the beginning of the debate, one senator (Rand Paul) sought to introduce an amendment about U.S. policy toward Egypt—an important issue, but one that has very little to do with delivering mail in a speedy and cost-effective manner. As a result, the Senate spent three days debating the procedure for amendments during the Post Office debate, instead of getting to the merits of the matter at hand.[45]

43. *See id.* at 281, 300 ("If one adds a sufficiently divisive issue to other, less contentious questions and one requires joint resolution of them all, then agreement may be rendered impossible.").

44. *See* Manu Raju, *Senate Dems Brace for "Poison Pills,"* POLITICO, Mar. 23, 2010, http://www.politico.com/news/stories/0310/34837.html (last viewed Apr. 4, 2012) ("Senate Republicans are planning an onslaught of politically sensitive amendments to a health care reconciliation bill, searching high and low for any way to derail the final legislation")

45. *See* Carl Levin & Lamar Alexander, *Fighting Senate Gridlock through Self-Restraint*, WASHINGTON POST, April 2012, at 27, http://www.washingtonpost.com/opinions/

Another problem with issue linkage is actually finding an unrelated issue to link with the issue one already wishes to negotiate. After all, if the issue were obvious, it would likely already be part of the discussions.[46]

Discussing multiple issues may also prove too complex for face-to-face negotiations; instead, multiple issues may force parties to resort to correspondence of some kind.[47]

In addition, forcing a linkage may place the parties on a more adversarial footing—a development that may not help the negotiation to conclude successfully.[48] For example, when negotiating the extension of the debt ceiling in 2011, congressional Republicans tried to add discussion of a controversial oil pipeline and reforms to unemployment insurance and Medicare to the resolution.[49] These additional issues were designed to attract more Republican votes for the deal (in other words, to bring constituents on board), but wound up alienating several Democrats who strongly opposed those issues.[50]

4.2.3 Subtracting Issues—Making Things Simpler

A party may also make progress in a multiple-issue negotiation by taking certain issues *off* of the table. For example, class action attorneys will often take specific discussions about fees off the table

fighting-senate-gridlock-through-self-restraint/2012/04/26/gIQAsUC0jT_story.html (last viewed Apr. 27, 2012).

46. *See* Tollison & Willett, *supra* note 27, at 425, 438 (pointing out that issue linkage is constrained by the ability of decisionmakers to process information about issues).

47. Janice Nadler, *Rapport in Legal Negotiation: How Small Talk Can Facilitate E-mail Dealmaking*, 9 HARV. NEGOTIATION L. REV. 223, 227–28 (2004).

48. *See* Sebenius, *supra* note 28, at 281, 306.

49. Paul Kane & Rosaline S. Helderman, *Congressional Leaders Reach Spending Deal to Avoid Government Shutdown*, WASHINGTON POST, Dec. 16, 2011 (http://www.washingtonpost.com/politics/congressional-leaders-negotiating-key-bills-to-avoid-government-shutdown/2011/12/15/gIQA6nPwwO_print.html) (last viewed Apr. 8, 2012).

50. *Id.*

when negotiating a settlement.[51] In other words, if certain issues are creating problems, the parties can agree to discuss them later, after they have reached agreement on the issues they can agree on.

The most obvious way to subtract an issue is to agree not to discuss it. One can also "subtract" issues by delegating them, that is, by giving them to team members with less responsibility or less perceived status.[52] (This can have the dual benefit of giving less experienced negotiators some experience, while also taking the pressure off of certain issues that might be resolved more easily when decoupled from the major issues. Trade negotiators used to do this with smaller issues, moving them further down the bureaucratic ladder.) Litigators might also "delegate" certain contentious issues (like attorneys' fees) to the court or an arbitrator.

Parties will not always agree to this tactic. But, where possible, it can work very well. Trying to force a subtraction—in other words, unilaterally refusing to discuss an issue—may also place the parties on a more adversarial footing.[53]

4.3 Agendas—The Secret Weapon

"Sire, [another battle] is not necessary. They have allowed me to set the agenda."

—TALLEYRAND[54]

The various issues in a complex negotiation may be strategically interdependent, meaning that the resolution of one issue will change

51. *See, e.g.*, *In re* Volkswagen & Audi Warranty Extension Litig., 2011 U.S. Dist. LEXIS 30881 (D. Mass. Mar. 24, 2011) (plaintiffs agreed not to seek more than $37.5 million in fees; defendant reserved right to oppose fee request).

52. *See* Sebenius, *supra* note 28, at 281, 303.

53. *See id.* at 281, 306.

54. *Cited in* P. V. (Sundar) Blakrishnan et al., *Toward a Theory of Agenda-Setting in Negotiations*, 19 J. Consumer Research 637, 637 (1993).

the manner in which a negotiator must approach other issues. As a result, even apparently simple administrative acts like developing an agenda can assume great strategic importance.[55] Deciding which issues are on the table can be important because some issues in a given negotiation may simply derail discussion, guaranteeing no agreement. This is one reason why subtracting issues can be so effective in some circumstances.

Indeed, political scientist and game theorist Bruce Bueno de Mesquita has written about one consultation in which, just by manipulating the order in which a board of directors considered possible successors for a departing CEO, he was able to ensure that a second-place choice would be selected over a more favored candidate the CEO detested. How did he do this? By looking at the way in which the candidates were considered. The detested candidate (de Mesquita calls him Mutt) and the less-favored candidate (Curly) were two in a field of five. Were the selection committee to vote on all five at once, Mutt would likely win. But "a specific sequence of head-to-head elimination contests" would put Mutt early in favor of another candidate (Moe), who would actually attract fewer votes head-to-head than Curly.[56]

Agendas do have some limitations: in particular they are vulnerable to time constraints.[57] After all, if there is a limited amount of time to negotiate, the parties may not have time to discuss all issues. Or they may be forced to agree on the most important issues and place those first. Agreement on which issues are most important, however, may not be easy. Leaving aside genuine differences of opinion, some negotiators may argue certain issues are more important because considering them first will lead to a better outcome for that side.[58] In

55. SCHELLING, *supra* note 9, at 31–32; Blakrishnan et al., *supra* note 54, at 637, 639.

56. DE MESQUITA, *supra* note 11, at Kindle location 945–1026.

57. Blakrishnan et al., *supra* note 54, at 637, 642.

58. DE MESQUITA, *supra* note 11, at Kindle location 945–1026.

other cases, a negotiator may have become so emotionally invested in a certain issue that its importance becomes inflated to her.[59]

Issues that are pushed to the end of the agenda may not be addressed as fully, or at all.[60]

Negotiating over the agenda—much like other negotiations over the course of the negotiations—is essentially a game about a game, or "meta-game." It can also be incredibly frustrating.[61]

The type of agenda one adopts will affect the course of the negotiation. For example, the more rigidly sequential an agenda is, the more difficult it may be to trade one issue off against another.[62] By contrast, broad, general agendas may make it more difficult for parties with deep, fundamental disagreements to reach an agreement.

4.3.1 Sequential vs. Simultaneous Negotiations—Chess vs. "Rock, Paper, Scissors"

The primary question when negotiating multiple issues is whether to negotiate the multiple issues all at once, or one by one in a predetermined order. There are solid reasons for trying each approach.

Parties may prefer simultaneous negotiation when they will be negotiating over a number of linked issues, since it will be easier to track trade-offs if they discuss the issues at the same time.[63]

Parties may prefer sequential negotiations under several conditions. First, they may gain some strategic advantage from having one issue heard first. Second, some issue may be sufficiently controversial that it must be postponed if the parties are to reach any agreement

59. Blakrishnan et al., *supra* note 54, at 637, 647.

60. *Id.* at 637, 642.

61. FISHER ET AL., *supra* note 10, at 10. Litigators may be familiar with this tactic, which is often referred to as "litigating the litigation."

62. Blakrishnan et al., *supra* note 54, at 637, 639.

63. *Id.*

at all. Finally, ordering the issues in a certain way may tell a party whether the negotiation is worth pursing and allow it to pull out quickly if it is not.

4.3.2 Strategic Ordering

The order in which negotiators consider multiple issues—or decide the merits of multiple options—matters. It matters a great deal, in fact.

One way to illustrate the structural issue involved in agenda control is the *doctrinal paradox*. The most popular illustration involves a three-judge panel, much like a federal appeals court, that is trying to decide whether Defendant Company breached its contract to Plaintiff Company. Doing so requires deciding three issues:

1. Defendant Company bought widgets from a third party.
2. Defendant Company had an obligation *not* to buy widgets from a third party.
3. Defendant Company is liable for breach of contract.

These are contingent issues. In other words, deciding 1 and 2 in a certain way dictates a particular decision on 3.

In this case, the first judge believes both 1 and 2, and therefore believes 3. The second judge believes 1, but not 2, and therefore not 3. The third judge believes 2, but not 1, so not 3. And there lies the problem: even though two of the judges don't believe that Defendant Company is liable, depending on the order in which the judges vote, they may still conclude that it is liable. If the judges vote on liability first and then go back over their reasoning, there should be no problem: someone will wind up changing their mind, or they will find the company not liable. But if they vote on whether Defendant Company bought from a third party, then two judges (the first and second) will vote yes. Then, when they vote on whether Defendant Company had an obligation not to do so, a different two judges (the first and third) will vote yes. The end result is that Defendant Company loses the lawsuit, even though a majority of the judges do not believe it breached the contract.[64]

But, in addition to the structural issue, agendas are important because the order in which parties decide issues may implicate some of the quasi-rational effects we discussed in chapter 2. *Anchoring effects*, for example, mean that the values discussed earlier in a negotiation may have effects on later valuations. So if the parties begin by discussing an issue important to one side, its concerns may predominate in discussions on later issues. Conversely, the *sunk-cost fallacy* (a form of *loss aversion*) means that if a party gets her counterpart to agree to an easy issue early in negotiating, he may be more committed to the negotiations, because he will not want to lose the agreement he has already reached.[65]

When there are multiple issues, *some* issues have to come first.[66] It may very well be that the party with the most leverage will be the one to determine the priority of the items on the agenda.

Moreover, because initial decisions can have an effect on later decisions, the order of the agenda may encourage path-dependence effects.[67]

64. Christian List, *A Model of Path-Dependence in Decisions over Multiple Propositions*, 98 Am. Pol. Sci. Rev. 495, 495 (2004).

65. Blakrishnan et al., *supra* note 54, at 637, 641 ("Anecdotal evidence (Cohen 1980; Nieremberg 1968) suggests a bargaining strategy in which a less important issue is discussed first in order to get the other party committed to the deal. Once a certain amount of investment in time and money is made, the sunk-cost fallacy affects the negotiators.").

66. *Id.* at 637, 642.

67. List, *supra* note 64, at 495, 496 ("Unsurprisingly, path-dependence may enable an agenda-setter to manipulate the outcome by controlling the decision-path (Riker 1982). More surprisingly, the mere existence of an alternative decision-path that would change the outcome—even if that path is never adopted—may create incentives for strategic expression of untruthful views.").

4.4 Practical Applications

Make a map. Not all issues are equally important. And some issues can be resolved at the same time. Therefore, it is vital to know if "there are many things that need to be decided" versus "these decisions are all tied together." Separating issues that are genuinely and practically linked or issues that are largely stand-alone helps to focus the parties. The stand-alone issues can be agreed to and give some momentum to the negotiations. The linked issues can be processed in batches. By illustrating to the other side this flow, it helps bring clarity to the negotiation and brings you the advantage of setting the agenda.

Build filters. So how does one deal with the problems posed by multiple options? The same way one deals with the problem of ten million search results in Google: by filtering. (In fact, this is how artificial intelligence experts have long treated the problem of negotiation when programming software.)[68] Certain options will simply not be attractive because they lack some important feature central to the final agreement. So negotiators can discard those options without too much worry. As a result, organizations can use the data at their disposal to rid themselves of less attractive options, taking them off the table entirely.

One drawback to filtering is that it is based on one's current frame of knowledge. So many organizations will view anything that delivers new or unique value with extreme suspicion because it does not fit their preexisting frame of reference. To use an example common to business school graduates, Chester Carlton, the developer of dry photocopying, began by shopping his idea to the technology giants of his day: RCA, IBM, A.B. Dick, and Kodak. None of them embraced the technology because they conceived of it only as

68. Oliver, *supra* note 20, at 49–50.

a clunky, high-tech replacement for the already-effective product carbon paper.[69] Rigid filters can backfire in another way: if the organization spends too long searching for the optimal mix of options. One alternative to filtering is to employ a third party, like a lawyer or consultant. These can be helpful either because they are better trained to sift through complicated packages of options,[70] or just able to offer a third-party perspective.

Issue experts. Once one knows which issues are likely to arise in a given negotiation, one can begin looking for team members who are qualified to talk about these issues. This is one of the areas where the advantages of negotiating teams becomes clear: there are more opportunities to bring specific expertise to bear.

Inventory the deal beforehand. Before walking into the room to negotiate a deal, it is important to know which issues the deal will comprise. A negotiator cannot anticipate *every* possible permutation of a deal, but the more that has been worked out beforehand, the better prepared one will be for the unanticipated events that occur later on.

Test extreme outcomes beforehand. Once you have an inventory, test your team's position against the extreme result on the range of issues. Since it is impossible to anticipate the permutations, by understanding your position on the extremes of each issue, it brings confidence to the "acceptable range."

Identify your expendable issues. Often, one can move forward on negotiating complex issues by postponing agreement on certain contentious issues. This can work with either large abstract principles or small details. The Federal Sentencing Guidelines, for example, were

69. *See* John H. Dessauer, My Years with Xerox: The Billions Nobody Wanted 21 (1971); John Seely Brown, *Changing the Game of Corporate Research: Learning to Thrive in the Fog of Reality*, *in* Raghu Garud et al. (eds.), Technological Innovation: Oversights & Foresights 97–98 (1997).

70. *See* Guthrie, *supra* note14, at 606 (suggesting lawyers might be better trained to "maximize the benefits and minimize the costs of option generation in negotiation").

negotiated offense by offense without reaching agreement on the underlying principles.[71] The result was not a masterpiece of coherence, but it was enacted into law.[72] By contrast, the Constitutional Convention would reach agreement on large issues, but leave blanks for contentious details like the number of delegates.[73]

4.5 Conclusion

The addition of multiple issues to a negotiation provides both an opportunity and a danger. The opportunity lies in the firm's renewed ability to find agreements: the more options it has, the more chances there are of finding common ground with the other side. But the danger lies in the fact that people do not operate well with too many choices. The more options there are, the more chance there is for paralysis, or for getting sidetracked by urgent issues that are inessential to the larger deal.

Adding issues also slows down a negotiation, as the negotiating team must weigh the options presented to it. And slowing down negotiations creates a host of separate challenges. It is these challenges that we address in the next chapter.

71. Cass R. Sunstein, *Incompletely Theorized Agreements*, 108 HARV. L. REV. 1733, 1743–45 (1995).

72. *Id.* at 1745.

73. Dana Lansky, *Proceeding to a Constitution: A Multi-Party Negotiation Analysis of the Constitutional Convention of* 1787, 5 HARV. NEGOTIATION L. REV. 279, 325 (2000).

5

Transactions Over Time

"Time is what prevents everything happening at once."

—JOHN WHEELER

In the late 2000s, Verizon Wireless faced a class action lawsuit alleging that it had violated the Fair and Accurate Credit Transaction Act (FACTA), a statute that required merchants to obscure credit card information on receipts.[1] The statute was intended to prevent identity theft, but proved controversial in class action litigation because it allowed plaintiffs to sue for staggering damages even when the violation was technical and no consumer could have been harmed. In this case, for example—- *Ehrheart v. Verizon Wireless*[2]—the plaintiffs alleged that Verizon Wireless had continued to print expiration dates on credit card receipts in violation of FACTA. They did not claim that they had been harmed in some way by this practice, but they did not have to, a technical violation was enough.

1. 15 U.S.C. § 1681, *et seq*.

2. 609 F.3d 590 (3d Cir. 2010).

Faced with the prospect of massive liability, Verizon began settlement negotiations with the *Ehrheart* plaintiffs through a mediator. After considerable back-and-forth, it reached a final agreement with the plaintiffs and got preliminary (but not final) approval from a federal district court in Pennsylvania.

After the trial court had given preliminary approval, but before the final approval hearing, Congress—at the urging of various businesses—passed another law known as the Clarification Act. The Clarification Act said that merchants who had technically violated FACTA but not caused any harm to a consumer were not liable for violations under the statute.[3] Now that it was no longer liable, Verizon moved to vacate the preliminary approval order (which the court granted), and then to dismiss the case (which the court also granted). The plaintiffs, who had just watched a very lucrative settlement vanish before their eyes, appealed to the Third Circuit Court of Appeals.

The primary issue on appeal was when a classwide settlement became binding. The plaintiffs argued that once they had an agreement with Verizon, it was binding regardless of whether or not it was finally approved. Verizon disagreed, arguing that the agreement could not bind it until the court had issued its final approval order.[4] While Verizon's argument had convinced the trial court, the Third Circuit did not accept it. Instead, it held "that changes in the law after a settlement is reached do not provide ground for rescission of the settlement."[5] So Verizon had to pay the plaintiffs, even though they no longer had a viable lawsuit.

Why didn't Verizon know the Clarification Act was about to pass? It is hard to say. Usually a corporation that size will have

3. 15 U.S.C. § 1681n(d).

4. For more on the mechanics of class action settlements, *see* chapter 6; *see also* Brian Anderson & Andrew Trask, The Class Action Playbook § 8 (2d ed. 2012).

5. *Ehrheart*, 609 F.3d at 593.

people whose sole job is to track shifts in the law that might affect its business deals or outstanding lawsuits. (For more about this, see chapter 9.) In this case, it may be that the lawsuit was an outlier. Or it may be that Verizon did not believe that the Clarification Act would be passed while the lawsuit was still pending. Regardless of why Verizon adopted the strategy it did, the *Ehrheart* case illustrates a fundamental truth about complex negotiations: the longer they go on, the more complex they get.

For a negotiator, time has three important qualities that affect strategy: it is unidirectional (it only moves forward, never backward), it is finite (there are only twenty-four hours in each day), and it is uniformly distributed (everyone gets the same twenty-four hours). In fact, it is this final characteristic that has led some to consider time to be the "fundamental scarce resource in the economy," since no one can receive more than twenty-four hours, and much of that we spend sleeping, eating, or with our friends and families.[6]

Time may seem like an abstract concept for negotiation strategy, but, because of these limitations, it has very real effects on every aspect of negotiations, effects that are more pronounced in complex negotiations that involve multiple issues or multiple parties. For example, a number of social scientists have shown that genuine time pressure can have an effect on negotiations. For example, parties under time pressure bluff less frequently and expect less out of the negotiation.[7] And it is possible to create conditions of limited time, by setting deadlines.

6. *See* F. Thomas Juster & Frank P. Stafford, *The Allocation of Time: Empirical Findings, Behavioral Models, and the Problem of Measurement*, 29 J. ECON. LIT. 471, 474 (1991).

7. P.V. (Sundar) Blakrishnan et al., *Toward a Theory of Agenda-Setting in Negotiations*, 19 J. CONSUMER RESEARCH 637, 643 (1993) ("Empirical support for the influence of time pressure is also provided by Pruitt and Drews (1969), who demonstrated in a laboratory experiment that increased time pressure produced lower aspiration levels and less bluffing.").

More important, the fact that negotiations may take place over longer periods of time can by itself change a negotiator's strategy, often for the better.[8] To begin with, parties' preferences change over time.[9] If parties know that they will encounter each other again, they are more likely to engage in long-term negotiating strategies. For example, they can engage in strategies that reward cooperative behavior over time.[10] They can also propose more controversial strategies gradually, allowing the other side to come to accept them.[11]

But engaging in many negotiations over a longer period of time also poses particular strategic dilemmas. Negotiations that take place over longer time periods may entrench some of the nonrational components involved in complex negotiations; for example, they can institutionalize animosity between fierce competitors.[12] They can also lead to further investment in the negotiation.

8. HERBERT GINTIS, THE BOUNDS OF REASON 102 (2009) ("The extensive form of a game is informationally richer than the normal form since player gather information that allows them to update their subjective priors as the game progresses."); *see also* Larry Crump, *A Temporal Model of Negotiation Linkage Dynamics*, 23 NEGOTIATION J. 117 (2007).

9. GINTIS, *supra* note 8, at 10 ("The central theorem on choice over time is that time consistency results from assuming that *utility is additive across time periods and that the instantaneous utility function is the same in all time periods, with future utilities discounted to the present at a fixed rate*. This is called *exponential discounting* and is widely assumed in economic models.") (emphases in original).

10. *See generally id.* at § 5.1.

11. Crump, *supra* note 8, at 117 138 (2007) (describing how changes in tariff classifications among Pacific Rim countries were introduced and then adopted over twenty-year period).

12. ROBERT MNOOKIN, BARGAINING WITH THE DEVIL: WHEN TO NEGOTIATE & WHEN TO FIGHT 107 (2010) (discussing how prolonged conflict can lead to parties establishing difficult preconditions for negotiation); Charles J. Hunt, Jr., *Mediator Tactics: Strategies and Behaviors Utilized in Labor-Management Negotiations*, 6 APPALACHIAN J. L. 263, 266–67 (2007) ("personal animosities between the parties can continue and involve management supervisors and company employees at the implementation level. If such is the case when the next round of negotiations starts, the attitudinal makeup of both parties will get off to a bad start.").

As a result, many business strategists have observed that the most effective strategic plans will build in time to respond to unforeseen change.[13]

This chapter describes five specific effects the passage of time has on complex negotiations. Path dependence—the tendency of later steps in a negotiation to follow even randomly chosen starting points—means that even early decisions can have large effects on the outcome of the negotiation. Discounting—the preference for gains now and losses later—can lead to friction over the pace of a negotiation. Sequential strategies, in which one party may see and respond to another's moves, promotes cooperative behavior over time. The role of exogenous shocks—random events that occur over the course of a negotiation—increases uncertainty, which increases the cost of negotiating. And finally, parties' capacity for learning means that the longer the negotiation goes on, the fewer gains there will be from private information.

This chapter also identifies practical measures a company can take to reduce the risks from long-term negotiations, including the importance of agendas and of interim agreements.

5.1 Path Dependence—Starting Points Matter

"Let me ask you a question, you, you never really remember the beginning of a dream do you? You always wind up right in the middle of what's going on."

—DOM COBB,
Inception (Warner Bros., 2010)

The passage of time shapes the way a negotiation proceeds in unexpected ways. The most common phenomenon affecting this process

13. Herbert A. Simon, *Strategy & Organizational Evolution*, 14 STRATEGIC MGMT. J. 131, 135 (1993) ("Effective strategic planning seldom calls for accurate estimates of the time paths of new trends. It calls for approximate estimates of time horizons in order to provide adequate lead time for planning responses.").

is known as "path dependence." Taken from the social sciences, the term means that each step in the development of an idea or product has a unique effect on the outcome.

The concept of path dependence was originally used to explain why the vast majority of English-language computer keyboards sport the QWERTY configuration, even though other keyboard layouts (like the Dvorak Simplified Keyboard) have better ergonomics or would lead to faster typing. Computer keyboards were based on electric typewriter keyboards, which also used QWERTY. Electric typewriters in turn followed the layout of manual typewriters. Manual typewriters actually had a reason for adopting QWERTY: the layout prevented jams caused by fast typists hitting keys too quickly. The QWERTY keyboard is not strictly necessary for computer keyboards. In fact, it may very well be suboptimal. But people were used to the QWERTY keyboard after learning to type on it on their electric typewriters. And they were used to the QWERTY layout on electric typewriters because a previous generation had learned it on manual typewriters.[14] In short, path dependence describes the phenomenon where early choices have magnified effects on later outcomes.

Over time, these choices get "locked in" for both parties. What is particularly interesting is that this is not a purely social phenomenon; there is an inexorable mathematics behind it as well.[15] Essentially, each choice along a path that reinforces the path makes the next choice to continue along that path less expensive. After a while, it costs nothing to stay on the path, but it will cost a great deal to diverge from it. After all, which will most people take while hiking in the woods: the worn path with little undergrowth, or the one that requires a machete?

14. Paul A. David, *Clio & the Economics of QWERTY*, 75 AM. ECON. REV. 332, 335 (1985).

15. *Id.*

When organizations negotiate with each other over long periods of time, they are subject to path dependence as well; essentially, the structure of the first set of negotiations between parties will shape any subsequent negotiations between them.[16] In this way, path dependence is closely related to the phenomenon of *anchoring* that we discussed in chapter 2.[17] Both of these phenomena rely on the fact that early decisions, even seemingly minor ones, will echo for a long time over the course of many subsequent decisions.[18]

In fact, starting points may matter long after they are known. As we described in chapter 2, social psychologist Muzafer Sherif conducted a series of experiments in which he showed groups of people in a dark room a pinpoint of light, then moved it and asked them to estimate the distance it had traveled. The experiment provided an excellent example of herding behavior: people would not just conform their guesses to what they heard others guess, they would do so even when some of the guesses were wildly divergent. More important for our purposes in this chapter, though, is what happened next. Sherif gradually replaced members of the group, but he found that the consensus on how far the light had traveled remained constant over time. In other words, institutions, like people, have memory, and that memory may outlast the people who were present for the original event.[19]

16. Crump, *supra* note 8, at 136 (noting that "field data" indicates that parties who have engaged in "prior relevant negotiation" are more likely to present a "preferred text" as a starting point in subsequent negotiations). For more on the phenomenon of path dependence, *see generally* David, *supra* note 14, at 332, 332; W. B. Arthur, *Competing Technologies, Increasing Returns, and Lock-in by Historical Events*, 99 Econ. J. 116 (1989); S. J. Liebowitz & S. E. Margolis, *Path Dependence, Lock-in and History,* 11 J. L. Econ. & Org. 205 (1995); Lucian Arye Bebchuk & Mark J. Roe, *A Theory of Path Dependence in Corporate Ownership and Governance*, 52 Stan. L. Rev. 127 (1999).

17. *See* § 2.1.1.

18. *See* Dan Ariely, Predictably Irrational: The Hidden Forces That Shape Our Decisions 38 (rev. ed. 2009).

19. *See* Neal Kumar Katyal, *Conspiracy Theory*, 112 Yale L.J. 1307, 1309 (2003).

So how does this apply in negotiations? First, it means that those who make the first few moves may have an inordinate effect on later negotiations. Economists have formally demonstrated this phenomenon with a game called the "take it or leave it" game. The "take it or leave it" game does just what it says. There are two players, one owns a book he values at $5; the other would like to buy the book, which she values at $15. Both sides know each other's valuations. One party is allowed to make a single "take it or leave it" offer. Under these circumstances, it is easy to predict that the book will sell for either $5.01 (if the buyer makes offer) or $14.99 (if the seller does). If the game is extended out over several moves, the price stays closer to preferred price of whoever made the first offer. In other words, the starting point for the negotiation matters a great deal; changing the order of the events changes the outcome in significant ways.[20]

In addition, agreements made before the current negotiation can wind up having significant effects on future agreements, even when the prior agreement was with a completely different party. As Duke Law School professor Ben Depoorter has demonstrated, settlements in certain kinds of high-stakes litigation (like class actions and products liability cases) can exert "peer pressure" on similar cases with different defendants. In other words, if General Motors settles a defective-brakes case for a large sum, then the next time Ford Motor Company is sued in a similar case, it may find that the General Motors case has set a floor for the settlement. The negotiated settlement operates as the same kind of precedent that a case litigated to a jury verdict (or an appellate opinion) would.[21]

How do lawyers find out about these settlements? People talk, and they observe. So, given large law firms (where, leaving aside

20. *See* Avery Katz, *The Strategic Structure of Offer and Acceptance: Game Theory & the Law of Contract Formation*, 89 MICH. L. REV. 215, 240 (1990).

21. *See* Ben Depoorter, *Law in the Shadow of Bargaining: The Feedback Effect of Civil Settlements*, 95 CORNELL L. REV. 957, 960 (2010).

firewalls, lawyers can share shoptalk safely) and the extensive networks plaintiffs' lawyers use, news of sizable or novel settlements disseminates quickly.

This same phenomenon also operates for business deals. Numerous newspapers, like the *Wall Street Journal*, the London *Financial Times*, and the *New York Times*'s "Dealbook" blog, cover the daily ins and outs of corporate deal making. Even before daily coverage of deal making became common, investment bankers and merger lawyers were a sufficiently tight-knit community that they frequently shared information on recently consummated deals, including the personnel retained to help and the terms of the agreements.[22]

5.2 Time Asymmetries—Why Someone Prefers to Go Slow

"'For a while' is a phrase whose length can't be measured. At least by the person who's waiting."

—HARUKI MURAKAMI,
South of the Border, West of the Sun

Another effect of negotiating over longer periods of time is that different parties will want to move at different speeds. In litigation, this is often very clear: plaintiffs like to move fast; defendants prefer to take their time. But this observation also holds true in business negotiations: offerors prefer movement; offerees are more comfortable with deliberation.

What causes these disjuncts between parties? It turns out that they stem from the way most people experience thinking about the future.

22. Bryan Burrough & John Helyar, Barbarians at the Gate: The Fall of RJR Nabisco 189 (2003) (describing back-channel communications through the "merger bar").

Classical economists have long assumed that people discount their future income (or the goods they will buy in the future) by some rationally predictable rate. In other words, the average person will prefer money today to money tomorrow, but you can get him to accept money tomorrow by giving him slightly more money then. (As the old adage goes: "a bird in the hand is worth two in the bush.")

If anything, these economists tended to understate the case. As it turns out, people tend to discount future benefits by much more than one might expect. They also do not discount everything the same way. While they want gains now, they are (consistent with what we know about loss aversion) happy to postpone losses of equivalent value. In other words, people *really* prefer to collect gains now, and they *really* prefer to postpone losses until later. This phenomenon is known as the *gain-loss* asymmetry. People also experience a related phenomenon known as the *delay-speedup asymmetry*: they feel the loss from waiting an extra day for a reward (like $100) more keenly than they feel the gain from receiving that same reward a day early.[23]

These asymmetries have real effects in both complex litigation settlements and large business transactions. In litigation, it leads to a situation where plaintiffs are far less patient than defendants. There is a common perception in complex litigation that time favors the defendant. Defendants often counsel clients not to react too quickly: situations that may provoke a fight-or-flight response in the moment often present more strategic opportunities as they unfold. And plaintiffs tend to agree; they often complain that defendants' primary strategy is just to delay litigation for as long as possible. Given the effects of these two asymmetries, it appears that plaintiffs value the gains they might receive less the further away they appear, and the mere fact of delay feels like a loss to them.

23. Philip Streich & Jack S. Levy, *Time Horizons, Discounting, & Intertemporal Choice*, 51 J. CONFLICT RESOLUTION 199 (2007).

By contrast, the defendant still anticipates that any anticipated loss will be close to the amount it hurts today, and it experiences comparatively less gain from the day.

The effects of this asymmetry also means that defendants have some leverage in negotiating how the litigation will proceed. All else being equal, delays are more immediately painful to plaintiffs than they are immediately helpful to defendants. So, when defendants need important concessions in other areas of the litigation (perhaps in the scope of discovery), they may be able to trade less-valuable (to them) scheduling concessions.

These same dynamics play out in business deals as well, particularly in the different ways that companies will treat acquisitions and divestments. For example, a company proposing to buy another company usually has a plan to improve the target company. As a result it wants to act on that plan quickly and so move quickly to lock in those perceived gains. They want to lock in value now. In contrast, the target company would tend to prefer to wait to negotiate a higher price because they see that the proposed buyer has great need and is placing value on the near-term benefits. So their position is to go slow in order to negotiate a more favorable purchase price or better terms.

Conversely, in a divestment, the company putting itself up for sale typically has reached the limit of what it can deliver in its current form. Its goal is to sell for that highest value it has created at this moment, and it will discount the future value that it might create as a stand-alone company. In this case, the selling company wants to lock in value immediately. By contrast, prospective buyers need time to understand what they might do with this company up for sale and so it is in their interests to delay in order to study and understand what the benefit is and how they might unlock value. The prospective buyers, in this case, are much more willing to wait to see what value the company can create on its own and how well it fits in with the buyer's overall strategy. The one exception to this pattern is if the seller can, through a private auction, identify multiple potential buyers.[24] The auction process is designed to increase competition between potential buyers, thereby increasing the seller's bargaining power and improving their offer terms. If the seller and associated banker can create enough excitement and potential concern that the company for sale might be bought by competitor and used to create significant market gains. In this case, a prospective buyer would be motivated to try to lock in gains now through acquiring the company for sale. That will give them capabilities and strengths ahead of their other competitors and so win more in the market sooner with these newly acquired capabilities.

A private auction is typically a more complicated and costly process than a negotiated sale. Even though all dissemination is private and to a prescreened group, it does make the sale more widely known and increases the potential risk of other people finding out, causing disruption to the company's operation and hurting its sales and profitability prospects. Additionally, certain companies might not want to participate in an auction process. This could be because it is unfamiliar, or because it is more complicated and with a pressured timeline.[25]

McKinsey consultants Lee Dranikoff, Tim Koller, and Antoon Schneider studied nearly fifty of the largest divestitures completed in the late 1990s, and found that most of them occurred only after long delays, when problems with the company or the decision became so obvious that action became unavoidable.[26] The loss resulting from the divestiture's final sale value versus the value that the seller had on its balance sheet needs to be recorded on the seller's income statement. These losses tend to be significantly larger than if they had not postponed action. Companies tend to move or lose the most valuable leaders from business units that are struggling, only compounding

24. For more on auctions, *see* chapter 3.

25. ClearRidge Capital, http://www.clearridgecapital.com/business_sale_auction_negotiated.htm.

26. Lee Dranikoff, Tim Koller, & Antoon Schneider, *May 2002—Divestiture: Strategy's Missing Link*, HARV. BUS. REV., http://hbr.org/2002/05/divestiture-strategys-missing-link/ar/1.

the problem over time. There is a strong tendency to believe that a new leadership team or a new set of initiatives will "fix the business." Most likely, it only delays the inevitable.

Overall, these asymmetries mean that it is more challenging to cooperate over time than one might think, because the passage of time itself will create friction in most negotiations.

5.3 Exogenous Shocks—What Happens When Stuff Happens

"Winter does not last forever. Spring comes. Snows melt."

—MARK ANTONY, *ROME EPISODE 1.2*,

"How Titus Pullo Brought Down the Republic"

Things happen. People die. Companies go bankrupt. New information comes to light that changes the balance of power between negotiating parties. These are unavoidable facts in life, and in negotiations. And this particular issue has received new currency in the 2000s with the surge in discussions about "black swans": unforeseen events that expose the shallowness of some risk evaluations.[27]

When negotiations take place over time, the negotiators must account for changes in factual circumstances that may affect the negotiations. These "exogenous shocks" (as political scientist Bruce Bueno de Mesquita calls them)[28] can add or remove parties from the negotiation, add or remove issues, or even change the parties' preferences. Each of these effects can upset already-achieved agreements,

27. *See generally* NICHOLAS NASSIM TALEB, THE BLACK SWAN (2008). Google's Ngram viewer (which provides an excellent view of how books use buzzwords) shows a sharp spike in the use of the phrase "black swan" between 2003 and 2008. *See* http://books.google.com/ngrams/graph?content=%22black+swan+%22&year_start=1800&year_end=2012&corpus=15&smoothing=3&share= (last viewed Jan. 1, 2013).

28. BRUCE BUENO DE MESQUITA, THE PREDICTIONEER'S GAME, Kindle location 2357 (2009).

or change points of possible future agreement. In other words, allowing for transactions over time increases the risk that random events will influence the negotiation, for better or (more likely) for worse.

These changes can affect even the negotiators themselves. People do not remain the same over time. Their preferences may change, or their circumstances.

Economists and social scientists have spent years investigating the problem of inconsistent personal preferences over time; they usually refer to it as the problem of "multiple selves."[29] People's emotional states can also change over time; so, to the extent their negotiating style depends on an emotional state (for example, convincing displays of anger), negotiations may become easier if they are stretched out over a longer time period.[30] Or, in other cases, it may be worth shortening a negotiation if one knows that one's counterparty is particularly volatile, since doing so may limit the opportunities for a tantrum to derail otherwise successful negotiations.

Circumstances also change. Due to promotions, transfers, deaths, and a whole host of other possibilities, the composition of the negotiating team on one or both sides may change. The longer the negotiation takes, the greater the chance of this happening. As team members change, there is a possibility the new members will want to revisit previously agreed elements. Because they lack the context that led to the interim agreements or agendas, they can potentially derail the negotiation. They may have different values or perspectives. They may have been injected into the negotiation precisely to change the dynamic and challenge the flow of the process, or they may be testing the limits of their own influence.

Changes in negotiating teams are often inevitable, even if—and sometimes especially if—the negotiation is progressing successfully. While the negotiation may have started with just a handful of people

29. *See, e.g.*, George Ainslie, *Beyond Microeconomics: Conflict among Interests in a Multiple Self as a Determinant of Value*, *in* JON ELSTER (ED.), THE MULTIPLE SELF (1986).

30. For more on the effect of emotional states on negotiation, *see* § 2.3.

on each side, if it gains momentum, it will migrate outside that original team. There will be others that are needed to progress discussions, perform due diligence, or provide guidance to the management teams. New people are typically brought in for two reasons: (1) the original team needs additional resources given the day-to-day requirements of the negotiation, or (2) specific expertise is required on different parts of the negotiation.

Paul Seabright has theorized that outside events have affected negotiations since communities of farmers and bands of hunter-gatherers first attempted trade. (In those cases, the availability of food, which depended heavily on weather and other exogenous factors, would affect whether the hunter-gatherers traded in the first place.)[31]

A common modern form of exogenous shock is a proposed change in law. Proposed legal changes can generate pressure to settle complex litigation before the legal regime changes for the worse for one party.[32] This may also dictate the use of certain terms in either settlements or deals. Indeed, Robert Mnookin and Lewis Kornhauser, in their influential study "Bargaining in the Shadow of the Law," observed that changes in legal rules governing divorce changed the relative bargaining power of divorcing husbands and wives.[33]

When negotiations take place over a short span of time (a day to a week), the odds that outside events will have some effect are slim. The longer those negotiations continue, however, the more likely it becomes that outside events (market fluctuations, conclusions of competing deals, changes in personnel) will affect the negotiation.

31. Paul Seabright, The Company of Strangers: A Natural History of Economic Life 273–74 (rev. ed. 2010).

32. *See, e.g.*, *In re* Corrugated Container Antitrust Litig., 643 F.2d 195, 203 n.8 (5th Cir. 1981) (defendant negotiated antitrust settlement in shadow of change to statutory liability).

33. Robert H. Mnookin & Lewis Kornhauser, *Bargaining in the Shadow of the Law: The Case of Divorce*, 88 Yale L.J. 950, 978 (1978).

To take another example, consider one of the most protracted and difficult negotiations ever: the attempts of the British East India Company to penetrate the markets of China in the eighteenth century. The Chinese empire was notoriously closed to Western outsiders. The British East India Company's mission was to open trade in Asia to enrich British merchants. In 1759, James Flint, a member of the company who spoke Chinese, traveled to the Qing court in Peking (now Beijing) to carry complaints about unfair trade restrictions and corrupt Chinese officials in the southern province of Canton. Once he had brought the complaints to Peking, he appeared to convince the emperor of the need to investigate the corruption; the emperor agreed to send a commission to investigate his allegations. Flint sent his ship—the *Success*—back to Canton while he returned on his own. The *Success* was lost at sea. And once Flint arrived back in Canton, he was arrested and received a three-year prison sentence for breaking various regulations, including those against sailing north, presenting petitions, and learning Chinese in the first place.[34]

Another form of exogenous shock may be the appearance of other agreements in analogous cases. In legal negotiations, for example, the settlements of similar cases on terms that favor either the plaintiff or the defendant may embolden the parties in a particular case to ask for more themselves.[35] As we discussed earlier in this chapter, previous agreements in either law or industry can affect the terms of a current negotiation. So, to the extent that similar agreements occur during a negotiation, their terms may lend additional bargaining power to one side over the other.

These changes in circumstances over time—few of which are predictable—create uncertainty.[36] And uncertainty is a factor that

34. *See* JONATHAN D. SPENCE, THE SEARCH FOR MODERN CHINA 121 (1990).

35. *See* Depoorter, *supra* note 21, at 957, 960.

36. *See, e.g.*, Richard A. Posner, *Let Us Never Blame a Contract-Breaker*, 107 MICH. L. REV. 1349, 1362 (2009) ("In addition, contract negotiations and choice of terms

businessmen and lawyers alike work very hard to control in negotiations. Uncertainty can surround any number of circumstances. There can be uncertainty about the state of the law. There can be uncertainty about the people who are important on the other side of the negotiations. The longer the time horizon for a deal, the more uncertainty will accrue before the end of the negotiations.

5.4 Learning—Why Some Conflict May Not Be So Bad

"Rommel... you magnificent bastard! I read your book!"

—GENERAL GEORGE S. PATTON, JR.,
Patton (20th Century Fox, 1970)

Negotiators learn over time. They gain a deeper understanding of the subject they are negotiating and the people they are negotiating with. Peoples' understanding of events and other people changes over time as well. Lawyers, for example, will come to a greater understanding of the complexities of a given lawsuit, information that will inform their sense of how much a settlement is worth.[37] That understanding may come from new information. But it can also come from the decay of certain information: issues that seemed simple at first may reveal themselves to be more complicated on reflection, or facts that seemed clear may be contradicted by new facts that are discovered.

But, in addition, as the negotiation progresses, the moves each side makes will provide the other side with more information, whether or not they intend to. In the standard economic model

(including price) are heavily influenced by the lawyers' and clients' understanding of the legal framework. Changing a common-law rule creates a period of uncertainty, as courts explore the boundaries of the rule in case-by-case adjudication.").

37. *See* Geoffry C. Hazard, Jr. & Dana A. Remus, *Advocacy Revalued*, 159 U. PA. L. REV. 751, 761 (2011) (discussing effect of time on understanding of litigation).

of bargaining, economists envision a buyer and a seller, and some private information (the true value of the object to the buyer). The buyer has an incentive to hide the true value, and the only real indication of the true value of the object is the buyer's willingness to keep negotiating or walk away.

Should the bargaining lead to any conflict, however, it will provide another source of private information (the distribution of power), and another way of learning about it (the fighting). Fighting will reveal some information that's not as prone to strategic manipulation. For example, actual litigation will reveal one's resolve to litigate, as well as provide some idea of the resources one has at his disposal.[38] Political scientist Robert Powell has proposed a model that explains how this dynamic works, and while he was specifically studying nations that might war against each other, the model also applies to opposing parties in litigation and to companies that compete in the same industry.

In the model Powell proposes, there is a satisfied party (we can call them the defendant for our purposes) and a dissatisfied party (the plaintiff). The plaintiff registers a complaint or a threat, and the defendant makes an offer. The more the defendant concedes, the more likely there will be a settlement without a fight, but the worse the terms become for the defendant. If the plaintiff rejects the offer, then there is conflict. But the bargaining doesn't have to end there. Instead, at the end of each round of conflict (here, those might be when motions are decided or discovery is released), each side knows a little more about the other side's capabilities and about the likely outcome of the conflict.

In the standard economic model of bargaining, there is really only one source of uncertainty (the price of the object), in negotiation that leads to conflict, there are two. One is the price; but the other uncertainty is the distribution of power, which will dictate who would win

38. Robert Powell, *Bargaining & Learning While Fighting*, 48 AM. J. POL. SCI. 344 (2004).

in a conflict. For lawyers, this can be any number of things: the state of the law, the relative talent for each firm, the resources available to each firm, even the rhetorical advantage for each position. For competing companies, this could be the difference in available capital, or a planned product launch. "This difference in types of uncertainty suggests that crises arising out of uncertainty over costs or resolve are likely to be settled more quickly and short of large scale fighting than are crises arising out of uncertainty over the distribution of power."[39]

In other words, bargaining, even adversarial bargaining between two parties locked in conflict, is primarily an exchange of information. So for litigators who continue to keep negotiation open as a strategy, it is important to watch how their opponents are actually fighting the case: doing so can provide vital information about what kinds of offers they might entertain, and which ones they are certain to reject.

5.5 Sequential Strategy—Why It Pays to Be Nice

"Don't get mad, get even."

—ROBERT F. KENNEDY

Game theorists distinguish between two different kinds of games—*simultaneous* games, where both sides make their choice at the same time and so do not have knowledge of the other side's move (think "rock, paper, scissors") and *sequential* games, where each side takes turns, so each side can see what moves the other side makes (think chess).

Simultaneous games may, based on the rules and the payoff structures, encourage parties to act competitively. The classic version of this, taught to most college students at this point, is the Prisoner's

39. *Id.* at 344.

Dilemma. Because neither party gets the opportunity to communicate with the other, and because neither party may observe the other's moves, it becomes more important to play for immediate advantage, which means informing on one's fellow prisoner.

Sequential games can be either competitive or cooperative. But social scientists have learned that longer-term sequential games tend to enable cooperation.[40] In fact, a number of scholars have found that the longer negotiations progress, the less parties bluff, and the less they demand.[41] How does this occur? In part, because each party can observe at least part of the other party's moves. (Remember, any action, whether communication or something else, leaks information.)

The fundamental point here is that the more interactions one party expects to have with another, the more likely it is to act in a cooperative, value-generating manner. This may sound like an obvious point, but given the assumptions involved in classical economics and game theory, it is anything but. In other words, the longer a series of negotiations go on, the more likely the negotiators are to cooperate.[42] A number of studies have shown that negotiators who encounter cooperation are more likely to cooperate in future exchanges.[43]

One explanation for this effect is that repeated interactions create some semblance of a working relationship, and it is difficult to demonize a known counterparty.[44] (Not impossible, just difficult.) Repeated interactions also create an investment in the agreement.[45]

40. Peter D. Taylor & Troy Day, *Stability in Negotiation Games and the Emergence of Cooperation*, 271 PROC. ROYAL. SOC'Y LONDON BIO. SCI. 669, 673 (2004).

41. Blakrishnan et al., *supra* note 7, at, 642.

42. Taylor & Day, *supra* note 40, at 669.

43. Blakrishnan et al., *supra* note 7, at 646. This, of course, is in line with the recent findings that most humans engage in behavior that exhibits strong reciprocity. (*See* § 2.3.1.)

44. ROGER FISHER ET AL., GETTING TO YES: NEGOTIATING AGREEMENT WITHOUT GIVING IN 157 (1991).

45. *Id.*, at 19.

(This is consistent with our discussion of loss aversion and sunk costs in chapter 2.)[46]

Another explanation is that, when negotiators repeatedly interact, they train each other to cooperate. Economists have observed that, in repeated bargaining games, "tit-for-tat" strategies perform extremely well.[47] A "tit-for-tat" strategy is one in which a party matches the moves of its counterparty. Each time the counterparty cooperates, the party matches that move with cooperation. Each time the counterparty defects or cheats, the party matches that move with a defection of its own. Economists have shown, through long times spent in front of computers simulating these exchanges, that tit-for-tat strategies tend to encourage cooperation (and therefore larger joint gains) over the long run. This conclusion makes intuitive sense. Wouldn't we all rather deal with someone we believe we can trust? And what better way of establishing trust than to show that both our promises of mutual cooperation and our threats of mutual destruction are credible?

This idea that negotiators learn over time apparently applies even to artificial negotiators, like software designed to bargain over the Internet.[48]

These tit-for-tat strategies may not work in shorter games with fewer turns, because most tit-for-tat strategies require several concessions by one side to draw out concessions by the other[49] (or, similarly, several punishments of noncooperation to encourage a change in behavior). The longer the tit-for-tat games runs, the more trustworthy the tit-for-tat strategy becomes.

46. *See* § 2.1.3.

47. *See, e.g.*, George Bunn & Rodger A. Payne, *Tit-for-Tat & the Negotiation of Nuclear Arms Control*, 9 ARMS CONTROL TODAY 207, 207 (1988); Taylor & Day, *supra* note 40, at 669, 673.

48. Jim R. Oliver, *Artificial Agents Learn Policies for Multi-Issue Negotiations*, 1 INT'L J. ELECTRONIC COMMERCE 49, 52 (1997).

49. Bunn & Payne, *supra* note 47, at 207, 211 ("Overall, the correlation between a single concession and a responding concession (which would be quite like TFT) was not strong. However, a trend of concessions or a group of concessions on one

5.6 Practical Implications

There are a number of lessons we can learn about how to conduct negotiations from the problems that arise when they are conducted over longer periods of time.

Scheduling Matters

Getting out in front of the process and laying out a timeline to provide urgency and expectations to each side is in itself a negotiation. There are both practical and substantial issues that need to be addressed and time allotted for. However, once you agree to the major milestones, then the sides have made a commitment to pull together the resources required to meet them.

Getting key meetings or hearings on the calendar focuses a team. People want to be prepared for challenges by the other side and also demonstrate their proficiency and value to their own team. A series of known deadlines, both major and minor, will help drive the collective team to deliver on the required elements for the negotiation.

Understanding the practical elements of how long certain elements of work will take or meetings based on travel schedules and holidays are very valuable in avoiding disconnects on expectations. Knowing U.S.-based team members will not be traveling on the Fourth of July or that Asian team members will be gone for Golden Week helps to manage expectations and avoid an unnecessary loss of trust.

Just as no battle plan ever survives first contact with the enemy, no schedule or timeline ever survives intact from the first draft. Practical or material issues will cause shifts to any schedule. However, this is not an excuse to not have one. Rather, having a consistent view of what are the required actions or meetings and revising them based on new information is a valuable tool to keep both sides on task.

side seemed to make a difference to the other—though it did not always produce cooperation.").

Note that if the other side consistently chooses not to align on a schedule at all or consistently misses agreed upon milestones, that is valuable information in itself. Meetings being delayed or key people being "unavailable," despite the sincerity of the apology, can be quite telling. It reveals information either about their position or the priority that this has within their organization.

If there is an external requirement to meet a certain timeline, that creates a distinct dynamic in the negotiations. This requirement can be based on a range of reasons:

- Financial calendar—a company needs to sell this business in this financial quarter for earning or tax purposes.
- Board meetings—there are set times when major agreements can be approved or that the company's operational cycle makes easier.
- Hearing date—requirement to settle before a court imposes one.

These deadlines can be either helpful or hurtful, depending on your position. In any negotiation, it is always a mix of time, value, and terms. If time becomes fixed, then either or both sides need to be ready to compromise on both value and terms. Understanding that walking in to the negotiation is critical.

Use Interim Agreements

Interim agreements are often a way of "locking in" progress during negotiations. Because both sides may have different interests in the pace and timeline of negotiations, an interim agreement is a method to create a meeting point to both confirm what has been agreed but also outline what still needs to get done—allowing both sides to claim success.

Another thing parties can do is change the time horizon of their agreement. Few agreements are permanent; most come with an implicit or explicit expiration date. Contracts with shorter durations do not have to worry about predicting the far future.[50] Contracts with longer durations, by contrast, either are more certain of future events or are between parties willing to bear that risk.

Parties can also create options, which place the risk of certain future events occurring on one or the other of the parties. The most visible of this kind of agreement is the "force majeure" or "Act of God" clause, which usually states that a party is not liable for future nonperformance if some unforeseen future event interferes. Force majeure clauses have been used to excuse nonperformance in cases involving gas explosions,[51] disputes with labor unions,[52] promulgation of new regulations, and even economic downturns.

Interim agreements are more common than most people realize, even the people making them. They can be simple and informal, such as writing a confirming e-mail that summarizes the agreements reached during a phone conversation. While these e-mail exchanges may not be legally enforceable as contracts,[53] they are certainly effective placeholders during longer, more complicated negotiations. The specific form of the interim agreement—a memorandum of understanding, a letter of intent, a term sheet—does not necessarily matter. Each are methods of confirming agreement on the major points of the negotiation and documenting that fact.

Interim agreements can also shorten the time horizon of certain aspects of a deal. Events in the near future are easier to predict than those further out. Interim agreements can lock in the more

50. Richard A. Posner, *The Law & Economics of Contract Interpretation*, 83 TEX. L. REV. 1581, 1584 (2005).

51. *See* Millennium Inorganic Chems. Ltd. v. Nat'l Union Fire Ins. Co., 686 F. Supp. 2d 558 (D. Md. 2010).

52. *See* Aleris Aluminum Canada L.P. v. Valeo, Inc., 718 F. Supp. 2d 825 (E.D. Mich. 2010).

53. *See, e.g.*, Orteck Int'l Inc. v. Transpacific Tire & Wheel, Inc., 704 F. Supp. 2d 499, 514, 515 (D. Md. 2010) (granting summary judgment to defendants on breach of

easily-negotiated short-term terms, while leaving some of the more difficult longer-term terms for later dates.[54]

These can also provide additional incentives to keep dealing. Each interim agreement gives an incentive to continue negotiation, because you become invested in the interim agreement as well. They also give greater clarity on what else needs to happen for the deal to happen.

There are some risks to interim agreements. First, if not defined properly, interim agreements themselves can become the subject of additional fights. Second, because of path dependence, an interim agreement that has not received the same strategic scrutiny as a final deal may wind up affecting that deal. In that case, one party or the other may have to explain a final agreement to its constituents that is based on a number of interim agreements. The constituents may be mystified at the fact that a term survived into the final agreement, and the party may not be able to justify the term except by reference to the complete history of the negotiations. Why would that matter? Because, in those cases, the constituent may not agree to the final term, even though the parties had—because they had seen it day to day—not considered it to be controversial.

Walk-away rights. Another way of limiting the risk that events will overtake a negotiation is to agree on walk-away rights for either party. (These are also sometimes called "blow-up" clauses.) Walk-away

contract claims because underlying e-mail exchanges were not enforceable contracts). In this particular case, the trial court found that the e-mail exchange did not meet several of Maryland's requirements for the Statute of Frauds (an old common-law doctrine requiring contracts to be reduced to a single writing) and that the e-mail exchanges did not contain finalized terms. *But see, e.g.*, Sands v. Helen HCI, LLC, 945 N.E.2d 176 (Ind. App. 2011) (reversing dismissal of breach-of-contract claim because e-mail exchange was enforceable agreement to settle case). For more about when e-mail exchanges may be considered enforceable contracts, *see* chapter 6.

54. *See* Posner, *supra* note 50, at 1581, 1584 ("Persons contemplating a transaction can reduce the potential error costs arising from imperfect foresight by shortening the duration of their contract (consider employment at will, or spot markets), since the near future is more predictable than the distant future. Similarly, they can agree on just a few things and leave the rest for a future negotiation by 'agreeing to agree.'").

rights allow one party or the other to abandon the negotiation (or the agreement) should certain events come to pass. For example, if one of the principals in the negotiation dies, or if certain earnings targets are not reached during the period when negotiations occur, then the parties would be able to abandon the agreement without worrying about adverse consequences.[55]

Start Nice, and Match Your Counterparty's Behavior

When entering into a negotiation, there is typically very little downside by starting off on a cordial note. In fact, perceived openness and kindness will generally be rewarded with information and insight into the other parties. The initial trust built provides a basis for the negotiation's success. Conversely, beginning as combative, arrogant, or presenting a siege mentality breeds instant distrust. The negotiations are already in a hole before you have ever gotten to substantive issues. As time progresses, you will want multiple tools to deal with the conflict and challenges that come forth in any negotiation. Trust and kindness can be just as valuable tools as ultimatums and threats.

Actively manage transitions. Changes in personnel can affect not just the substantive discussion of issues but intangibles such as trust or the rapport between negotiating teams. Prior to bringing the new members into contact with the other side, make sure they understand the history and context of the negotiation. The project manager for negotiation should maintain a regularly updated summary of the negotiation that includes:

- Why are the current issues being discussed the right issues?
- What has already been covered and agreed to?
- What has been agreed to that is not be a material issue?

55. *See* Albert Choi & George Triantis, *Strategic Vagueness in Contract Design: The Case of Corporate Acquisitions*, 119 YALE L.J. 848, 857–58 (2010).

If a team member walks into a discussion or drafts any material to be shared with the other side that is contrary to what is known in these questions, several bad things happen. First, the other side becomes either confused or frustrated by what is communicated, and time is wasted. Second, the new team member starts off with a credibility deficit because of her misguided actions and so becomes less useful. As a result, it is critical to make sure team members understand the current landscape when they join the discussions.

To formally introduce team members to the other side, there are a couple of options:

- For central players, try to bring them on at an in-person meeting to give them opportunities to illustrate their credibility and compatibility so that they can immediately build trust visibly
- For issue-specific experts who will only have limited direct engagement, it is valuable to have one of the trusted central players from your team join phone calls or meetings done with the other side. While these can be time-consuming, it is typically more efficient than dealing with damage control on the back end.

One method to deal with changing people is to provide them with an "on-boarding" to the current status of the negotiation. This would be a side meeting with the principal negotiators from each side to help orient the new team member to provide the context for how the team reached the point in the process that they did. By doing it out of the normal flow of meetings, the new member's inquiries do not distract or disrupt the rest of the team.

If the new team member is disrupting the current path of the negotiations, this is a time to invoke a back-channel discussion (for more on this, see chapter 9) to understand the influence and direction the new member was given. Depending upon what is learned, it may be necessary to escalate to a discussion among the executive sponsors from each side to either reset the new team member or revisit the course of the negotiation.

5.7 Conclusion

Despite what shows up in movies, negotiations are not concluded at a table in one sitting. Time is a critical element that must be embraced and planned for. Understanding what the starting points are for each of the parties and why some prefer to go quickly versus slowly is just as much a part of the negotiation as the specific issues of any agreement.

During that time, there are events that continue to happen in the world that may change negotiating positions on either or both sides of the table. Also during the process, each of the parties learns more about itself and the other party, which will cause the negotiating dynamic to change.

Because of all of these facts, what we have found is that it pays to be nice and work with the other team through the process, because no one ever does know what exactly is going to happen next and how it may affect the negotiation.

In the next two chapters, we will explore the rules that go with negotiation, both the written regulations and the unwritten rules of culture.

6

Regulated Negotiations

Jerome Van Gorkom, the chairman of credit-reporting agency TransUnion, faced an unusual problem. The company's taxable income was not large enough to take advantage of certain investment tax credits. So Van Gorkom approached his friend (and corporate takeover specialist) Jay Pritzker about buying the company. (Van Gorkom had decided against a leveraged buyout by management, even though the board was open to one, because he feared the conflicts of interest it would generate.) Based on calculations he performed himself, Van Gorkom suggested a price of $55 per share to Pritzker when they met. Pritzker counter-offered with a lower price and asked that the terms of the deal prevent TransUnion from shopping around for a better offer. (He was worried that he was just a "stalking horse" for better offers.)

Two days after their meeting, Pritzker called Van Gorkom and told him he was interested in TransUnion at $55 per share. Van Gorkom met with Pritzker several more times during the next few days, hammering out the details of the deal. Finally, in mid-September, Pritzker told Van Gorkom that the TransUnion board would have to act on the proposal within days, in order to beat the opening of the English stock exchange. Van Gorkom hastily convened two meetings, one of the senior management of the TransUnion on September 19, and one of the board on September 20. The September 19 meeting was a disaster for Van Gorkom. Almost no one in senior management liked the proposed merger: they thought that the price was too low, that the deal was moving too quickly, and that there had not been enough chance to shop around for other buyers.

The September 20 board meeting also went badly. Because lawyers were still drafting the merger agreement (remember, they had been given only a weekend to put it together), there were no documents available for review. Instead, all the board could rely on was a twenty-minute presentation from Van Gorkom and statements by some other members of management. Van Gorkom briefly rehearsed the problem he was trying to solve (accelerated depreciation of assets coupled with insufficient investment tax credits) and talked about his reasons for approaching Pritzker. He did not tell the board that he was the one to propose the $55 price, or how he had reached that number. As the Delaware Supreme Court later put it:

> The Board meeting of September 20 lasted about two hours. Based solely upon Van Gorkom's oral presentation, Chelberg's supporting representations, Romans' oral statement, Brennan's legal advice, and their knowledge of the market history of the Company's stock, 9 the directors approved the proposed Merger Agreement.[1]

1. Smith v. Van Gorkom, 488 A.2d 858, 869 (Del. 1985).

The board reconvened on October 8 and approved a series of amendments sight unseen. (The amendments were actually delivered two days later and differed significantly from what Van Gorkom had told the board they would contain. In particular, they limited the board's ability to withdraw from the deal or make a better one.) It did solicit other offers during this period as a "market test," but no one else would make an offer unless TransUnion backed out of its current merger agreement.

The merger (into a Pritzker-owned entity, New T Company) resulted in a shareholder class action in Delaware state court that sought to undo the entire transaction, or, failing that, for significant money damages. The defendant directors won a bench trial, where the chancellor (the Delaware term for a judge in a court of equity) found that they had been fairly informed and had properly exercised their business judgment in approving the merger. (More on this later.) But the Delaware Supreme Court reversed the judgment, resulting in a damages award of millions of dollars for the plaintiff class, and a lesson for subsequent business executives that Delaware courts would examine the conduct of business negotiations very carefully to make sure officers and directors upheld their duties of loyalty and care.

Any negotiation—no matter how simple—takes place against a backdrop of legal rules.[2] Every time a consumer walks into a store and buys a computer, her purchase is governed by the laws of contract (she agrees to pay money, she gets a computer), warranty (her computer may come with separate contracts that govern what happens if she bought a defective computer), fraud (the store cannot lie to her in order to sell the product), taxation (if she can claim the computer as a work-related expense on her own taxes), and various other laws. In fact, many laws exist specifically to shift

2. *See generally* Robert H. Mnookin & Lewis Kornhauser, *Bargaining in the Shadow of the Law: The Case of Divorce*, 88 YALE L.J. 950, 951 (1979) (examining effect of family law on divorce negotiations).

the leverage within a negotiation.[3] So changes to legal rules will change the balance of power in a negotiation.[4]

Even more than a consumer buying a computer, however, negotiations involving large organizations take place against a heavily regulated backdrop. (Indeed, Congress and state legislatures have passed a number of laws, such as the Sherman Act and the Clayton Act, specifically to regulate the behavior of large organizations when they interact with each other.)

The specific content of these laws varies from state to state and from country to country. And enforcement of those laws may even vary from court to court within a specific jurisdiction.[5] Nonetheless, certain basic principles remain relatively constant, and those who negotiate on behalf of organizations should be familiar enough with those principles to know when their specific negotiation is treading close to legal trouble.

The level of regulation is a moving target. Because government regulation affects how organizations negotiate (and how lucrative their deals may be), many firms make efforts to change influence regulations an important part of their overall corporate strategy.[6] Similarly, while common law (that is, the law made in U.S. courts) tends to be stable, there is a constant influx of new precedent that may change the nuances in various jurisdictions.

3. Robert S. Adler & Eliot M. Stephenson, *When David Meets Goliath: Dealing with Power Differentials in Negotiations*, 5 HARV. NEGOTIATION L. REV. 1, 28–29 (2000) ("statutory or common law provisions may shift the power balance by prohibiting either side from overreaching").

4. *See generally* Mnookin & Kornhauser, *supra* note 2, at 950, 978 (discussing effects of change in family law on divorce negotiations). For more on the effects of changes in governing law, *see* chapter 5.

5. *Id.* at 950, 969 ("Legal rules are generally not as simple or straightforward as is suggested by the last example. Often the outcome in court is far from certain, with any number of outcomes possible.").

6. Amy J. Hillman & Michael A. Hitt, *Corporate Political Strategy Formulation: A Model of Approach, Participation, and Strategy*, 24 ACAD. MGMT. REV. 825, 825 (1999)

Most of these rules are enforceable in one of two ways: prosecution by a government, or litigation by private parties. The type of private party ranges widely; contract actions are litigated by parties to a contract,[7] antitrust suits may be brought by competitors or customers,[8] suits invoking corporation law are usually brought by shareholders,[9] and all of these may also be brought by entrepreneurial class action lawyers.[10]

There is no way a book this short, let alone a single chapter in it, could cover every area of the law that might arise in a complex negotiation. There are simply too many, and they change too frequently. Instead, we will provide a rough approximation of each of the bodies of law that touch on most complex business negotiations, and focus on how these rules affect the conduct of negotiations. In the process, we will also try to highlight the question of when it is wise to bring in the lawyers.

We also will not attempt to address certain types of law—like tax or bankruptcy—even though they have an undeniable effect on complex negotiations. (Most corporate deals are affected by tax laws, for example; and many complex lawsuits, at some point, must account for the possibility that the corporate defendants may go bankrupt.) The reason for this is that these are complex areas of law all on their own and will usually require the services of specialists. Suffice to say that

("Because government policies have significant effects on the competitive environment of firms, many firms are expanding their efforts to affect public policy decisions.").

7. Richard A. Posner, *The Law & Economics of Contract Interpretation*, 83 TEX. L. REV. 1581, 1582 (2005). Judge Posner does note that most contracts are enforced informally through the maintenance of business reputation. *Id.* at 1606.

8. *See, e.g.*, Pac. Bell Telephone Co. v. Linkline Commc'ns, Inc., 129 S. Ct. 1109 (2009) (antitrust suit brought by competitor).

9. *See* Stephen M. Bainbridge, *Why a Board? Group Decisionmaking in Corporate Governance*, 55 VAND. L. REV. 1, 42 (2002) (discussing effects of shareholder litigation on board decisions).

10. *See* BRIAN ANDERSON & ANDREW TRASK, THE CLASS ACTION PLAYBOOK § 3 (2010).

our general advice that it is usually a good idea to consult an expert goes double for these situations.

6.1 Information and Disclosure—Basic Concepts

"Information wants to be free."

—STEWART BRAND

The most important rules that influence complex negotiations are those that govern the disclosure of information. The amount (and kind) of information available to parties in a negotiation can have a very real effect on how it is conducted. There are various levels of protection for information that may be used in a negotiation. Among them are the following.

Public domain. Some information is simply in the public domain, which means it is available to anyone willing to put in the work to collect it. Individuals may trade on this information without fear of government prosecution. And courts, relying on the assumption that investors are quick and thorough researchers, deem information in the public domain to be almost instantaneously incorporated into a stock's price.[11] In all, it is surprising how much information sits in the public domain. As Malcolm Gladwell reported for *The New Yorker* back in 2002, much of the information necessary to identify Enron as a bad long-term investment was publicly available. Indeed, a group of Cornell students, as part of a class project, had already posted a "Sell" recommendation on the Web; their analysis was based in large part on the same flaws that would later bring down the company's stock price.[12]

11. *See* Basic Inc. v. Levinson, 485 U.S. 224 (1988).

12. *See* Malcolm Gladwell, *Open Secrets*, NEW YORKER, Jan. 8, 2007, at 44, 46–47.

However, just because information is in the public domain does not mean that everyone knows it. It can take a great deal of work to collect raw data and process it into usable forms. As a result, companies will often leave a lot of information in the public domain because, in its raw form, it poses no competitive threat.

Business confidential information. Some information is so vital to maintaining a business's competitive edge that the law offers it additional legal protection. For example, some information may be classified as *trade secrets*. What is a trade secret? KFC's specific blend of eleven herbs and spices is one; so is the recipe for original formula Coca-Cola.[13] But trade secrets involve far more than just lunch ingredients. A company's manufacturing process may be a trade secret, or the specific protocols it uses to address customer service programs. According to most states' laws, a trade secret is information that derives economic value from the fact that it is not publicly known and that the company has taken pains to keep private.[14]

In addition to trade secrets, companies treat certain other kinds of information as business confidential. Pricing information may be business confidential. (In fact, as discussed in greater detail in section 6.3 below, the law may actually prohibit businesses from sharing pricing information.) Corporate strategies may also be treated as business confidential, although some executives reason that if a company's core strategy is not apparent from its public actions, it may not be worth protecting in the first place.

Privileged information. Some information receives even greater protection than we have already described. For example, information that an individual shares with her lawyer in order to get legal advice is protected by the attorney-client privilege.[15] The privilege can become

13. *See* KFC Corp. v. Marion-Kay Co., Inc., 620 F. Supp. 1160, 1172 (S.D. Ind. 1985); Coca-Cola Co. v. Joseph C. Wirthman Drug Co., 48 F. 2d 743 (8th Cir. 1931).

14. *See, e.g.*, Seng-Tiong Ho v. Taflove, 648 F. 3d 489, 504 (7th Cir. 2011) (applying Illinois law); Contour Design, Inc. v. Chance Mold Steel Co., 794 F. Supp. 2d 315, 322 (D.N.H. 2011) (applying New Hampshire law).

15. Upjohn Co. v. United States, 449 U.S. 383, 389–90 (1981).

more complicated in application. (For example: Does the privilege apply when a member of an organization speaks to an organization's attorney?[16] What if the attorney also provides business advice on occasion?)[17] A person can also waive the attorney-client privilege, by revealing the content of the communications told to her attorney.

The law protects certain other kinds of information from disclosure in litigation as well. An attorney's mental impressions about his case are protected as *attorney work product*.[18] And an attorney's communications with other parties on the same side of a lawsuit may be protected under the *common interest rule*.[19]

Required disclosures. Finally, the law requires that certain information must be disclosed even during the course of a negotiation. For example, *securities laws* require the disclosure of material facts when issuing a security.[20] Since corporate mergers (and some other transactions) often require issuing new securities, those provisions may well apply, and may require disclosure of any ongoing negotiations.[21] And, in many negotiations, public disclosure that parties are talking may have an effect on the course of the negotiation itself by, for example, attracting competitors.[22] Disclosures of a proposed acquisition

16. *See, e.g.*, Tucker v. Fischbein, 237 F. 3d 275 (3d Cir. 2001).

17. *See, e.g.*, *In re* County of Erie, 473 F. 3d 413 (2d Cir. 2007).

18. Hickman v. Taylor, 329 U.S. 495 (1947).

19. *See, e.g.*, US v. Schwimmer, 892 F. 2d 237 (2d Cir. 1989).

20. *See, e.g.*, 15 U.S.C. § 77a, *et seq.*, 15 U.S.C. § 78a, *et seq.*, 17 C.F.R. 240.10b-5.

21. J. Robert Brown, Jr., *Corporate Secrecy, the Federal Securities Laws, and the Disclosure of Ongoing Negotiation*, 36 CATH. U.L. REV. 93, 93–94 (1986).

22. *See, e.g.*, Lyondell Chem. Co. v. Ryan, 970 A.2d 235, 237 (Del. 2009) (Schedule 13D disclosure by company resulted in buyout firm contacting Lyondell board to suggest leveraged buyout); BRYAN BURROUGH & JOHN HELYAR, BARBARIANS AT THE GATE: THE FALL OF RJR NABISCO 8 (1990) ("Lifting the veil of secrecy was ordinarily enough to kill a developing buyout in its cradle: Once disclosed, corporate raiders or other unwanted suitors were free to make a run at the company before management had a chance to prepare its own bid.").

may also prompt the target company to take defensive action.[23] As a result, it becomes important to know which disclosure laws will affect a given negotiation. If the party knows that it must disclose a possible acquisition, its negotiation strategy should account for the possibility of having to deal with competitors or with a board whose interests may diverge from the counterparty's interests.

6.2 Obligations/Duties to Constituents (Corporate Law)

For certain purposes (such as holding property or entering into contracts), the law may treat an organization as a person.[24] In fact, economists have theorized that corporations (the most common private organizational form) exist in part to cut down on the effort and expense of contracting with everyone for everything. As Nobel Laureate Ronald Coase wrote:

> The main reason why it is profitable to establish a firm would seem to be that there is a cost of using the price mechanism. The most obvious cost of "organising" production through the price mechanism is that of discovering what the relevant prices are. The cost may be reduced but it will not be eliminated by the emergence of specialists who will sell this information. The costs of negotiating and concluding a separate contract for each exchange transaction which takes place on a market must also be taken into account.[25]

23. Lyondell Chem., 970 A.2d at 237 (Lyondell board convened in response to Schedule 13D disclosure of intent to buy stock).

24. *See, e.g.*, Dartmouth College v. Woodward, 17 U.S. 518 (1819).

25. Ronald H. Coase, *A Theory of the Firm*, 4 Economica 386, 390–91 (1937).

In reality, however, an organization is a collection of people, with differing motivations, differing loyalties to the organization and differing abilities to influence the conduct of the organization. As a result, any organization—whether business corporation or non-profit—has to deal with various questions: How will it deal with contracts with other bodies? How will it retain its personnel? What will it do with the ideas that its people generate? To whom is it ultimately responsible? Organizations do not have to be formed as corporations,[26] nor must they exist only to generate profits. Nonetheless, we will focus on the for-profit corporation here because it tends to be more heavily regulated than other forms, and because it tends to serve as a template for other organizational forms.

6.2.1 The Corporate Form

"Let me explain to you how this works: you see, the corporations finance Team America, and then Team America goes out . . . and the corporations sit there in their . . . in their corporation buildings, and . . . and, and see, they're all corporation-y . . . and they make money."

—TIM ROBBINS,

Team America: World Police (Paramount, 2004)

The first way in which corporate law regulates negotiations is by regulating the shape the organization takes. In chapter 3, we offered a brief, functional overview of the corporation, focusing mainly on how it creates a constituency within the organization (shareholders and a board of directors) that serves as an additional party to any negotiations. Now, we will look at the law that governs that form. In examining corporate law, we will look primarily at Delaware law. First, Delaware has the most developed body of corporate law

26. *See* Frank H. Easterbrook & Daniel R. Fischel, The Economic Structure of Corporate Law 2 (1991) (discussing alternate organizational forms, including trusts, partnerships, mutuals, and cooperatives).

available, because many corporations incorporate there.[27] Second, other states tend to look to Delaware for guidance on how to handle thorny issues of corporate law when they arise.

Corporate law primarily defines the relationships between those who lead the corporation (managers and directors) and those who own it (shareholders).[28] It also defines the relationship between management and the board of directors that monitors the activity.[29]

6.2.1.1 *Board of Directors*

While the management tends to make the day-to-day decisions affecting a corporation, theoretically the board of directors outranks the managers.[30] (We say "theoretically" because the CEO often exerts extensive influence over the board.) As a result, both the management (officers) and the board (directors) tend to owe certain legal duties to the shareholders of a firm.

What does a corporate board look like? The directors are often leaders of other companies.[31] Ordinarily, they make decisions by

27. E. Norman Veasey & Christine T. D. Guglielmo, *What Happened in Delaware Corporate Law & Governance from 1992–2004? A Retrospective on Some Key Developments*, 153 U. PA. L. REV. 1399, 103 (2005).

28. Of course, the law is more nuanced; it also governs relationships with lenders, bondholders, and preferred stockholders. *See* Douglas G. Baird & M. Todd Henderson, *Other People's Money*, 60 STAN. L. REV. 1309, 1311 (2008). But for our purposes, the relationship with shareholders is enough.

29. Bainbridge, *supra* note 9, at 1, 33.

30. *Id.* at 1, 10 ("In any event, the institutional structure created by corporate law allows, but does not contemplate, one-man rule. If it comes to overt conflict between the board and top management, the board's authority prevails as a matter of law, if not always in practice. Indeed, it is the necessity for retaining dismissal of senior management as a potential sanction that explains why the board is at the apex of the corporate hierarchy rather than functioning as an advisory committee off to the side of the corporate organizational chart.").

31. *See, e.g.*, Lyondell Chem., 970 A.2d at 237 ("Dan Smith ('Smith') was Lyondell's Chairman and CEO. Lyondell's other ten directors were independent and many were, or had been, CEOs of other large, publicly traded companies."); Gantler v. Stephens,

consensus.[32] In fact, legally, a corporate director cannot act alone for the corporation; he may act *only* as part of the board.[33] As a result, we are less concerned about the actions of individual directors.

There is no central government agency ensuring that corporations fulfill their duties to shareholders. Instead, the law that governs managers and directors is usually enforced through private, shareholder-filed lawsuits.[34] As a result, a corporation may at times deviate from these principles if it believes the likelihood of getting sued is low. However, larger corporations with many shareholders run a higher risk of lawsuits, so they are more likely to adhere to corporate law

In fact, the threat of litigation from private parties like shareholders—either through derivative actions or class actions—may also influence whether a corporate board will agree to certain concessions or certain deals. For example, the threat of shareholder litigation may make directors more risk-averse and therefore more likely to drag their feet when presented with new opportunities.[35] (As a result, when guessing how a counterparty's board may react to a proposal, it makes sense to know which state's laws govern their deliberations.)

Depending on the stakes of the negotiations, and the resulting likelihood of lawsuits if the parties cannot successfully conclude an agreement, corporate law can have a significant effect on

965 A.2d 695, 699 (Del. 2009) (describing occupations and business relationships of various directors on board).

32. Bainbridge, *supra* note 9, at 1, 45 ("The board of directors is a collegial body that, for the most part, makes decisions by consensus.").

33. Del. Code § 131(b); *see also* Bainbridge, *supra* note 9, at 11 ("Why this emphasis on collective rather than individual action? The MBCA's drafters offer the following answer: 'The underlying theory is that the consultation and exchange of views is an integral part of the functioning of the board.'").

34. Geoffrey P. Miller, *A Modest Proposal for Fixing Delaware's Broken Duty of Care*, 2010 Colum. Bus. L. Rev. 319, 322.

35. Bainbridge, *supra* note 9, at 42 ("[E]xternal review may skew director decision-making in undesirable ways. Shareholder litigation encourages directors to be risk

relationships between negotiators and directors. Or, as a corporate lawyer advised then RJR Nabisco CEO Ross Johnson (who was notoriously cozy with his board of directors) as he prepared for a leveraged buyout of the firm:

> As soon as you start this . . . [the board are] not your friends anymore. They can't be. Don't expect favors from them; they won't come. They'll be under the control of Wall Street advisers, people you don't even know. They'll be sued by thirty different people for millions of dollars. The pressure will be intense . . . and they will resent you for it.[36]

In some cases, it is possible that the form a corporation takes may magnify some of the cognitive errors we discussed in chapter 2. For example, a corporation that concentrates control in the hands of the CEO may amplify CEO overconfidence.[37] (Some of these cognitive errors may also take the form of corporate culture.)[38]

In general, when an acquisition is likely, Delaware law imposes only one duty on the board of the target company: get the best price possible.[39] However, when deals go wrong and litigation results, the

averse. In turn, risk-averse directors take excessive precautions and avoid risky decisions.").

36. BURROUGH & HELYAR, *supra* note 22, at 2 (2d ed. 2003).

37. Troy A. Paredes, *Too Much Pay, Too Much Deference: Behavioral Corporate Finance, CEOs, & Corporate Governance*, 32 FLA. ST. U.L. REV. 673, 680 (2005) ("My theory is that CEOs are emboldened and more confident as a result of the great deal of corporate control concentrated in their hands, as well as the fact that their business judgment is deferred to and their exercise of control is for the most part unchallenged. In sum, my hypothesis is that deference to the CEO can bolster CEO confidence.").

38. For more on corporate culture, *see* chapter 7.

39. Lyondell Chem., 970 A.2d at 242 ("There is only one *Revlon* duty—to '[get] the best price for the stockholders at a sale of the company.' No court can tell directors exactly how to accomplish that goal, because they will be facing a unique combination of circumstances, many of which will be outside their control.") (internal footnote omitted).

boundaries of other duties, such as the duty of loyalty and the duty of care, may become important.

6.2.2 The Duty of Loyalty

"Fidelity purchased with money, money can destroy."

—SENECA,
The Conquest of Happiness

Both directors and officers owe a duty of loyalty to the corporation that requires them to refrain from benefiting themselves at the expense of the corporation's interests.[40] This duty of loyalty may sound like simple common sense, but as a legal concept, it is notoriously tricky. In particular, it can be extremely difficult to prove loyalty in court.

When the facts allow a court to infer that an officer or director has acted from personal financial interest instead of the interests of the shareholders, he has breached the duty of loyalty. A breach of the duty of loyalty can manifest itself in any number of ways. For example, a failure to provide due diligence for a pending corporate deal may be a breach of loyalty. [41] What does a breach of the duty of loyalty look like? For an example, we can look at the case of *Gantler v. Stephens*.

Gantler was a lawsuit challenging a leveraged buyout of First Niles, a holding company for an Ohio bank. In 2003, the First Niles board of directors (which included company CEO and President William L. Stephens) met and decided that, since First Niles was growing slowly but acquisitions of banks were "brisk," the company should put itself up for sale. Once it decided on the sale, the board retained both an investment bank and a law firm to advise it. The board received four

40. *See, e.g.*, Gantler, 965 A.2d at 708–709.

41. *See, e.g.*, *id.* at 709 ("From these alleged facts it may reasonably be inferred that what motivated Stephens' unexplained failure to respond promptly to Cortland's due diligence request was his personal financial interest, as opposed to the interests of the shareholders.").

offers: one, from the First Niles management, proposed "privatization" (essentially a leveraged buyout); two others, from Farmers National Banc Corporation and Cortland Bancorp, were within the acceptable range for share offers, but both companies indicated that they would fire the current board; the final offer, from First Place Financial Corporation, was within the acceptable range and made no mention of the board's fate.

The board sat on these offers for several weeks and then took steps to learn more about First Place's offer. When First Place went to conduct its due diligence, however, Stephens did not provide the information it requested. First Place wound up making a revised offer that included a lower share price, although since First Niles's stock price was falling, it still represented a substantial premium. At the board's next meeting, Stephens argued for waiting on responding to the offer and scheduled a special meeting to discuss the offer. At that meeting, the board voted 4–1 to reject First Place's revised offer; then Stephens presented management's buyout plan and instructed the lawyers to investigate it further.

Five weeks after the board had rejected the First Place proposal, Stephens presented a full management proposal to the board. The most important feature of this proposal was that it converted a large amount of common stock into "preferred" stock that would still pay dividends, but would not afford its owners the right to vote. The board approved the proposal 3–1, and the vote was followed by a board shake-up, although none of the three "pro" votes lost their seats. Several months later, the board voted unanimously to amend First Niles's certificate of incorporation to allow for the stock reclassification program.

The *Gantler* lawsuit followed. The plaintiffs—a group of shareholders that included one of the ousted directors—challenged the board's proxy statement for the stock reclassification, alleging that it contained a number of material misstatements and that the board had breached its fiduciary duties to the shareholders both by rejecting First Place's proposal to buy the company and by accepting the management stock reclassification proposal. The defendants moved to dismiss the case (a legal procedure that asks the court to recognize that the claims have no legal support), and the Delaware Chancery Court granted the motion. The plaintiffs appealed to the Delaware Supreme Court.

So, among other issues involving more technical aspects of the duty of loyalty, the Delaware Supreme Court had to decide whether turning down what appeared to be a good offer for shareholders—but not for the board—constitutes disloyalty.

The court held that rejecting the offer was disloyal. It was careful to point out that a plaintiff cannot simply allege that a director is disloyal when he rejects an offer that might cost him his place on the board (what it called an "entrenchment motive"), because "[b]y its very nature, a board decision to reject a merger proposal could always enable a plaintiff to assert that a majority of the directors had an entrenchment motive."[42] But, the court also observed that the plaintiffs had alleged additional evidence of self-dealing. Stephens, for example, had discouraged buyers by not responding to due diligence requests. Two other directors—Kramer and Zuzolo—were businessmen for whom the bank was a major client; if the bank changed management, they might lose significant business.

So to be disloyal, a director or officer must take action that benefits them at the expense of the shareholders. Stephens stood to reap a huge financial windfall if he could sabotage offers other than his own; Kramer and Zuzolo both stood to protect their independent business interests if they kept the bank's ownership in its current hands. Each of these individuals was promoting his own financial interest over that of the people who actually owned the bank at the time.

Why require a legally enforceable duty of loyalty? Because without it, directors face strong temptation to commit (and little oversight to prevent) acts for their own benefit, rather than the corporation's. And while the board technically oversees the organization's management, there is no one (but the shareholders, to the extent they

42. Gantler, 965 A.2d 707.

can) watching over the board. Requiring a duty of loyalty that can be enforced through lawsuits turns the shareholders into the watchdogs for the board. Should the board betray investors' interests, the investors can force a course correction in a court of law.

6.2.3 The Duty of Care

"Being responsible sometimes means pissing people off."

—COLIN POWELL

Directors and officers also owe a *duty of care* that requires them to act as an "ordinarily prudent person would... under similar circumstances."[43] The duty of care ensures that a board actually performs its job by acting as an independent adviser, rather than just rubber-stamping management's decisions. Or, as the Delaware Supreme Court put it in *Smith v. Van Gorkom*:

> fulfillment of the fiduciary function requires more than the mere absence of bad faith or fraud. Representation of the financial interests of others imposes on a director an affirmative duty to protect those interests and to proceed with a critical eye in assessing information...[44]

The *Van Gorkom* case (described in greater detail at the beginning of this chapter) provides a good illustration of what situations

43. *See* AM. LAW INST., PRINCIPLES OF CORPORATE GOVERNANCE ANALYSIS AND RECOMMENDATIONS 4.01 (1994) ("A director or officer has a duty to the corporation to perform the director's or officer's functions in good faith, in a manner that he or she reasonably believes to be in the best interests of the corporation, and with the care that an ordinarily prudent person would reasonably be expected to exercise in a like position and under similar circumstances."); *see also* Miller, *supra* note 34, at 322 ("The duty of care officially requires directors to exercise some degree of skill and diligence in the management of the companies they serve.").

44. Van Gorkom, 488 A.2d at 871.

might fall under the duty of care, and its effects show just how difficult it can be to incorporate respect for these duties into an actual negotiation.

The lawsuit began on December 19 and proceeded to trial before the Delaware Court of Chancery. The court found (among other things) that the board had been sufficiently informed for its decision to be protected by the business judgment rule and that the board had adequately informed the shareholders of the details of the deal. When the plaintiffs appealed, the Delaware Supreme Court overturned the verdict. It ruled:

> Under the business judgment rule there is no protection for directors who have made "an unintelligent or unadvised judgment." A director's duty to inform himself in preparation for a decision derives from the fiduciary capacity in which he serves the corporation and its stockholders. Since a director is vested with the responsibility for the management of the affairs of the corporation, he must execute that duty with the recognition that he acts on behalf of others. Such obligation does not tolerate faithlessness or self-dealing. But fulfillment of the fiduciary function requires more than the mere absence of bad faith or fraud. Representation of the financial interests of others imposes on a director an affirmative duty to protect those interests and to proceed with a critical eye in assessing information of the type and under the circumstances present here.[45]

The court expressed particular concern about the fact that, in its hurried meeting, the board had seen no documents—not even a summary of the deal—and were forced to rely only on Van Gorkom's presentation. The court also worried that there had been no independent valuation study to determine how much the deal was worth,

45. *Id.* at 872 (internal citations omitted).

and no independent fairness opinion. While it was careful to say that none of these were "required," it found the absence of any of them to be "that the Board accepted without scrutiny Van Gorkom's representation as to the fairness of the $55 price per share."[46]

However, given the language of the business judgment rule, which requires a court to presume that directors and officers act in good faith, in the best interests of the corporation, and with good information, it is unclear exactly how enforceable the duty of care is.[47] Over time, corporate law has evolved to require the board to consult more third-party advisers.[48] As we discussed in chapter 3, this adds yet another layer of complexity to the negotiation.

The duty of care may also—as a practical matter—require the board to spend a predetermined amount of time on decisions, no matter how simple they may seem at first.[49] From a practical standpoint, this means that negotiations in deals that require board approval must be prepared to address a number of logistical challenges. Assembling a quorum of a board of directors (as well as any necessary advisers) is difficult to do on a moment's notice. As a result, complex negotiations may necessarily take longer not just because of the complexity of the agreement but because of the logistical challenges of getting all of the right people into the right places at the right times.

46. *Id.* at 874–77.

47. *See* Bainbridge, *supra* note 9, at 42 (noting tension between duty of care and business judgment rule).

48. *See* Charles M. Elson, *The Duty of Care, Compensation, and Stock Ownership*, 63 U. Cin. L. Rev. 649, 683 (1995).

49. Lyondell Chem., 970 A.2d at 237 (noting the "trial court expressed concern about the speed with which the transaction was consummated" may have "created a triable issue of fact on duty of care"). *See also* Elson, *supra* note 48, at 682–83 ("It is not unlikely that the proceedings have been informally, or even formally, scripted in advance by corporate counsel keenly aware of the *Van Gorkom* parameters and eager to create a protective paper record. Staged like a good play, such proceedings may evoke a recitation of the required emotions on the part of the actors that, in the final analysis, when the stage lights dim, have only been an illusion. Nothing is gained by such a charade.") (internal footnote omitted).

6.2.4 The Business Judgment Rule

"Wisdom consists of the anticipation of consequences."

—NORMAN COUSINS

The business judgment rule requires courts to presume "that in making a business decision the directors of a corporation acted on an informed basis, in good faith and in the honest belief that the action taken was in the best interests of the company."[50] In other words, unless there is credible evidence otherwise, a court should presume that a board's actions were correct.[51] The business judgment rule is important because it gives corporate officers and directors the freedom to make difficult decisions without worrying that they will be second-guessed in court.

Several legal scholars have pointed out that there is an unavoidable tension between the business judgment rule and the duty of care: after all, how can a court require directors to act prudently if the business judgment rule already presumes that they performed an act in good faith?[52] Some of this tension resolves itself if we recognize that judges are not businesspeople: they are experts in law, but not in business decisions. Therefore, they tend to be reluctant to second-guess decisions without clear evidence that directors or corporate officers threw caution to the winds.[53] Reluctance does not mean refusal, however. For example, in the *Van Gorkom* case,

50. *See, e.g.*, Gantler, 965 A.2d at 705–706 (internal quotations omitted).

51. City of Westland Police & Fire Ret. Sys. v. Axcelis Techs. Inc., 1 A.3d 281, 288 (Del. 2010) ("That conclusion must stand, because the record provides no credible basis to infer that the Board's rejections of those proposals, and its refusal to extend the deadline for SHI to submit a revised acquisition bid, were other than good faith business decisions.").

52. Bainbridge, *supra* note 9, at 42.

53. *See, e.g.*, Donald C. Langevoort, *The Behavioral Economics of Mergers & Acquisitions*, Georgetown Business, Economics & Regulatory Law Research Paper No. 10–17, http://ssrn.com/abstract=1692777, at 16 (Oct. 2010).

the Delaware Supreme Court held that the business judgment rule would not shield a company's directors from liability when the presumption it applied was "contrary to the record and not the product of a logical and deductive reasoning process."[54]

6.2.5 Other Duties to Constituents (Lawyers' Duty to Clients)

"No snowflake in an avalanche ever feels responsible."

—VOLTAIRE

There are other duties to constituents of an organization as well. For example, lawyers who negotiate on behalf of clients owe several duties to those clients, including a duty of loyalty.[55] But lawyers also have some duties that stem from their law licenses, including an ethical duty to conduct negotiations in a certain way. That way includes an ethical duty to tell the truth in negotiations. There is no denying the fact that sometimes people lie when negotiating; or at the very least they shade the truth.[56] This tendency to shade the truth makes sense: to the extent that negotiations are an exchange of information about what agreements will provide the most value to both sides, and to the extent that we all leak information without knowing it, it is just sound strategy to try to keep some information private. There are several ways one can do this. One is to outright lie; another is simply to use accurate information to mislead.

But, because of their unique position as licensed professionals, lawyers face additional duties. In addition to any laws that might prohibit fraud or other deceptive conduct in business negotiations, the law governing lawyers' professional duties has evolved to regulate some of this conduct as well. The best-known of these rules is

54. Van Gorkom, 488 A.2d at 871.

55. *See, e.g.*, Nix v. Whiteside, 475 US 157 (1986).

56. For more on lying in negotiations, *see* chapter 10.

probably the ABA Guidelines on Settlement Negotiations. And while these are not the last word to lawyers in negotiations, they do provide a good starting point.

First and foremost, the ABA Guidelines say that a lawyer cannot lie outright about a material fact.

> In the course of representing a client a lawyer shall not knowingly:
>
> (a) make a false statement of material fact or law to a third person; or
>
> (b) fail to disclose a material fact when disclosure is necessary to avoid assisting a criminal or fraudulent act by a client, unless disclosure is prohibited by Rule 1.6.[57]

Unlike the law governing fraud, these prohibitions against misstatements apply whether or not the counterparty relies on the statement. (In other words, it is the misrepresentation itself that is a problem, not the harm it does to the other side. The ABA has reason to be strict about this: lawyers have enough public relations problems without being thought to condone lying.) That said, the ABA has been quick to clarify that "misstatements" does not mean *all* misstatements, just the ones about provable facts: "The prohibition against making false statements of material fact or law is intended to cover only representations of fact, and not statements of opinion or those that merely reflect the speaker's state of mind."[58] The Guidelines point out that this prohibition allows a certain amount of "puffing," or strategic misinformation, during a negotiation. An attorney may still, for example, react with outrage to a settlement offer that is well within his range of acceptable offers, if he thinks doing so will encourage his counterpart to respond with a higher offer.

57. ABA Guideline 4.1. Rule 1.6 prohibits attorneys from revealing information under certain circumstances.

58. *Id.*

The rules governing legal ethics also impose a duty to disclose certain information, at least to correct misrepresentations by his client.

> The duty to disclose may arise in at least three situations: (1) a lawyer has previously made a false statement of material fact or a partially true statement that is misleading by reason of omission; (2) a lawyer learns of a client's prior misrepresentation of a material fact; and (3) a lawyer learns that his or her services have been used in the commission of a criminal or fraudulent act by the client, "unless such disclosure is prohibited by the ethical duty of confidentiality."[59]

Finally, ethical rules prohibit a lawyer from engaging in "extortionate" tactics or making unlawful threats when negotiating.[60] Threatening a valid civil claim is not considered extortionate; neither is "reminding" the party of the costs of fighting a civil claim in court. So there is some leeway for lawyers to use the threat of a lawsuit as leverage in negotiations.

6.3 Conduct of Negotiations

"A good conspiracy is unprovable. I mean, if you can prove it, it means they screwed up somewhere along the line."

—JERRY FLETCHER,

Conspiracy Theory (Warner Bros. 1997)

There are also specific sets of laws—both in the United States and elsewhere—that regulate the way in which the corporation can conduct its negotiations. These laws were originally intended to prevent

59. ABA Guideline 4.3.5. The language here tracks the language of Model Rule of Professional Conduct 3.3, which governs candor to the tribunal.

60. ABA Guideline 4.3.2 ("A lawyer may not attempt to obtain a settlement by extortionate means, such as by making extortionate or otherwise unlawful threats.").

powerful actors (like conspiracies or criminals) from combining forces to break the law.[61] To that end, they sought to limit the agreements these actors could reach. And aggressive enforcement of those laws also wound up limiting the way negotiations were conducted (since certain statements or tactics could serve as evidence of an illegal agreement).

The single largest category of laws like this regulates conspiracies. For our purposes, a conspiracy is an agreement between two or more parties to violate the law, either by doing something illegal (like murdering someone) or by accomplishing a legal end by illegal means (building a plant faster by bribing government inspectors). Conspiracy is usually not a freestanding cause of action; it must be accompanied by some kind of independently illegal conduct; and it punishes the agreement rather than the act.[62] In fact, there are several ways in which the law prohibits conspiracy. There are both criminal and civil penalties. In addition, the law prohibits specific kinds of conspiracy, such as criminal enterprises (often known as racketeering) and agreements to restrict competition. And, finally, the law prohibits certain kinds of negotiations with foreign companies, particularly those that involve incentives or payoffs.

These laws are most effective when enforced by the government; however, many statutes empower other parties, like competitors or consumers, to bring private lawsuits enforcing them as well. That said, the U.S. Supreme Court has begun to limit how easily plaintiffs may challenge allegedly conspiratorial conduct. Most specifically, the Court now requires that the plaintiffs' complaint describe a "plausible" conspiracy using specific facts, meaning that the plaintiffs may not just use the fact of discussion as their only evidence of a possible conspiracy.[63]

61. Neal Kumar Katyal, *Conspiracy Theory*, 112 YALE L.J. 1307, 1369 (2003) (describing how federal conspiracy law evolved to "take advantage of many of the pressure points" of groups).

62. *Id.* at 1307, 1309.

63. *See, e.g.*, Bell Atlantic Corp. v. Twombly, 127 S. Ct. 1955 (2007) (dismissing complaint that did not contain "plausible suggestion of conspiracy").

A specific subset of these laws also regulates negotiations and agreements that will have an adverse effect on business competition, thus driving up prices for consumers. Specifically, American *antitrust law* (such as the Sherman Act and the Clayton Act) discourages the formation of monopolies or cartels.[64] As a result, it is usually important for parties to understand the antitrust laws of their jurisdiction. However, antitrust laws change substantially from country to country, either in their intent, their substance, or their enforcement. The following overview provides only the most basic of the questions one must consider when engaging in business-related negotiations in a given jurisdiction.

United States. For many business deals, antitrust law constrains the available options for negotiation. Antitrust laws (in the United States and elsewhere) exist to ensure that companies compete with each other instead of joining forces to exploit consumers. As a result, certain kinds of agreements (such as agreements among competitors to fix prices) are prohibited no matter what the circumstances.[65] Other kinds of agreements (such as buying one of one's few competitors in a given market) are also viewed with great suspicion.[66]

64. *See generally* Richard A. Posner, Antitrust Law (2d ed. 2001); *see also* William H. Page, *Communication and Concerted Action*, 38 Loy. U. Chi. L.J. 405, 408 (2007).

65. 15 U.S.C. § 1 ("Every contract, combination in the form of trust or otherwise, or conspiracy, in restraint of trade or commerce among the several States, or with foreign nations, is declared to be illegal"); *see also* United States v. Socony-Vacuum Oil Co., 310 U.S. 150, 223–26 n.59 (1940) ("Whatever economic justification particular price-fixing agreements may be thought to have, the law does not permit an inquiry into their reasonableness. They are all banned because of their actual or potential threat to the central nervous system of the economy.").

66. 15 U.S.C. § 2 ("Every person who shall monopolize, or attempt to monopolize, or combine or conspire with any other person or persons, to monopolize any part of the trade or commerce among the several States, or with foreign nations, shall be deemed guilty of a felony . . ."). *See also* Northern Securities Co. v. United

The primary source of antitrust law in the United States is the Sherman Act, which forbids contracts, combinations, or conspiracies in restraint of trade.[67] The language of the Sherman Act is broad enough to encompass even tacit collusion among would-be monopolists.[68] However, most courts agree that a plaintiff must demonstrate an actual agreement to fix prices somehow.[69] The most important document for organizations that are considering merging, however, is the *Horizontal Merger Guidelines*, which outline the enforcement policies of the U.S. Department of Justice and the Federal Trade Commission.[70]

As a result, organizations engaging in talks of merger or acquisition must ask themselves whether the mere act of talking raises any competitive concerns. The state of the law, and the zealousness of government enforcers, may limit the information that the negotiators may share with each other. As George Spindler—an integral member of oil giant Amoco's negotiating team when it merged with BP—described the dilemma:

> Whenever you put two companies together, until the final closing, you are still competitors. The information you can exchange is still limited because there is always the possibility that the deal will not go through. You do not want to find yourself in the situation where you have all kinds of antitrust violations because you have been sharing the wrong kind of

States, 193 U.S. 197 (1904); Standard Oil Co. of New Jersey v. United States, 221 U.S. 1 (1911).

67. *See* 15 U.S.C. § 1.

68. *See* Page, *supra* note 64, at 405, 407.

69. *See In re* High Fructose Corn Syrup Antitrust Litig., 295 F.3d 651, 654 (7th Cir. 2002) ("it is generally believed... that an express, manifested agreement, and thus an agreement involving actual verbalized communication, must be proved in order for a price-fixing conspiracy to be actionable under the Sherman Act") (Posner, J.).

70. *See* UNITED STATES DEPT. OF JUSTICE & FED. TRADE COMM'N, HORIZONTAL MERGER GUIDELINES 1, Aug. 19, 2010.

data during that period between when you have announced and when you have closed.[71]

It is particularly important for negotiators to pay attention to antitrust laws because, at least in the United States, a perceived violation could lead to a preliminary injunction against a deal, a development that can stop some complex business deals cold in their tracks.[72]

The presence of antitrust laws in the United States that are enforced by government agencies introduces an additional level of negotiations to any deal. Indeed, as practitioners D. Daniel Sokol and James A. Fishkin have observed, discussions about the relative benefits and drawbacks of mergers occur between merging parties and the government at several stages, including during the filing of the pre-merger notification form, and going up through the conduct of an investigation into a merger.[73]

European Union. The European Union (EU) also has a robust antitrust regime in place. Indeed, at times, it appears that the EU may be more aggressive about enforcement than the United States. Some of this difference in enforcement stems from differing policy goals. Throughout its history, antitrust law in the United States has held a primary goal of protecting American *consumers*. By contrast, since most member nations of the EU have robust industrial policies, EU competition law holds a secondary goal of protecting European *competitors*.[74] In addition, left-center parties in various EU member states

71. George Spindler, *The Amoco BP Mega-Merger: An Insider's Reflections*, 13 DePaul Bus. L.J. 19, 31–32 (2001).

72. Jamie Henikoff Moffitt, *Merging in the Shadow of the Law: The Case for Consistent Judicial Efficiency Analysis*, 63 Vanderbilt L. Rev. 1697, 1732 (2011) ("preliminary injunctions are generally considered to be 'deal killers.'").

73. D. Daniel Sokol & James A. Fishkin, *Antitrust Merger Efficiencies in the Shadow of the Law*, 64 Vanderbilt L. Rev. En Banc 45, 48–49 (2011).

74. Adit Bagchi, *The Political Economy of Merger Regulation*, 53 Am. J. Comp. L. 1, 8 & n.31 (2005).

are particularly sensitive to threats posed by corporate takeovers, and so may be cautious about approving mergers or other acquisitions.[75] Finally, the EU does not have the same history of overlapping federal and state jurisdictions as the United States. As a result, EU antitrust authorities are more likely to investigate anticompetitive behavior by traditionally regulated industries, like banking and finance.[76]

China. At this point, China is considered a "state capitalist" society. In other words, it does not pursue the same unfettered capitalism as Western nations. Instead, it has sought to harmonize the demonstrated advantages of market capitalism with its preexisting social and political structures. As a result, China's antitrust laws, while they look similar to Western laws, contain some key differences. China's recent Anti-Monopoly Law has four basic sections, that

- forbid certain kinds of business agreements prohibited;
- state that a firm cannot abuse a dominant market position;
- provide merger review guidelines; and
- prohibit some anticompetitive government action (sometimes known as "administrative monopolies").[77]

While there is not yet much precedent to inform speculation, most informed followers believe that Chinese enforcement of the Anti-Monopoly Law will center on maintaining market stability.[78] The Anti-Monopoly Law has a very different definition of "market power"

75. *Id.* at 15.

76. Todd Fishman et al., *U.S. & EU Antitrust Enforcement: What Role in a More Heavily Regulated Financial Sector?*, 7 COMPETITION POL'Y INT'L 32, 33 (Autumn 2011).

77. For a good summary of the Anti-Monopoly Law's provisions, *see* Benjamin Ryberg, *Pro-Competitive or Protective? The Chinese Anti-Monopoly Law, Implications for the United States, and Bilateral Antitrust Cooperation as an Effective Response*, 18 CARDOZO J. INT'L & COMP. L. 527, 535 (2010).

78. *See, e.g.*, R. Hewitt Pate, *The Anti-Monopoly Law of the People's Republic of China*, 75 ANTITRUST L.J. 195 (2008).

than that used in the United States: anything over 11 percent market share is capable of abusing its dominance in the market.[79] (This lower threshold for "abuse of dominance" is likely to protect smaller, local companies.) The Anti-Monopoly Law also contains more exceptions than the Sherman Act does.[80] For example, it is more likely to give a pass to "administrative monopolies"—anticompetitive activities sponsored or condoned by local governments to favor local businesses over foreign interlopers.[81]

India. India recently implemented a number of merger control regime, which finally gives effect to its Competition Act of 2002. The Competition Commission of India (its antitrust authority) has wasted little time in stepping up its enforcement of the Competition Act. During the summer of 2012, it issued an order in *Builders Ass'n of India v. Cement Manufacturers' Ass'n.*[82] The investigation, which was touched off by a complaint from the Builder's Association of India, looked into collusive price-fixing and anticompetitive trade practices in cement industry.[83] It found the various cement manufacturers to have violated the Competition Act, and levied a fine equivalent to $1.1 billion.[84] As the American law firm Jones Day described in a client alert, the notable feature of the investigation was that, unlike most initial investigations by a new antitrust authority, which prefer to prosecute blatant violations with incontrovertible proof, this one "relie[d] wholly on circumstantial evidence to establish a cartel."[85] The reliance on circumstantial evidence signals that the Competition

79. Ryberg, *supra* note 77, at 542–43.

80. For a good summary of the Anti-Monopoly Law's provisions, *see id.* at 527, 543.

81. *See, e.g.*, Pate, *supra* note 78, at 195.

82. No. 29/2010 (Competition Comm'n India June 20, 2012).

83. *Id.* § 2.4.

84. *Id.* §§ 7.1, 7.3–7.6.

85. *Antitrust Alert: Competition Commission of India Imposes US$ 1.1 Billion Penalty in Cement Cartel Case*, Jones Day, July 2012, *available at* http://www.jonesday.com/an

Commission is likely to pursue aggressive enforcement, a conclusion supported by its recent announcement that it would next pursue an investigation into Internet giant Google.

Brazil. Since the beginning of the twenty-first century, Brazil has become a center for international deal making. In the first quarter of 2012, it had the seventh-largest volume of deals in the world.[86] As a result of its need to keep up with this increase in deal making, Brazil has overhauled its antitrust regime, enacting what has been referred to as the "New Law."[87] The New Law introduces a pre-merger notification system (like the one the United States has) and establishes new rules for Brazil's leniency program.[88] In general, the New Law allows Brazil to be more nimble in its enforcement of antitrust laws, reacting more quickly than its old "labyrinthine" legal system did.[89] However, it speeds up enforcement at the cost of delaying merger approval—what used to be a "merge first, ask questions later" system now may take up to 330 days to secure approval.[90]

Each of these antitrust regimes is subtly different, reflecting local priorities. However, these laws do have some common themes. One is that the government has an interest in agreements that may affect consumers or competitors in its markets. Another is that agreements should not take advantage of already-dominant market positions. As a result, negotiators are well advised to make sure that the content of their agreements will pass muster under local antitrust laws, and

titrust-alert—competition-commission-of-india-imposes-us-11-billion-penalty-in-cement-cartel-case-07-09-2012/ (last viewed Aug. 27, 2012).

86. Joe Leahy & David Gelles, *Brazil Launches Revamped Antitrust Regime*, FINANCIAL TIMES, June 4, 2012.

87. Krisztian Katona & Diego Herrera Moraes, *Reforms Achieved, but Challenges Ahead: Brazil's New Competition Law*, ABA NEWSLETTER 2011(3) at 11.

88. *Id.*

89. Leahy & Gelles, *supra* note 86.

90. *Id.*

that any documentation of the agreement does not evidence any improper motives.

6.3.1 Anticorruption Laws

"If you have integrity, nothing else matters. If you don't have integrity, nothing else matters."

—ALAN SIMPSON

For a small but growing number of countries in the developed world, corruption is also a strong public-policy concern. The problem—from a negotiation standpoint—with anticorruption laws is that sometimes bribery is an effective or even required tactic to complete an agreement. As anyone with a small child knows, sometimes, to secure the outcome one wants or needs, one has to sweeten the pot with candy or a small toy. The same holds true for other deal making; sometimes, one must provide something extra. These payments get different names, depending on their context and their purpose. A payment to a negotiating partner may be an "incentive." Payment to a third party to prevent interference may be "logrolling." A supplier might give a purchasing agent a "kickback." But when a payment is made to a public official (or to a private individual within an organization) in order to improperly influence the approval (or the conduct) of an agreement, it gets called a "bribe."[91]

Most jurisdictions in the United States have laws that prohibit the corruption of public officials. (Indeed, famed plaintiffs' lawyer Richard "Dickie" Scruggs was imprisoned for attempting to bribe a

91. *See* Patrick Conroy & Graeme Hunter, *Economic Analysis of Damages under the Foreign Corrupt Practices Act*, NERA Economic Consulting (May 5, 2011), at 2 ("The fact that a bribe is offered or paid presumably implies that winning the project was not certain without the bribe and that *the bribe is expected to increase the probability of winning.*").

federal judge.)[92] In the wake of the Watergate scandals in the 1970s, the U.S. Congress also passed the Foreign Corrupt Practices Act (FCPA). The FCPA prohibits payments to foreign officials, enforceable by fines (both civil and criminal) and prison sentences. It also imposes record-keeping requirements on companies that prevent them from disguising payments to foreign officials as other kinds of expenses. There can be severe consequences for even just the announcement of an investigation or an indictment under the FCPA. For example, companies that rely on government contracts may find their licenses suspended should they be indicted.[93] Similarly, an indictment may lead to civil lawsuits in the United States for violations of laws other than the FCPA.[94]

There are a few specific issues that are raised by anticorruption laws. First, anticorruption laws may affect the offers available in a given negotiation. For example, the specific scandal that sent Dickie Scruggs to jail involved bartering of political opportunities for judicial favors, with the specific concern being the corruption of the judicial process.[95] Second, anticorruption laws may affect the ways in which certain negotiations are conducted. For example, gift-giving may be an important component of deal making in certain cultures.[96] However, depending on the kind of gift, or its value, certain legal regimes may prohibit the giving of certain kinds of gifts. (In general, the FCPA only prohibits gifts or payments that are offered

92. *See generally* Curtis Wilkie, The Fall of the House of Zeus: The Rise and Ruin of America's Most Powerful Trial Lawyer (2010).

93. That said, it appears that government contractors are almost never debarred for violations of the FCPA. *See generally* Drury D. Stevenson & Nicholas J. Wagoner, *FCPA Sanctions: Too Big to Debar?*, 80 Fordham L. Rev. 775 (2011) (discussing lack of debarment with large government contractors found liable of FCPA violations).

94. *See, e.g.*, Glazer Capital Management, L.P. v. Magistri, 549 F.3d 736 (9th Cir. 2008); Conroy & Hunter, *supra* note 91, at 7–8 (discussing follow-on class actions in bribery cases).

95. *See generally* Wilkie, *supra* note 92.

96. *See* chapter 7.

"corruptly"—that is, with the intent of unduly influencing the recipient. Proving that corrupt intent, of course, is extremely difficult and can lead to investigations or indictments even where conduct may have been innocent.) Finally, some "red flags" for corrupt behavior—such as impositions of "special handling fees" or requests that payments be made to offshore or numbered accounts—may not be obvious to all members of a negotiating team.[97]

The FCPA, at least, does provide some flexibility for extreme situations. For example, it does allow companies to make *facilitation payments* under certain limited circumstances; by contrast, the United Kingdom's Bribery Act will not.[98] A facilitation payment (sometimes also called a "grease payment") is a payment to a public official to obtain services that should be routine. (In other words, it's a bribe to make the official do his job in the first place.) Similarly, the FCPA also allows an exception for payments that are extorted by the foreign official, or otherwise made under duress.[99] And it allows an affirmative defense for payments that are lawful in the other country.[100]

Finally, not all anticorruption laws cover the same conduct. For example, the United Kingdom's Bribery Act prohibits corruption of both public and private enterprises, while the FCPA only prohibits payments to foreign public officials.[101] The Bribery Act also prohibits *receiving* bribes as well as paying them out.

97. Rose Parlane, Adequate Anti-corruption Procedures: Can Your Team Identify "Red Flags"?, Bribery Library Blog, Nov. 16, 2011, http://www.briberylibrary.com/compliance-programmes/adequate-anti-corruption-procedures-can-your-team-identify-red-flags/ (last viewed Aug. 1, 2012).

98. *See* 15 U.S.C. 78dd-2(d)(b); Bribery Act 2010 (c.23).

99. United States v. Kozeny, 582 F. Supp. 2d 535, 540–41 (S.D.N.Y. 2008).

100. 15 U.S.C. § 78dd-2(c); *see also* Kozeny 582 F. Supp. 2d at 537.

101. For an excellent overview of the basic differences between the FCPA and the Bribery Act, *see* Adam Greaves, Is My FCPA Compliance Good Enough for the

6.3.2 Class Action Settlements

"Think about that for a second. Your odds of surviving a game of Russian roulette are better than winning a case at trial. Twelve times better. So why does anyone do it? They don't. They settle."

—JAN SCHLICHTMANN,
A Civil Action (Buena Vista, 1999)

One specialized area of high-stakes negotiation that is nonetheless of vital interest to many companies is the negotiation of settlements in class action litigation.[102] Unlike the settlement of other litigation, class action settlements are governed by an additional set of rules that ensure that the attorneys (and the class representatives) are adequately representing the absent members of the class. As a result, settlements of class actions require two additional steps where the court (1) preliminarily approves the terms of the settlement and orders notice to class members and other interested parties,[103] and (2) finally approves the settlement after all interested parties have a chance to be heard.[104] This process is governed by two sets of rules. Rule 23(e) of the Federal Rules of Civil Procedure provides the substantive requirements for a class action settlement. In addition, certain provisions of the Class Action Fairness Act impose additional restrictions on the terms of agreement and require the parties to inform appropriate government authorities of the existence of the settlement.

Bribery Act?, Bribery Library Blog, July 6, 2011, http://www.briberylibrary.com/associated-persons/is-my-fcpa-compliance-good-enough-for-the-bribery-act/ (last viewed July 31, 2012).

102. For more on the specific law and strategies governing class action settlements, *see* ANDERSON & TRASK, *supra* note 10, at § 8 (2d ed. 2012), from which this discussion is derived.

103. MANUAL FOR COMPLEX LITIGATION (FOURTH) § 21.632 at 320 ("First, counsel submit the proposed terms of the settlement and the judge makes a preliminary fairness evaluation."); PRINCIPLES OF THE LAW OF AGGREGATE LITIGATION § 3.03.

104. MANUAL FOR COMPLEX LITIGATION (FOURTH) § 21.634.

Rule 23(e) requires a court to determine whether the settlement is: (1) fair, (2) reasonable, and (3) adequate to the plaintiff class. The circumstances of particular settlements have prompted various courts to consider a number of other factors in evaluating a proposed settlement, but these tend to link back—even if only loosely—to the explicit requirements of fairness, reasonability, and adequacy.[105] Many courts use "fairness" as a loose synonym for all three Rule 23(e)(2) factors, although the *Manual for Complex Litigation* (which serves as a guide for federal judges) is more precise: "Fairness calls for a comparative analysis of the treatment of class members vis-à-vis each other and vis-à-vis similar individuals with similar claims who are not in the class."[106] The court's primary concern when determining reasonableness is whether the class will receive a comparatively good value in exchange for releasing its claims.[107] The adequacy requirement determines whether the settlement provides enough relief to the proposed class: "Adequacy of the settlement involves a comparison of the relief granted relative to what class members might have obtained without using the class action process."[108] To determine whether the settlement is adequate, the trial court must establish a "ballpark valuation" of the case, given both the value of the alleged claims and the risk of plaintiff's losing.[109]

105. *See* PRINCIPLES OF THE LAW OF AGGREGATE LITIGATION, § 3.5 Comment a ("The current case law on the criteria for evaluating settlements is in disarray. Courts articulate a wide range of factors to consider, but rarely discuss the significance to be given to each factor, let alone why a given factor is probative."); Nat'l Ass'n of Chain Drug Stores v. New England Carpenters Health Benefits Fund, 582 F.3d 30, 44 (1st Cir. 2009) (listing additional factors); City of Detroit v. Grinnell Corp., 495 F.2d 448, 463 (2d Cir. 1974) (same); *In re* Gen. Motors Corp. Pick-Up Truck Litig., 55 F.3d at 806–807 (same); Rodriguez v. West Publ'g Corp., 563 F.3d 948, 963 (9th Cir. 2009) (same); *In re* CP Ships Ltd. Sec. Litig., 578 F.3d 1306, 1318 (11th Cir. 2009) (same).

106. MANUAL FOR COMPLEX LITIGATION (FOURTH) § 21.62 at 315.

107. *In re* Gen. Motors Corp. Pick-Up Truck Litig., 55 F.3d at 807.

108. MANUAL FOR COMPLEX LITIGATION (FOURTH) § 21.62 at 315.

109. Synfuel Techs., Inc. v. DHL Express (USA), Inc., 463 F.3d 646, 653 (7th Cir. 2006).

6.4 What Written Agreement Looks Like (Contract Law/Rules of Evidence)

6.4.1 Contract Law

"It was all settled right here in this office. Remember? Danny and me signed a contract, and you witnessed it. You stood over there. I stood there, and Daniel stood here. Remember?"

—PEACHY CARNEHAN,
The Man Who Would Be King (Columbia Pictures, 1975)

At its base, contract law concerns agreements: how they are formed, what they may say, and how they are enforced.[110] Or, as the famed federal judge Learned Hand once put it:

> A contract is an obligation attached by the mere force of law to certain acts of the parties, usually words, which ordinarily accompany and represent a known intent.[111]

The entire body of contract law regulates how parties may enshrine their agreements so that they are enforceable later, or how to tell an agreement exists if the parties did not reduce it to writing.[112] From a practical standpoint, this is the single most important

110. *See* Lawrence M. Solan, *Contract as Agreement*, 83 NOTRE DAME L. REV. 353, 356 (2007) ("Actual agreement matters in the law of contracts. Promises are enforced when the parties have breached an agreement, and are not enforced when the parties have not actually reached an agreement . . .").

111. Hotchkiss v. Nat'l City Bank, 200 F. 287, 293 (S.D.N.Y. 1911); *see also* Solan, *supra* note 110, at 353, 368.

112. Avery Katz, *The Strategic Structure of Offer and Acceptance: Game Theory & the Law of Contract Formation*, 89 MICH. L. REV. 215, 216 (1990) ("At its broadest, my argument addresses all legal rules that answer two types of questions: First, which objectively verifiable actions or subjectively experienced intentions suffice to conclude a bargain and form a contractual obligation? Second, how do these actions and intentions affect the substantive content of any contract formed?").

feature of contract law.[113] Contracts prevent parties to an agreement from acting opportunistically toward each other.[114]

It is important to have a working knowledge of contract law while negotiating an agreement because, at some point, one party may breach the contract. That breach may be deliberate and strategic, as when parties seek to disavow contracts once circumstances have changed enough that the deal is no longer good for them.[115] Or the breach may be inadvertent. But in either case, the breaching party may choose to challenge the other party's interpretation of the contract rather than suffer the consequences of a breach.[116] (There is a third possibility, that the nonbreaching party may mistakenly conclude a breach has occurred; in that case, too, it is important to have contract law.)

In general, many scholars assume that parties to a contract have an incentive to formalize as many terms of their agreement as possible.[117] That said, even conscientious parties have strong incentive not to spell out every potential problem. After all, no one planning

113. BRETT COLE, M&A TITANS: THE PIONEERS WHO SHAPED WALL STREET'S MERGERS & ACQUISITIONS 58 (2008) ("If we ended up selling the company, we had to get things documented in a way to protect ourselves to make sure nobody could gazzump a deal they decided they wanted to do.").

114. *See* RICHARD A. POSNER, ECONOMIC ANALYSIS OF LAW § 4.5 at 103 (5th ed. 1998).

115. *See, e.g.*, TKO Equip. Co. v. C&G Coal Co., 863 F.2d 541, 542 (7th Cir. 1988) (Easterbrook, J.) (noting that parties in contract dispute "disavowed their own documents").

116. Posner, *supra* note 7, at 1581, 1582 (2005).

117. *See* POSNER, *supra* note 114, § 4.5 at 102–103 ("Someone known not to perform his side of bargains will find it difficult to find anyone willing to make exchanges with him in the future—a costly penalty for taking advantage of the vulnerability of another party to a contract, the vulnerability that is due to the sequential character of performance. There might even be more explicit definitions, either in writing or by reference to custom, of the undertakings of the parties to an exchange than there would be under a regime of enforceable contracts. Transacting parties would be particularly eager to minimize misunderstandings that might give rise to charges of bad faith, since someone against who such charges were lodged might find it more difficult to get people to make exchanges with him in the future . . .").

a wedding wants to dwell on the prenup.[118] And sometimes leaving deliberate ambiguities in a contract can be an effective way of closing a deal; deliberately bearing the risk of disagreement later in order to reach agreement now.[119]

But, given the infinite number of possible contingencies, the parties cannot formalize everything. Formalizing terms has a cost—even if it is just the time, paper, and ink required to write down easily-agreed terms.[120] To minimize these costs, contract law dictates certain terms the parties are likely to agree to.[121] Among other effects, this allows parties to insure themselves against unforeseen events.[122]

While contract law is based on a set of principles common among most common-law states, the application can differ widely from state to state.[123] We will focus on a few basic doctrines of contract law here, those which have the greatest effect on negotiations.

The doctrine of *consideration* requires that, for a contract to be enforceable, each party must exchange something of value. The exchange does not have to be an equal one, so long as each side receives something of value.[124] As a result, consideration serves as

118. Posner, *supra* note 7, at 1585–86 ("being reminded of the possibility of litigation is a downer for the prospective consumer").

119. *Id.* at 1583.

120. Avery Katz, *supra* note 112, at 215, 230 (discussing transaction costs involved in formalizing agreements).

121. *See* POSNER, *supra* note 114, § 4.1 at 104 ("[C]ontract law has another function but one intimately related to that of preventing opportunistic behavior: filling out the parties' agreement by interpolating missing clauses."); *see also* Posner, *supra* note 7, at 1585.

122. *See* Posner, *supra* note 7, at 1582; POSNER, *supra* note 111, § 4.5 at 115–21.

123. For example, while New York and California have adopted many of the same doctrines, New York has adopted a more formalistic interpretation, while California emphasizes questions of public policy. *See* Geoffrey P. Miller, *Bargains Bicoastal: New Light on Contract Theory*, 31 CARDOZO L. REV. 1475, 1478 (2010) (discussing implications of differences between New York and California interpretations of contract law).

124. *See, e.g.*, Weiner v. McGraw-Hill, Inc., 57 N.Y.2d 458, 463–64 (N.Y. App. 1982).

"proof" of a fresh round of negotiation, allowing the requirement to deter opportunistic behavior by one side or the other.[125]

The doctrine of *parol evidence* asks how much evidence outside the four corners of the contract a court may consider that contradicts the plain meaning of the contract.[126] It roughly states that, after a contract has been consummated, the plain language of the contract is the entire evidence of the agreement, rather than any extrinsic events.[127] (This is particularly important if the parties have included an integration clause.) As one might expect, the scope of the parol evidence rule is hotly contested in many breach-of-contract cases. The party who gains advantage from the contractual language will seek to confine the contract to its "four corners." The party who wishes to breach the contract as it stands will seek to introduce parol evidence that the contract means something other than what it says.

Why allow extrinsic evidence at all? Why not simply enforce the four corners of the contract, come hell or high water? Because language can be loose, and as a result, it does not always mean what the parties think it means. As then Judge Cardozo put it in deciding a contract dispute under New York law:

> The proper legal meaning, however, is not always the meaning of the parties. Surrounding circumstances may stamp upon a contract a popular or looser meaning. The words loans and discounts are not so clear and certain that circumstances may not broaden them to include renewals. They often have that meaning in the language of business life. . . . The triers of the facts must fix the sense in which the words were used in the contract now before us. To take the primary or strict meaning

125. *See* Posner, *supra* note 114, § 4.2 at 110.

126. Posner, *supra* note 7, at 1602.

127. *See generally* Eric A. Posner, *The Parol Evidence Rule, the Plain Meaning Rule, and the Principles of Contract Interpretation*, 146 U. Pa. L. Rev. 533, 533–34 (1998).

> is to make the whole transaction futile. To take the secondary or loose meaning, is to give it efficacy and purpose. In such a situation, the genesis and aim of the transaction may rightly guide our choice.[128]

A number of states' contract laws also recognize a *duty to negotiate in good faith*, generally understood to be a duty to negotiate with the intent of actually concluding a successful agreement.[129] There are other reasons to negotiate: a company might propose an acquisition or a merger with the intent of gaining more information about its competitors. Similarly, a defendant might choose to negotiate a settlement in order to buy itself time in heated litigation.

6.4.2 Evidence

"It doesn't matter what I believe, it only matters what I can prove."

—DANIEL KAFFEE,

A Few Good Men (Tri-Star Pictures, 1992)

Why care about the rules of evidence in a negotiation? Because if a deal later falls apart and a court allows extrinsic evidence, these rules dictate how the parties can prove what they actually agreed to. Also, in some cases, the mere fact of a negotiation may affect later liability for the parties.

The *hearsay rules* exist to ensure that evidence admitted into a trial is sufficiently trustworthy that a jury may rely on it.[130] This implies that, in negotiations, an organization should keep track of its negotiators, and possibly limit those who speak for each side.

128. Utica City Nat'l Bank v. Gunn, 222 N.Y. 204, 208 (1918) (internal citations omitted) (Cardozo, J.).

129. *See* Miller, *supra* note 123, at 1478 (comparing enforcement of duty in New York and California).

130. *See* Fed. R. Evid. 801–804.

There are certain exceptions to the hearsay doctrine that will affect negotiators. For example, the *statement against party interest*, which allows a statement by one of the parties into evidence, may color the statements made during a negotiation.[131] Similarly, the *business records exception* may affect the ways in which organizations record their impressions of how a negotiation is proceeding. Those who believe they may rely on documentation later may seek to create "business records"; those who wish to keep the negotiation separate from the agreement should make sure they have not kept routine notes or records, and may wish to limit their use of e-mail or instant messaging during the course of a negotiation.[132]

The Federal Rules of Evidence also prevent a party from introducing evidence of settlement discussions at trial.[133] By keeping settlement discussions confidential, the rule encourages parties to make overtures as early as possible.[134] Like with contracts, this rule is not really concerned with how parties arrive at settlements; instead, it is interested in protecting the agreement.

131. Fed. R. Evid. 801(d)(2). Technically, given its placement in the Federal Rules, the statement against party interest is "not hearsay" as opposed to an exception to the rule against hearsay. Even legal scholars find this distinction confusing. *See* Sam Stonefield, *Rule 801(d)'s Oxymoronic "Not Hearsay" Classification: The Untold Backstory and a Suggested Amendment*, 2011 FED. CTS. L. REV. 1, 3 ("Commentators have long criticized Rule 801(d)'s 'not hearsay' term, calling it 'awkward' (per Judge Henry Friendly in 1973), "unnecessarily confusing" (per Judge Edward Becker in 1992), 'wrong' (per Professor Faust Rossi in 1993), and 'Orwellian' (per Professor George Fisher in 2008).") (internal footnotes omitted).

132. *See* Michael H. Dore, *Forced Preservation: Electronic Evidence & the Business Records Hearsay Exception*, 11 COLUM. SCI. & TECH. L. REV. 76, 77 (2010) (discussing effects new communications technology has on business-records exception).

133. Fed. R. Evid. 408 (declaring evidence of "conduct or statements made in compromise negotiations regarding the claim" inadmissible).

134. *See* Fed. R. Evid. 408, Notes of Advisory Committee on Rules (1974).

6.5 Content of Deal (Tax/Specific Regulations)

Finally, there are areas of the law that govern specific aspects of any deal.

Taxation. There is no real debate that the structure of the tax code directly affects how companies structure transactions. After all, companies have a strong financial incentive to minimize their tax burdens.[135] And, as Ronald Coase recognized as far back as 1937, the mere existence of a sales tax might encourage a firm to produce goods or services on its own that it might otherwise buy from other providers.[136]

One of the most important sources of tax regulation that affects corporate negotiations is the set of rules governing corporate reorganizations, such as mergers or acquisitions. These rules have been called "quirky, excessively complex, and utterly inconsistent."[137] In fact, some legal scholars consider this quirkiness to be a feature, not a bug. The more baroque the tax rules, the more options sophisticated shareholders have to structure a corporate sale to avoid recognition of certain taxes.[138] At least one study has found that the tax benefits in S-corporation acquisitions (that is, a corporation that passes its income and losses through to its shareholders) are equal to approximately 12–17 percent of deal value.[139] These benefits can accrue to all types of acquisitions. As a result, negotiators will often

135. Ajay K. Mehrotra, *Mergers, Taxes, and Historical Materialism*, 83 IND. L.J. 881, 885–86 (2008) ("The reorganization tax rules have become exceedingly important with each succeeding M&A wave, especially as corporations continue to search for ways to minimize their tax burdens.").

136. Ronald H. Coase, *The Nature of the Firm*, 4 ECONOMICA 386, 391 (1937).

137. Herwig J. Schlunk, *Rationalizing the Taxation of Reorganizations and Other Corporate Acquisitions*, 27 VA. TAX. REV. 23, 24 (2007).

138. *Id.*

139. Merle M. Erickson & Shiing-wu Wang, *Tax Benefits as a Source of Merger Premiums in Acquisitions of Private Corporations*, 82 ACCOUNTING REV. 359 (2007).

consider specific deal structures based on the tax benefits they may allow. Among the structures one might consider:

- *Asset v. stock sales*. Is the acquirer taking on the entire legal entity, with all of its resulting assets and liabilities, or is it just buying the assets, both tangible and intangible?
- *The corporate form*. Is the target company an S-corporation, a C-corporation (taxed separately from its owners), or a limited liability company? Each is governed by different IRS regulations and may result in different tax burdens.[140] The jurisdiction in which the company is incorporated may also affect the tax burden the buyers and sellers face.
- *Carryovers*. Under some circumstances, the buyer can take advantage of tax credits for the target's net operating losses. In others, regulations may prevent these carryovers from being transferred. These rules may also affect the corporate form the transaction may take.[141]
- *Purchase price allocation*. The seller will want to allocate as much of the sales price to assets that generate capital gain, such as goodwill or land, or other assets with fair market values higher than original tax cost (thereby generating a gain). The buyer on the other hand will generally want to allocate as much as possible to short-lived assets such as machinery and equipment, inventory, prepaid expenses, and so forth rather than goodwill or covenants not to compete, which are amortized for tax purposes.[142]

140. *See* Blake Christian, *Top 10 Merger and Acquisition Tax Issues*, American Institute of CPAs, May 2008, *available at* http://www.cpa2biz.com/Content/media/PRODUCER_CONTENT/Newsletters/Articles_2008/CorpTax/Tax_Issues.jsp (last viewed Oct. 11, 2012).

141. *See id.*

142. *See id.*

These are only a few the tax-related issues related to an acquisition. Given the magnitude of the potential benefits or liabilities, consulting a tax specialist is not just smart, it is essential.

Trade regulation. Nation-states care about their economies. When their populations are gainfully employed, they tend to be more stable, and their leaders tend to be happier. So states often jealously guard their population's ability to reap the benefits of international trade (cheaper goods, export-related jobs) while seeking to minimize its downside (loss of jobs to other countries). How do they do this? By regulating. In fact, the earliest known trade regulations may have been export controls to forbid merchants from selling weapons to a state's military rivals.[143] As a result, if an organization has any international dealings, it is likely to be subject to trade regulations. In extreme cases, components of deals—such as the supply of parts for a manufacturing project—may be affected or prohibited by trade embargoes.

Intellectual property. Intellectual property laws evolved to protect creativity and innovation.[144] A corporation's intellectual property is often one of its greatest assets. Companies that make their money from advances in science or technology, like computer or pharmaceutical companies, rely on patents for their income. Entertainment companies rely on copyright and trademark law to protect their popular book or movie franchises, like *Harry Potter* or *Star Wars*. Even more traditional conglomerates rely on trademark law to protect their brands. An increasing number of complex deals also involve some degree of intellectual property. Either the corporation seeks out the deal for access to intellectual property, or it seeks to protect its own

143. Paul Seabright, The Company of Strangers: A Natural History of Economic Life 282 (rev. ed. 2010).

144. *Id.* at 240 ("Intellectual property is best understood, therefore, as an institution—combining a set of formal laws, such as patent and copyright laws, with a set of social conventions, such as those governing scientific citations—that tries to increase our trust in the willingness of others to reward our valuable ideas.").

intellectual property. In either case, it is important to know what laws govern a corporation's patents, trademarks, and copyrights.

Employment contracts. Organizations are made up of people, which means that for many organizations, human capital is their most valuable asset. (Think, for example, of how much a law firm would be worth without its lawyers.) As a result, employment contracts play a critical role in corporate negotiations, because an acquirer is often vitally interested in whether the company's people will stay with it. There are several ways of making sure that employees stay with a new merged firm. One is to pay them exorbitant amounts to stay, an option that is certainly attractive to the employees (which may include management), but is less so to the acquiring firm. The dangers of excess compensation hold true in both complex business deals and complex litigation. (In complex litigation, the part of the settlement that relates to compensation is the attorneys' fee provision, and an exorbitant attorneys' fee provision can easily scuttle a potential settlement, just as exorbitant compensation provisions can scuttle business deals.) The compensation may not even be for future work: business deals especially may include "golden parachute" provisions, which provide executives with large severance packages should they leave the company before a specified time.

If one cannot pay employees what they demand to stay, one alternative is to make it costly to leave. Many employment contracts contain provisions that raise the barriers to leaving a firm. One of the most popular is the *noncompete provision*. At its base, the noncompete provision is simply an agreement between the employee and the firm that the employee will not work for a competing firm within a specified period of time. While technically noncompete agreements only limit the ability to work with the competition, that is likely going to be the easiest source of alternative work for most employees. After all, what they have largely picked up is firm-specific or industry-specific knowledge and skills. Those will be far less valuable the further from the industry the employee strays. (Why would an employee agree to such a provision? Assuming that it is not an unconscionable agreement where the employee lacked any bargaining power whatsoever, then an employee would do so in order to induce an agreement with the employer. It is a guarantee that the employee will not walk off with valuable skills and firm-specific knowledge.)

Local operating requirements. In addition to the various laws that govern the formation and enforcement of contracts, many countries also have a series of local requirements that influence how a company is managed, and so the content of a given agreement.[145] These requirements usually reflect the country's goals for its economy. (This occurs in litigation as well, where different jurisdictions will have different "local rules" that may require settlement conferences or influence how settlements are conducted. In some cases, specific judges will have specific operating requirements for settlements.)[146] To provide just a few illustrative examples:

- *China.* As one might expect, the country with the world's largest population and second-largest economy, China, has a number of local licensing and tax requirements that make it a challenge for outsiders to conduct business smoothly. Business licenses are particularly important since they permit a company's specific business conduct in an area. As a result, when buying a Chinese company, most corporations are very concerned with which business licenses can be transferred from the target company to the parent. Further complicating the issue, there are usually two layers to this question: an official legal answer based on the reading of the

145. For a current reference on local requirements in different countries, the World Bank, in partnership with International Financial Corporation, regularly updates a website "Doing Business" (http://www.doingbusiness.org/), which provides summaries of the challenges of setting up as well as operating businesses in 183 economies around the world.

146. *See, e.g.*, Arellano v. T-Mobile USA, Inc., 2011 U.S. Dist. LEXIS 21441 (N.D. Cal. 2011) (standing order by Alsup, J. regarding requirements for class action settlements).

law, and the actual enforcement practices of the government agency or local jurisdiction. The most visible example of this disparity occurred in 2009, when the Chinese government rejected a $2.6 billion bid by Coca-Cola to buy the Huiyuan Juice Group, a move that mystified industry-watchers at the time.[147] China is particularly sensitive to transfer of business licenses and acquisitions in the food sector on the basis of domestic security.

- *Saudi Arabia*. Saudi Arabia is very concerned with local unemployment, which was roughly 35 percent in 2011 and which is compounded by the hiring of cheap foreign labor.[148] As a result, it has imposed a series of regulations, known as the *Nitaqat* system, that require any business to significantly increase the hiring of local Saudi citizens. Complying with the *Nitaqat* rules can be a significant challenge, because Saudi Arabia's educational and training systems have not developed the necessary talent for many sectors of the economy; moreover, local citizens have significantly different expectations for their pay and performance (in some cases three to five times higher than what expats are being paid).[149] The situation is further complicated by the fact that Saudi enforcement of these regulations has been uneven over time.
- *Brazil*. Brazil has—justifiably, given its population and infrastructure—gained a reputation as a country that will likely outperform the rest of the global market over the next

147. Bill Powell, *China Says "Keep Out" to Coca-Cola*, TIME, Mar. 18, 2009, *available at* http://www.time.com/time/business/article/0,8599,1886024,00.html (last viewed Oct. 17, 2012).

148. *Saudi Arabia: Out of the Comfort Zone*, THE ECONOMIST, Mar. 3, 2012, *available at* http://www.economist.com/node/21548973 (last viewed Oct. 17, 2012).

149. Sanket Mohapatra, *Implications of "Nitaqat," Saudi Arabia's Indigenization Program, Likely to be Modest for Migrants*, PEOPLE MOVE, Sept. 28, 2011, *available at* http://blogs.worldbank.org/peoplemove/implications-of-"nitaqat"-saudi-arabias-indigenization-program-likely-to-be-modest-for-migrants (last viewed Oct. 17, 2012).

> decade. However, it also presents several unique operational pitfalls. More so than other countries, Brazilian law is concerned with the social impact of business operations. As a result, Brazil's rules around contract law, company formation, visas, jurisdiction of different governmental departments, and tax law all add new layers of complications for companies to navigate.[150]

Government-owned businesses. Many of the largest developing countries today—chiefly China, India, and other parts of Asia—have histories of communism or state ownership of major companies. Sometimes the government would step in to control key industries for domestic political or security reasons; other times it would do so to drive employment and maintain local harmony. Regardless of the reason, government ownership of a business entity can complicate either a business deal or a lawsuit. While the most obvious examples of government ownership usually involve federal governments (the Russian-owned Gazprom, the Industrial Commerce Bank of China, Indian Railways), local or regional governments have far more involvement in various companies. There is no obvious categorization that limits these companies: they can manufacture appliances, develop property, or provide logistical services.

Government involvement in these companies can take many different forms. The government may be a silent partner while the company generates revenue similar to taxes to fund social infrastructure programs. It may also take a more active role, where various government officials also serve as company board members or officers. Regardless, dealing with a government-owned entity poses a new set of challenges to manage. In particular, because the government is

150. Michael Diaz, Jr., *The Top 5 Corporate Compliance Issues Facing Brazil*, CORPORATE COMPLIANCE INSIGHTS, June 13, 2011, *available at* http://www.corporatecomplianceinsights.com/the-top-5-corporate-compliance-issues-facing-brazil/ (last viewed Oct. 17, 2012).

also the executive authority in a given area, it has the opportunity to change the rules of the game even in mid-negotiation.

These complications can extend to privately owned companies that are customers of government-owned entities. When looking for potential partners in the Chinese energy efficiency market, one of the authors (DeGuire) discovered that though the companies were small and independently owned, roughly half of their revenue came from either the Chinese People's Liberation Army or was used in managing the food chain within China, both sectors that do not allow foreign companies. As a result, any transaction would have been pointless because that revenue would have—by law—disappeared following the first day of acquisition. Similar issues exist for those seeking to sue government entities. Leaving aside the issue of sovereign immunity (cases when a government simply does not allow itself to be sued in local or foreign courts), a government-owned entity may simply shut down to avoid litigation. For example, in 2008, when milk tainted with melamine, a toxic chemical used in making plastics, killed six infants and injured at least a thousand more in the Gansu province of China, the government recalled the milk and shut down the state-owned distributor Sanlu Group, preventing any litigation.[151]

Similarly, companies that are targets of state-owned firms may also find themselves in unusual negotiating situations. Most obviously, their home governments may raise objections, such as when Chinese oil company CNOOC Ltd. tried to buy American oil company Unocal Corp.[152] When home governments do not object, targets may find that negotiating with state-owned companies provides some distinct advantages (the firm may be less concerned with share price; government regulations may be less of a problem) and some distinct

151. *China's Baby-Milk Scandal: Formula for Disaster*, The Economist, Sept. 18, 2008, *available at* http://www.economist.com/node/12262271/ (last viewed Oct. 17, 2012).

152. Matt Pottinger et al., *CNOOC Drops Offer for Unocal, Exposing U.S.-Chinese Tensions*, Wall St. J., Aug. 3, 2005, *available at* http://online.wsj.com/article/SB112295744495102393.html (last viewed Oct. 17, 2012).

challenges (integration may be more difficult; there is the distinct possibility of espionage).[153]

6.6 Practical Implications

Hire a lawyer. This suggestion may seem self-serving, especially since one of the co-authors (Trask) is a lawyer himself. But it is hard to deny that when this many legal issues are at stake, someone with legal training can be useful (if not essential) to have on the negotiating team. And most organizations either have full-time lawyers in-house, or a good, continuous relationship with an outside lawyer.

Do the homework. If there is one thing that the various Delaware cases on fiduciary duty show, it is that careless decisions are not just bad for business, they may also expose one to legal liability. As a result, it often makes sense to make sure that one has taken all of the necessary steps to prepare for the legal issues that may arise during a negotiation. Similarly, when dealing with different countries' local operating requirements, it is important to understand the business impact they will have on the final agreement. Even though aspects of a deal may work well in the United States or the United Kingdom, they may have the opposite impact in Brazil, Saudi Arabia, or China.

Know when to ask questions. One of the most significant tensions between lawyers and businesspeople in complex negotiations exists over how often the team should consult its lawyer. Lawyers are not without ego and so may try to insert themselves in more of the negotiation than is strictly necessary. Businesspeople prize efficiency and may avoid consulting a lawyer when they believe all it will do is slow down a deal or provide an answer they do not want to hear. As a result, knowing which issues are really worth the lawyer's advice is

153. *See Chinese Takeovers: Being Eaten by the Dragon*, THE ECONOMIST, Nov. 11, 2010, *available at* http://www.economist.com/node/17460954/ (last viewed Oct. 7, 2012).

an important skill. Similarly, a lawyer who understands how to help business teams focus on the material issues is invaluable.

The size of some issues that have eluded legal scrutiny until a deal is well underway is staggering to laypeople, and embarrassing to some companies. For example, in the 2000s, Disney looked to acquire Fox Family, a basic cable channel. The Disney executives hoped to use the channel to "repurpose" Disney and ABC programming that had already run on other channels, a strategy that promised to increase their annual revenues by more than 20 percent. However, the Disney executives involved in the transaction were not aware that they lacked the intellectual property rights to do what they wanted. (Simply put, it was the studios that produced the programming, not the network that broadcast them, that retained those rights.) ABC's lawyers learned of the plan only days before it was to be consummated, too late to advise against a costly acquisition that proved to be a large liability.[154]

Know whom you're negotiating for. Many of the legally enforceable duties on negotiators (at least those unrelated to fraud) stem from the fact that the negotiator is supposed to represent the organization, which usually means its stakeholders. The duty of loyalty makes sure that the negotiator is not really working for herself. The duty of care makes sure that the negotiator works as hard for her constituents as she would for herself. As a result, it is vital to remember in a given negotiation who the actual "client" is. Is it the board? The chief executive? The sales department?

Know whom you're negotiating with and know their requirements. It is critical to also understand the requirements and approval process of your counterparty. Otherwise, even if you agree in a negotiating room, if the other side cannot deliver on its agreements because of the hurdles or requirements it faces (say, because of the Chinese prohibition on foreign companies providing material to the military), then the negotiation is for naught.

154. James Stewart, Disneywar, Kindle location 7151–84 (2005).

Think about how you would defend your actions in court. A common adage people hear is that you should think about how your actions would look if splashed across the front page of the newspaper. From a legal standpoint, it always helps to wonder how your actions would appear if you had to defend them in court. And that means envisioning them with two twists: (1) assume you cannot actually introduce all of the mitigating circumstances surrounding the actions, and (2) assume that someone is available to put the worst possible spin on those actions. In those circumstances, if a particular negotiating stance or tactic still appears worthwhile, one should absolutely pursue it. But if it appears unclear, it may be time to question whether some other tactic would work better.

There is a serious tension on this point between the business and legal takes on negotiation. As a lawyer, Trask would advocate documenting every part of the negotiation: it maintains transparency and creates an excellent record of what happened should there be a dispute later. As a businessman, DeGuire advocates the opposite: *not* documenting every part of the negotiation preserves flexibility, increases the openness to discuss a range of options, and minimizes the chances of a third party imposing a different interpretation on records later. Of course, the right answer is some kind of balance between these competing concerns, but where that balance exists will depend upon the situation. Hopefully the context and range of tools presented in this book gives understanding and detail to both businesspeople and lawyers to help them interpret and efficiently navigate the range of challenges and questions that they must effectively answer.

6.7 Conclusion

In every negotiation, it is important to play by the rules. It builds trust with the other party, and it prevents problems later that could undo a deal. The challenge in a complex negotiation is identifying all of the rules that apply to a given deal and then navigating them to a successful conclusion. But this is easier said than done. Simply managing the flow of information and making the proper disclosures at the proper times trips up many negotiating teams, let alone doing so without falling afoul of antitrust or anticorruption laws. Doing so while also complying with one's fiduciary duties to shareholders and clients only makes a negotiation more complex.

Assuming both sides have acted properly, they still must set down an enforceable agreement, one that accurately reflects the agreement they intended. Otherwise, certain missing words or clauses can cost potentially millions of dollars, years of litigation, or both.

Complying with written rules is hard enough. In the next chapter, we will discuss something even more difficult: negotiating while complying with the unwritten rules imposed by corporate and national cultures.

Intercultural Negotiations

On May 7, 1998, when German manufacturing conglomerate Daimler-Benz (which made the upscale Mercedes) and embattled American automobile company Chrysler announced that they were merging, new co-CEO Jürgen Schrempp told journalists that the primary reason for the merger was to "bring[] together two cultures, American and German. The real result will be a better solution."[1] Schrempp and his American co-CEO Bob Eaton hoped that they could marry American ingenuity and efficiency with German quality and precision, boosting the attractions of each of their brands.

Daimler-Benz and Chrysler were bringing together two cultures in more than one way. Certainly, they were combining two national cultures, with different expectations about negotiations and about how corporate structures integrated into the society around them. But they also were combining two corporate cultures that were as plainly different as their dress codes. Chrysler's business casual open collars reflected their focus on flexibility and efficiency, while Daimler

1. Bill Vlasic & Bradley A. Stertz, Taken for a Ride: How Daimler-Benz Drove Off with Chrysler 247 (2009).

executives' starched collars and business suits reflected their attention to detail and formality. As might be expected, the merger was not quite as smooth as Schrempp made it sound. As auto analyst Maryann Keller said shortly after the deal was announced, "When it comes to the cultures of these two companies, they're like oil and water."[2]

The cultural differences between the two firms complicated the negotiations at several points. There was significant disagreement over the name of the final company, specifically over which firm's name would be first: Chrysler had a long and storied history in the United States, but the Germans at Daimler-Benz considered themselves to have invented the automobile.[3] The deal almost collapsed after the Daimler board met in Stuttgart, when it appeared that the Germans were willing to leave various issues unresolved before merging.[4]

The issues continued after the merger. Chrysler, an American company through and through (and especially after the U.S. government had bailed it out in the 1970s), had difficulty dealing with the German corporate style, which was simultaneously more hierarchical, but contained murkier chains of command that led to more protracted strategic debates. That was complicated enough, but the Americans also had to get used to the *Aufsichsrat*, or Supervisory Board, which contained elected representatives of the employees, and which had the power to replace managers or executives.[5] The Germans, on the other hand, had to acclimatize themselves to the American concept of executive compensation.[6]

Smaller issues bode poorly as well. While both companies agreed on the importance of brand separation (not advertising workmanlike Jeeps with luxury Mercedes), the Mercedes executives balked

2. *Id.* at 248.

3. *Id.* at 225.

4. *Id.* at 232.

5. *Id.* at 254–55.

6. *Id.* at 267.

at sharing a factory with Chrysler in order to increase production of their popular M-class sedans, worrying that it would compromise their brand's quality (the Jeep actually had better quality ratings at the time).[7] Schrempp was often fidgety at meetings or social occasions in the United States because he needed a cigarette and his new American colleagues did not smoke.[8]

The marriage between Daimler-Benz and Chrysler lasted only eight years, much of it rocky. During that time, Daimler managed to alienate a number of Chrysler's distributors by slashing incentives (compromising a key strength it had brought to the relationship), and Chrysler began losing money quickly.[9] Key Chrysler executives fled to other companies or were fired.[10] By 2004, investors were calling on Schrempp to resign.[11] In 2007, Daimler finally sold an 80 percent stake of Chrysler to private equity firm Cerberus Capital Management for $7.4 billion, absorbing roughly a 75 percent decline in value for the company. (By the terms of the deal, Cerberus effectively accepted $670 million to take Chrysler off Daimler's hands.)[12]

It is a common saying in the business world that "culture eats strategy."[13] Even most meticulously planned corporate strategies can fall prey to unanticipated clashes between corporate or national cultures.

7. *Id.* at 265.

8. *Id.* at 261.

9. *DaimlerChrysler: Marital Problems*, THE ECONOMIST, Oct. 12, 2000, *available at* http://www.economist.com/node/393076/ (last viewed Oct. 13, 2012).

10. *The DaimlerChrysler Emulsion*, THE ECONOMIST, July 27, 2000, *available at* http://www.economist.com/node/341352/ (last viewed Oct. 13, 2012).

11. *DaimlerChrysler: The Wheels Come Off*, THE ECONOMIST, Apr. 29, 2004, *available at* http://www.economist.com/node/2630460/ (last viewed Oct. 13, 2012).

12. *Chrysler: Divorced*, THE ECONOMIST, May 17, 2007, *available at* http://www.economist.com/node/9196298/ (last viewed Oct. 13, 2012).

13. *See, e.g.*, Deloitte, *"Culture Eats Strategy for Breakfast": Executing Your Strategy More Successfully*, *available at* http://www.deloitte.com/assets/Dcom-UnitedKingdom/Local%20Assets/Documents/UK_C_CultureEatsStrategyForBreakfast.pdf (last viewed Oct. 18, 2012).

But understanding the effect of culture on negotiation is important not so much because it helps avoid embarrassing misunderstanding, but because it helps negotiators understand how decisions get made at the highest level of companies, and how the rest of the company will accept and implement those decisions. Once a negotiator understands that process, she can answer critical questions about the negotiation, including:

- Who are the main decisionmakers vs. influencers in their organization?
- What is the pace and process for decision making in their organization?
- How can she build trust with the other side?
- What modes of communication (e.g., writing, presentation, drunken dinners) will have the greatest impact on the other side?
- What types of information (e.g., hard data, personal anecdote) will motivate a decision by the other side?
- Who will be the best match for the other side's lead negotiator?
- If the negotiation is successful, what will be critical elements or next steps to align the organization to ensure effective implementation?

"Culture" is a tricky, amorphous term. Because it is not written down anywhere, culture can be difficult to talk about in a precise fashion.[14] We will use it to mean certain patterns of thinking and acting

14. *See, e.g.*, Lynn Spillman, *Enriching Exchange: Cultural Dimensions of Markets*, 58 AM. J. ECON. & SOC. 1047, 1048 (1999) (explaining economists' difficulty in discussing culture); FONS TROMPENAARS & MAARTEN NIJHOFF ASSER, THE GLOBAL M&A TANGO 8 (2011) ("The problem with organizational and national cultural issues in general is that the underlying basic assumptions remain largely implicit and unspoken."); *When Something Is Rotten*, THE ECONOMIST, July 25, 2002 ("culture is a concept that many business leaders find difficult to grasp.").

that, once established, work as a default operating system for an individual.[15]

(That is, they provide a set of unspoken assumptions that the individual can quickly plug into new situations.)[16]

Culture changes the way we process information. The same facts can mean different things to different parties from different cultures. As a result, when negotiating across cultures—corporate or national—parties must take care that their actions are consistent with the message they want to send. It is also important to make sure that they are properly interpreting the information that they receive.

The effect of "culture" can be particularly complex because it can operate along more than one layer.[17] To take the examples most relevant to our discussion, every organization has a unique corporate culture, but two organizations in the United States will share the same national culture. If an organization from the United States negotiates with one from China, they will have to negotiate two national cultures as well. To make matters even more complicated, cultures do not stay still. They are always evolving, incorporating aspects of other cultures they encounter and reacting to changes in technology, the

15. GEERT HOFSTEDE, CULTURES AND ORGANIZATIONS: SOFTWARE FOR THE MIND, at Kindle location 174 (1997) (describing culture as "certain patterns of thinking, feeling and acting [that] have established themselves within a person's mind, [that] (s)he must unlearn . . . before being able to learn something different, and unlearning is more difficult for her than learning for the first time"). Hofstede also pioneered using software as a metaphor for culture.

16. Herbert A. Simon, *Strategy & Organizational Evolution*, 14 STRATEGIC MGMT. J. 131, 137 (1993) (defining organizational culture as "a set (possibly a large set) of premises that reside in the minds of the decisionmakers of the organization"). If this sounds suspiciously like heuristics to you, you're not alone. For more, *see* chapter 2.

17. HOFSTEDE, *supra* note 15, at Kindle location 243 ("As almost everyone belongs to a number of different groups and categories of people at the same time, people unavoidably carry several layers of mental programming within themselves, corresponding to different levels of culture."); *see also* Spillman, *supra* note 14, at 1047, 1048 (explaining economists' difficulty in discussing culture); TROMPENAARS & ASSER, *supra* note 14, at 8 ("The problem with organizational and national cultural issues in general is that the underlying basic assumptions remain largely implicit and unspoken.").

political environment, and the economy.[18] (American culture during the Depression, for example, was not the same as in the Sixties, or during the Internet boom of the Nineties.)

As a result, any negotiation between two organizations will involve the interaction of two different sets of expectations, and two different worldviews, along a cultural layer not present when two individuals negotiate.

In this chapter, we will examine the various effects that differing levels of organizational and national culture can have on a negotiation, as well as strategies to—if not avoid—then at least account for those effects.

7.1 Organizational Culture—The Personality of the Organization

It is an unavoidable fact that each organization has a particular culture.[19] As merger consultants Fons Trompenaars and Maarten Nijhoff Asser describe it:

> Culture is to the organization what personality is to the individual—a hidden yet unifying theme providing meaning and direction that exerts a decisive influence on the overall ability of the organization to deal with the M&A [Merger &

18. *See, e.g.*, Damian Zhang & Kenji Kuroda, *Beware of Japanese Negotiation Style: How to Negotiate with Japanese Companies*, 10 NW. J. INT'L L. & BUS. 195, 206 (1989) (discussing Japanese adaptation to international business negotiations).

19. *See* Daniel R. Denison & Aneil K. Mishra, *Toward a Theory of Organizational Culture & Effectiveness*, 6 ORG. SCI. 204, 204 (1995) ("The relationship between the culture and functioning of social organizations has been a recurring theme in the social sciences for over 50 years."); Anthony F. Buono, *When Cultures Collide: The Anatomy of a Merger*, 38 HUMAN RELATIONS 477, 479 (1985) ("Just as culture is a central factor which influences the ways in which people act and interact in a given society, indigenous cultures evolve over time in organizations which affect individual and group behavior in predictable though subtle ways.").

> Acquisition] challenges and dilemmas. Corporate culture has a profound effect on an organization's effectiveness, because it influences how human resources are used, and how the organization responds to the environment.[20]

Culture can have a positive effect on organizations. Google, for example, is famed for a corporate culture that promotes creativity and job satisfaction.[21] It can also have a decidedly negative effect. Enron's star-focused corporate culture, for example, encouraged manipulating performance statistics over substantive improvements, an emphasis that presaged the problems that led to its downfall.[22]

That said, no corporation has a monolithic culture, just as no country does. There will be "conservatives" and "liberals," groups and outsiders. Many of these divisions will evolve naturally. However, if the company grew through acquisition, there may already be several distinct cultures within the company, depending on how recent those acquisitions were made and how geographically dispersed they are.

As Trompenaars and Asser describe the problem, most mergers involve a central cultural dilemma: one corporate culture will take over, the other will be overtaken. If the acquiring company does not allow the target's culture room to breathe, it may stifle the very strengths the acquirer wanted to buy. On the other hand, if the target remains too independent, it can monopolize the parent company's resources.[23]

20. *See* TROMPENAARS & ASSER, *supra* note 14, at 57.

21. *Google's Corporate Culture: Creative Tension*, THE ECONOMIST, Sept. 17, 2009, *available at* http://www.economist.com/node/14460051 (last viewed Oct. 17, 2012).

22. *See* Malcolm Gladwell, *The Talent Myth: Are Smart People Overrated?*, NEW YORKER, July 22, 2002, at 31–32 (experiments show people praised for talent will lie to protect self-image).

23. TROMPENAARS & ASSER, *supra* note 14, at 17; *see also When Something Is Rotten*, THE ECONOMIST, July 25, 2002 ("Many of America's downfallen (Tyco, Global Crossing, WorldCom) were hastily bundled together amalgamations of companies that lost their distinctive ways and found nothing to replace them.").

7.1.1 Values—The Principles that Guide

Values (or tendencies to prefer certain circumstances over others) help to dictate each organization's priorities in a negotiation.[24] For example, one firm may value stable, long-term profits, while another emphasizes taking advantage of shorter-term arbitrage opportunities. These two values would likely conflict in any negotiations over a merger or joint venture.

Looking at an organization's values gets to the root of what each side perceives is most important. Some organizations embrace risk, promoting or paying leaders who are willing to take aggressive positions. Others may value a deliberative process that focuses on properly vetting options; in a corporate culture like this, getting the "right" answer is prized, though it likely comes at a slower pace. Significant corporate values also tend to show up in corporate policies. Many corporations claim they prize creativity, but only Google is known for holding regular meetings in which employees can pitch ideas to the co-founders and the CEO.[25]

These values have a strong influence on how executives serve the needs of their corporations. While there are dozens of different ways to describe organizational cultures, one good first pass is Competing Values Framework, developed by executive consultants Jeff DeGraff and Bob Quinn, which offers a useful perspective how different values may affect negotiations.[26] DeGraff and Quinn focus on four different kinds of corporate culture:

- *Collaborate*. Collaborative organizations prioritize teamwork and consensus. In a negotiation, these organizations will

24. Jeswald W. Salacuse, *Ten Ways that Culture Affects Negotiating Style: Some Survey Results*, 14 NEGOTIATION J. 221, 222 (1998) (noting definitions of culture are "numerous" and "vague").

25. *Google's Corporate Culture: Creative Tension*, THE ECONOMIST, Sept. 17, 2009, *available at* http://www.economist.com/node/14460051 (last viewed Oct. 17, 2012).

26. Jeff DeGraff & Bob Quinn, Competing Values Framework, http://competingvalues.com/.

tend to want to include a broad set of representatives from across the organization early in the process to ensure that there is appropriate buy-in and alignment. Scheduling discussions tend to be challenging because of the number of people engaged, and, to an outsider, it may appear to be unclear who exactly is the decisionmaker(s). However, once there is agreement, then organizational acceptance tends to be high as the team built the foundation from the start.

- *Create.* Creative corporations seek out innovation and encourage risk-taking. Speed is almost tangible within these organizations. There is typically a "deal team" that can drive negotiations, and a portion of the organization already championing the cause. However, implementing a completed agreement may be more challenging because other corporate teams were not part of the negotiation process and will have to be brought on board. Cisco and Google would stand out as examples of a "create" culture, as would the pre-merger Chrysler.
- *Control.* Controlling organizations focus on rules and procedures. Leaders strive to be good organizers who maintain efficient, smooth-running organizations. As a result, leaders often focus on process and decision rights so they "don't screw up," and keep a tight leash on negotiators. Negotiations are likely to be well documented, with frequent review and sign-off requirements. Like in a "collaborate" culture, decisions will take longer; unlike in a "collaborate" culture, the delay comes from sending decisions up and down the hierarchy rather than achieving consensus. Negotiators may have less flexibility to agree to terms that do not mesh with existing internal rules. Many parts of the utility industry would have this type of culture, as would Daimler.
- *Compete.* Competitive organizations tend to be goal-oriented, with demanding, hard-driving leaders. Their focus on specific goals is similar to that in creative organizations, but usually

> involves more reduction of risk. (In other words, the leaders will insist on additional terms in a negotiation, or other actions to mitigate any potential problems.) Competitive organizations usually have clear leaders and motivated teams.

In each case, getting a good feel for the kind of corporate culture provides insight about how the company will negotiate.

7.1.2 Practices—How to Go to the Bathroom

Sometimes, the difference in corporate culture is as plain as the dress code. One could sense the difficulties facing Daimler-Chrysler just by looking at its executives. Daimler required formal business dress, in keeping with its hierarchical nature and emphasis on formalism and detail. Chrysler, on the other hand, favored the tie-free business casual style, which reinforced its hard-charging focus on efficiency and results.[27] In this case, the dress code policy imparted important information about the culture of each company and how difficult they would be to merge.

Corporate culture often finds expression in company practices, and those practices will infect an individual's approach to any number of other tasks. Organizations transmit shared practices in a number of different ways. In some cases, they will share rituals of some kind. Gentle Giant, a moving company in Somerville, Massachusetts, makes its new hires run the steps of nearby Harvard Stadium with the boss; chiropractic products manufacturer Foot Levelers ensures that, within ninety days of joining the firm, everyone has watched *Rudy*, the 1993 Sean Astin vehicle about a Notre Dame senior who walked onto the Fighting Irish football team.[28]

27. Vlasic & Stertz, *supra* note 1, at 248.

28. Leigh Buchanan, *Bizarre Hiring Rituals*, Inc. Magazine, Mar. 1, 2010, *available at* http://www.inc.com/magazine/20100301/bizarre-hiring-rituals.html (last viewed Oct. 18, 2012).

Organizations also may tell common stories. Business professors Dan and Chip Heath spend a chapter of their bestselling book *Made to Stick* describing the importance of storytelling in communicating ideas. In particular, they point out the importance of "shop talk," the phenomenon of swapping stories with co-workers that one would never share at a dinner party (their examples include Xerox repairmen relating how they spent four hours chasing down a burned-out dicorotron when they had been misled by a false E053 code—something we can surely all relate to). The Heaths say that such stories, which depend on shared knowledge and experience for interest, are essential to maintaining both expertise and a sense of community among skilled workers.[29]

Practices influence the way in which negotiations are conducted. One organization, for example, may prefer long formal sessions in conference rooms, while another may see back-channel communications as an essential method of getting at what parties truly want.[30] Clearly, when these two kinds of practices intersect, there are opportunities for misunderstanding.

Practices will also create norms (unwritten rules understood by other members) that can affect the conduct of negotiations.[31] For one organization, it may be understood that subordinates defer to superiors, while in another everyone is expected to defend their ideas against all comers. While there is no one "correct" corporate practice, obvious differences may raise questions behind the negotiating table. Among them:

- Why is this issue important to them? Are we giving away something that should be more valuable to us?

29. *See* DAN HEATH & CHIP HEATH, MADE TO STICK, Kindle location 3537 (2007).

30. HOFSTEDE, *supra* note 15, at Kindle location 139.

31. *Id.* at Kindle location 245. *see also* Buono, *supra* note 19, at 479–80 ("Subjective organizational culture also encompasses what may be termed a managerial culture, the leadership styles and orientations, mental frameworks, and ways of behaving

- Why do they need to get agreement on this issue now? We have others that we think are much more pressing.
- One of the junior members of our team just got a call from their side looking for a specific piece of information. What are they after?

Without an understanding that differences in corporate culture may lead to differences in practice, issues like these can trip up otherwise sound negotiations. Even worse, differences in practices can easily be misinterpreted for mismatched goals of the negotiation. One side's insistence on progressing in a specific way (because that is what its negotiators are used to) may be interpreted as an unwillingness to reach agreement.

7.1.3 Language—The Dangers of In-Jokes

When French automaker Renault merged with Japanese Nissan in 1999—only a year after the Daimler-Chrysler deal—it tried one surprising reform to bridge the culture gap: "It is by no means easy for people at Renault or Nissan," wrote CEO Carlos Ghosn in 2005, "but we have embraced English as a language that allows us to communicate effectively with each other and with customers around the world."[32] He reasoned that it would allow the two companies to communicate with each other (both had a number of English speakers already), as well as attract the best and brightest new talent from a global marketplace. By contrast, American executives often felt alienated in the merged Daimler-Chrysler when their German

and solving problems that are influenced by the organization. While some aspects of managerial culture are, of course, shared across organizations, crucial but subtle facts are indigenous to particular organizations.") (internal citations omitted).

32. Carlos Ghosn, *Managing across Cultures*, The Economist, Nov. 18, 2005, *available at* http://www.economist.com/node/5156760 (last viewed Oct. 17, 2012).

compatriots would break into their native language to discuss key points, effectively excluding the Americans from the discussion.[33]

Language plays a formative role in organizational culture, and language differences do not have to be as stark as between French and Japanese (or English and German) to cause miscommunications. The labels an organization assigns to concepts—or even just physical objects—can have a distinct effect on how people frame issues. Social scientists Roberto Weber and Colin Camerer performed an experiment that showed just how quickly, and how decisively, this process can occur. They started with pairs of volunteers, one of whom they designated a "manager," the other an "employee." They then showed the volunteers a set of sixteen pictures of people in offices. While the subject matter was the same, the specifics were not. The number of people differed, the actions differed, and physical objects like furniture and clothing differed. The manager's job was to get the employee to select eight of the pictures correctly in a predetermined order. Quick and correct selection was rewarded with cash. Each pair played twenty rounds of this selection game. After twenty rounds, Weber and Camerer "merged" pairs into foursomes, "fired" one of the managers, and had them play again.

The result? The threesomes were much less efficient than the pairs had been when they started out. Much of the inefficiency stemmed from the need to educate the new "employee" in the shorthand they had developed after only twenty rounds of play. The conclusion we can draw from this is that language (even just in the form of shorthand) develops quickly and changes the way different groups communicate about issues.[34]

33. VLASIC & STERTZ, *supra* note 1, at 361.

34. *See* Roberto A. Weber & Colin F. Camerer, *Cultural Conflict & Merger Failure: An Experimental Approach*, 49 MGMT. SCI. 400 (2003).

7.2 National Culture—You Can Take the Boy Out of Iowa...

An increasing number of organizations are multinational.[35] And many more (particularly in business) are engaging in multinational negotiations that either create new business opportunities or have some effect on other areas of the company's business operations (for example, negotiating over buying a new business may necessarily require additional negotiations over the rights to sell a new product or technology in another country of operation). As a result, these organizations are engaging in negotiations that will often involve not just multiple organizational cultures, but multiple national cultures as well.[36]

Just as organizations will develop their own cultures, distinct nations (which may share a common language and history) will have distinctive cultures as well.[37] Discussing national culture presents a number of real difficulties. Most obviously, it encourages one to fall back on stereotypes, which are usually lazy and overgeneralized, and so do not convey much useful information.[38] The concept of a "nation" has long been a problematic one.[39] Equally problematic, discussion of national cultures can encourage one to treat national cultures as "black boxes," irreducibly unique, and therefore useless to

35. Stephen E. Weiss, *Analysis of Complex Negotiations in International Business*, 4 Org. Sci. 4 Org. Sci. 269, 269 (1993).

36. Hofstede, *supra* note 15, at Kindle location 131 (explaining difference between national culture and organizational culture).

37. We recognize that many nations will encompass numerous subcultures, but we don't believe this changes our analysis.

38. *See* Trompenaars & Asser, *supra* note 14, at 34 (discussing dangers of reinforcing national stereotypes).

39. *See generally* Benedict Anderson, Imagined Communities: Reflections on the Origin and Spread of Nationalism (New ed. 2006).

even try to understand.[40] Focus too much on the uniqueness of each culture, and negotiations among cultures begins to seem impossible.[41] However, it is difficult to deny that certain groups share specific assumptions of acceptable behavior, or specific understandings of certain behaviors.

We will not focus on specific national cultures (except as examples). Instead, we will focus on several distinct areas of negotiation where the abstract idea of national culture can have a nonetheless concrete effect. In fact, the different cultures do not even have to be national cultures. Specific regions of a particular country, like New England or the American Southeast, may have some of their own cultural expectations, scripts, and "legitimate tactics"—a Southerner might be lost trying to order a cup of coffee in a Boston Dunkin' Donuts (where the line moves fast, shouting is encouraged, and a "regular" coffee has cream and two sugars), while the Boston native might inadvertently offend his Southern hosts by asking for things too bluntly.

7.2.1 Signaling Behavior

As we have already discussed, people's behavior can communicate distinct information to others. But certain kinds of signaling behavior—such as body language—may actually change meaning from national culture to national culture. This is not surprising. Linguistic drift is a well-known phenomenon. When sites are geographically isolated from one another, language evolves in different directions. Body language is subject to the same pressures, and path dependence makes those alternate meanings sticky.

To take one example, Americans often share information to get information, so sharing information operates as a signal that it's time

40. *See* Spillman, *supra* note 14, at 1051 (explaining hesitance to rely on "cultural" explanations of differences among national economies).

41. *See, e.g.*, Zhang & Kuroda, *supra* note 18, at 195, 196–97 (discussing characteristics "unique" or "intrinsic" to national negotiating styles).

for sharing in return. Japanese negotiators, by contrast, are used to more indirect methods of gleaning information and so don't attach the same reciprocal importance to sharing.[42] Another important signaling behavior is gift exchange. Gifts of different sizes or types may act as an important social lubricant in different cultures. And differing cultural norms may dictate appropriate ways of offering or receiving gifts. Certain gifts may appear respectful, but be calculated to insult.

Signaling behavior does not have to be intentional. Often, miscommunication results from behavior that was not consciously designed to send a signal, but which does so nonetheless. During the Paris peace negotiations in 1919, American President Woodrow Wilson was "surprised and somewhat shocked" to find that the Europeans would break for tea and macaroons most afternoons at a specified time; he first thought that it betrayed a lack of seriousness, although he later reported that he came to accept it as a foreign custom.[43]

7.2.2 "Legitimate" Tactics

Cultures may, as part of their "software," include scripts or schemes for "appropriate" negotiation.[44] As a result, one's national culture may also dictate what one perceives to be "legitimate" negotiating tactics. For example, as discussed in greater detail in chapter 6, what is considered legitimate gift-giving in one culture may be considered corrupt behavior in another.

Similarly, national culture may carry with it expectations of when it is acceptable to break form in negotiation. In some cultures, appearing to lose one's temper may be acceptable or even expected,

42. *See, e.g.*, Jeanne M. Brett & Tetsushi Okumura, *Inter- & Intracultural Negotiation*, 41 Acad. Mgmt. J. at 497, 503 (1998) (negotiation experiment confirms use of different scripts for information sharing among American and Japanese negotiators).

43. Margaret MacMillan, Paris 1919: Six Months that Changed the World, Kindle location 1226 (2007)

44. Brett & Okamura, *supra* note 42, at 495, 496.

while in others it may be considered a serious breach of protocol. For example, in October 1943, when Averell Harriman first arrived in the Soviet Union to serve as the ambassador from the United States, he had the following exchange with Soviet Minister of Foreign Affairs Vyacheslav Molotov:

> "We have found you a very tough man to deal with," . . .
> "I have come as a friend," Harriman responded.
> "Oh, I know that," Molotov said. "I intended my remarks to be complimentary."[45]

The Soviets (a unique combination of both a national and an organizational culture) prized tough negotiators and did not take "tough" stances personally—good news for Harriman.

The "tactics" we refer to here more often have to do with process than specific negotiating points. One common process in Asia, particularly Japan, is the "meeting before the meeting." This is where junior representatives from each side gather before senior-level leaders from opposite sides meet. While they do not necessarily negotiate, they do get an understanding from each side of what are the critical issues and main points, so that each side's senior leader is properly prepared for what will be discussed in the meeting. As a result, in the meeting, the senior leaders from both sides appear knowledgeable, thoughtful, and well prepared. This reinforces their image as being the leader of the business and well in control of their operations as opposed to needing to make decisions and judgments on the spot that may need to be renegotiated later.

Similarly, resort to legal mechanisms is far more common in the United States than it is in other, less litigious cultures.[46] As a result,

45. WALTER ISAACSON & EVAN THOMAS, THE WISE MEN: SIX FRIENDS AND THE WORLD THEY MADE 221 (1986).

46. *See* James R. Maxeiner, *When Are Agreements Enforceable? Giving Consideration to Professor Barnett's Theory of Contract*, 12 IUS GENTIUM 92, 94 (2006) (describing American failure to develop comprehensive code governing contracts rather than litigation).

American negotiators may be more comfortable threatening litigation (or treating litigation as a default) than negotiators from other countries. In this vein, when negotiation specialist Robert Mnookin mediated a long-standing dispute between American computer giant IBM and Japanese technology firm Fujitsu, he found that some of the animosity stemmed from differing perceptions of how much a contract could control subsequent negotiations. The two companies reached an understanding they enshrined in a settlement agreement: IBM treated any agreement as a legally enforceable contract designed to be the last word on any future dispute; Fujitsu, on the other hand, treated the agreement as a commitment to repair a damaged relationship through reasonable discussion and worried less about the precise terms. As a result, when later disputes arose, IBM was frustrated by Fujitsu's unwillingness to stick to the settlement agreement, while Fujitsu was bewildered by IBM's refusal to sit down and talk things over.[47]

7.2.3 The Meanings of Actions

Culture can also impose radically different meanings on the same actions. Most groups of people develop their own shorthands that can be expressed in distinct words (or neologisms), idioms, or gestures. Often, those shorthands require some degree of cultural context to decode effectively. For example, when negotiating in Iraq during the recent occupation, U.S. soldiers frequently found that locals interpreted some statements as promises even when they were not intended as such.[48]

These differing interpretations tend to magnify the further removed cultures are from one another. To take one example that

47. Robert Mnookin, Bargaining with the Devil: When to Negotiate, When to Fight 153 (2010).

48. David M. Tressler, *The Soldier & the Sheik: Lessons from Negotiating in Iraq*, 13 Harv. Negotiation L. Rev. 67, 84–85 (2008).

has become so common it is often used by consultants in role-play: "hai" in Japanese signals acknowledgment (much like some people nod and say "uh-huh" to indicate they have heard a statement); nonetheless, in English, we tend to translate it as "yes," which we take as agreement. As a result, many American negotiators get tripped up by seeming agreements that are actually just acknowledgments of position. Digging a bit deeper into these, there are often local expressions and idioms that may further complicate understanding. Tokyo residents tend to use something from the old British style as a conversation starter, referring to the weather—"Soreni sitemo atsui desu ne?" ("Hot day, isn't it?"). Osaka businessmen tend to take a more direct approach starting a conversation—"Konichiwa... Moukatte makka?" ("Hello... How is business?").

7.3 Practical Applications

Be aware of how both sides use language. As the experiments we discuss above indicate, for many people, language *is* culture, and culture is language. As a result, careful use of language becomes extremely important, even with those who share a native tongue. It usually makes sense to finish a meeting by explicitly discussing tangible next steps, and immediately assigning resources so the parties can work out any potential miscommunications. The potential for miscues from different understandings of the same language also counsel both sides to be patient with each other. Miscommunications are often not attempts to take advantage, but actual misunderstandings based on how each side usually works.

Do due diligence on company culture in your counterparty. Most organizations—unless they are brand new—have different ways of "leaking" their culture. There may be alumni. There may also be profile articles that specifically refer to company culture. And a negotiator may have contacts with people in the other organization.

Learning a counterparty's culture can provide important insights into how a deal is progressing. Without that knowledge of culture, even the simplest of transactions may prove baffling. Finance writer Michael Lewis famously began his career at the Salomon Brothers investment bank, a job he lucked into after being seated next to one of the managing director's wives at a fund-raising event. After impressing the wife, Lewis went in for a formal interview. While he thought it had gone well, no one made him a formal job offer. It was only after he spoke to a fellow student at the London School of Economics (where he was studying) that he learned that the firm:

> never made job offers. It was too smart to give people the chance to turn it down. Salomon Brothers only gave hints. If I had been given a hint that it wanted to hire me, the best thing for me to do was call [the head recruiter] in New York and *take* the job from him.
>
> So I did. I called him, reintroduced myself, and said "I want you to know that I accept."
>
> "Glad to have you on board," he said, and laughed.[49]

Had Lewis not done even this small bit of due diligence—checking with one of his fellow students—he might have missed the fact that Salomon considered it the recruit's responsibility to close the deal. Salomon's coyness about recruiting was more than just a cultural characteristic, it was a cleverly designed screening mechanism: it protected its reputation for not getting turned down and ensured that Salomon bankers were aggressive enough to close important deals. Those were important characteristics to know if one worked at Salomon Brothers, but just as important to know if one worked *with* the firm.

Try to learn the "rules." For any given culture, there are unwritten rules about what is acceptable in interaction and what is not. English

49. Michael Lewis, Liar's Poker 25 (1989).

anthropologist Kate Fox, author of *Watching the English*, points out that the stereotypical English obsession with "weather" has a grain of truth to it. But it is not *weather* that the English care about; the subtleties of the cold and damp are just a convenient subject that allows strangers to acknowledge each other. ("Cold, isn't it?" "Yes it is, really.")[50] Violating this norm can result in awkwardness and set up further miscommunications.

Where possible, use "local experts." Adding a person to your team who has experience with either the other nation, region, or company can be extremely important when negotiating. The importance of a local expert "in the room" to interpret both verbal and nonverbal signals is hard to deny. But a local expert will also have great value "outside the room." A good local expert can advise the team on logistics (where are the convenient hotels? how does one get to the airport?), context (how is this company perceived locally? why do people work there?), and even opportunities to rest and recharge (how is the nightlife? where are the good restaurants?).

Eat dinner. Humanizing the other side can be key to building trust. All people need to eat and drink. Sharing meals or a drink (or several) brings context outside of the negotiation room. It brings an opportunity to discuss other topics. These, again, are valuable as they can bring insight into what is of value to the other side both as people and as an organization.

There is often a tendency to meet for a "formal dinner" between the leaders of both sides. However, these are typically scripted affairs that are largely a continuation of the negotiation room. Opportunities to meet in less formal settings provide more of an opportunity for team members to be themselves and discuss issues openly.

See the sights. Most business travelers—lawyers and consultants in particular—will note that business travel is not necessarily that glamorous: all cities look the same from the inside of a conference room.

50. Kate Fox, Watching the English: The Hidden Rules of English Behaviour 25–36 (2005).

To the extent one can remove oneself from the conference room, however, and experience even small doses of new areas, one can gain some level of understanding about one's counterparts. Visiting local shops or markets can give one an excellent idea how people transact day-to-day business—do they haggle? is there banter? is everyone a regular?—an insight that will often pay dividends back at the conference table.

Look in the mirror. Another difficulty with culture is that not only do other entities have reputations and identifiable characteristics, but one's own organization does as well. Some of these will be very general. Americans are often viewed as brash, direct, and concerned with money. Corporations are often viewed as greedy and conniving; plaintiffs' lawyers as greedy and overly prone to outrage. So, at the same time as one is trying to interpret signals from the other side, one has to be very careful about the signals that one is sending out about oneself, and how they interact with the counterpart's perceptions.

People rely on cultural stereotypes when they lack further information. But, like many other nonrational judgments that are used in the absence of information (more about which see chapter 2), these stereotypes can become ingrained. As a result, people are not always aware of when they are actually employing stereotypes.

One of the authors (Trask) once had the experience of litigating in a local court in Oklahoma, where the opposing counsel began by referring to him as "one of those tall-building lawyers." By the end of a series of depositions, the two sides had found common ground for negotiating various discovery disputes. But the initial posture—on both sides—was slightly more adversarial based on the assumptions—again, on both sides—that the other side might be less trustworthy in part because of the geographic area they hailed from.

So the complex negotiator must take special care both to avoid allowing unnecessary stereotyping to influence his own strategy, and to understand what stereotyping may be influencing the negotiation strategy of the other side.

7.4 Conclusion

Culture is everywhere. It is on the streets that we walk. It is in the companies where we operate. These cultures intermix, sometimes for the better and sometimes for the worse. The main point for negotiations is that cultures are critical for how things get done and how decisions are made.

Along the way for any successful negotiation, you will need interpreters. They will be able to interpret both corporate as well as national culture issues so that you can effectively navigate the pitfalls and speed the building of trust and connections. If not, cultures will wreak havoc on the best laid plans.

Over the last seven chapters, we have taken you through a range of issues including nonrational behavior, multiple decisions, multiple parties involved in negotiations, how regulation is injected into the process, how time affects negotiations and where cultures have their sway. In chapter 8, we will show you how they all begin to wrap together and focus on what are the primary goals and issues in a negotiation.

8

Grand Strategy

"Take your time. See the whole board."

—JED BARTLETT,
The West Wing, "Hartsford's Landing"

For the past seven chapters, we have discussed the various challenges that can arise from complex negotiations. While we have offered practical suggestions for addressing each of these complications individually, it is critical to tie together all of these elements to be successful.

There are certain processes in both business and litigation that one can follow to minimize the risk from complex negotiations. This chapter and the next two chapters will outline these processes, most of which include making sure that one has the best possible information about the negotiation, both about oneself and about one's counterpart.

First, we turn to the importance of developing an overall strategy, one that dictates not only the next moves in the negotiation itself but also some of the larger strategic questions, like when negotiation is worth entering in the first place, and how to deal with unanticipated changes to the business and legal terrain.

What we are really talking about here is what diplomats and military strategists call "grand strategy." As B. H. Liddell Hart, one of Britain's premier strategists during World War II, defines it:

> [T]he role of grand strategy—higher strategy—is to co-ordinate and direct all the resources of a nation, or band of nations, towards the attainment of the political object of the war—the goal defined by fundamental policy.
>
> . . .
>
> while the horizons of strategy is bounded by the war, grand strategy looks beyond the war to the subsequent peace. It should not only combine the various instruments, but so regulate their use as to avoid damage to the future state of peace—for its security and prosperity.[1]

Put more simply, "grand strategy" is the larger set of goals that govern any particular strategic action. Very few deals are ends in themselves. Instead, they each serve a larger purpose for the organization, such as a plan for strategic growth. For example, between 2002 and 2010, IBM acquired seventy companies, spending $14 billion as part of its overall growth plan. While each individual deal was important by itself, there was an overlapping focus to all of them: IBM was building a business platform to accelerate growth in the rest of its software portfolio. The acquisitions of Cognos (a firm that made business intelligence and performance management software), SPSS (a statistical software firm), and ILOG (a firm that made supply chain software) aimed squarely at building a platform in business intelligence and analytics. According to forecasts, that

1. B. H. Liddell Hart, Strategy 335 (1967).

business analytics software platform should contribute 20 percent to IBM's growth through 2015.[2]

Similarly, the specific settlement of a large piece of litigation (not to mention the litigation itself) may fit into a larger plan for the organization. Litigation over intellectual property like the Apple-Samsung lawsuit over smartphone designs for example, is often part of a larger set of business negotiations over the licensing of new technologies.[3]

Grand strategy can also be thought of as strategic design. Few organizations—either corporations in a competitive environment or loose collections of litigants who have banded together for a common purpose—can survive for long simply reacting to new events. Indeed, they need a plan for forward motion. This need for design is important at several different levels of strategy. It is important for defining the overall mission of the organization (what we will call its "primary purpose"), as well as in determining what comparative advantages may exist in a given set of circumstances.[4]

The purpose of this chapter is to explain the role that "grand strategy" plays when conducting a particular negotiation. Once the parties understand their own (and their counterparties') grand strategies—or the fact that the counterparty lacks a grand strategy—it becomes easier to reach an agreement that both parties can live with.

2. Mark Loughridge, IBM 2010 Investor Briefing—Financial Model, 11–13, 34. http://www.ibm.com/investor/events/investor0510/presentation/pres3.pdf.

3. *Apple v. Samsung: Swipe, Pinch & Zoom to the Courtroom*, THE ECONOMIST, Sept. 1, 2012, *available at* http://www.economist.com/node/21561912 (last viewed Oct. 16, 2012).

4. *See* Herbert A. Simon, *Strategy and Organizational Evolution*, 14 STRATEGIC MGMT. J. 131, 138 (1993) ("In the domain of corporate strategy, design enters at several levels. At the most general level, defining the company mission and identifying its sources of comparative advantage are themselves design activities. At a more concrete level, the search for new products, the search for new markets and the interactions of products with markets are all design activities.").

8.1 Primary Purpose

"A man got to have a code."

—OMAR LITTLE,
The Wire, "Unto Others"

Many strategy books will focus on a "mission statement," or stress the importance of goals. While these concepts are clearly useful, they have been overused to the point where they have become abstract and meaningless. "Mission statements," for example, have become a subject of parody: it is easy to find "Mission Statement Generators" on the Internet that will string together buzzwords into plausible-sounding mission statements for cheap laughs.[5] The problem with buzzword mission statements goes beyond cheap laughs, however. If an organization does not clearly articulate its goals, and understand how to pursue them, it operates at a competitive disadvantage to those organizations that have good guiding policies.

A good guiding policy is the 30,000-foot view of the solution, the one that everyone can hold in their head easily as they come up against new permutations of the problem. This is rare, rare enough that Professor Rumelt has observed that "[a] good guiding policy itself can be a source of [competitive] advantage."[6]

We find it simpler to refer to this guiding policy as a "primary purpose." The advantage of this term is that it simplifies the inquiry. Instead of gathering a committee to compose a "mission statement" that is clouded with dozens of different concepts (usually as the result of compromise among the primary purposes of many different subgroups within the organization), the primary purpose of an organization identifies exactly what the organization seeks. For example,

5. *See, e.g.*, The Corporate Mission Statement Generator, http://www.netinsight.co.uk/portfolio/mission/missgen_intro.asp (last viewed Sept. 29, 2012).

6. Richard Rumelt, Good Strategy/Bad Strategy: The Difference and Why It Matters 85 (2011).

the primary purpose of Amnesty International is to campaign for the protection of human rights.

By definition, an organization can have only one primary purpose. That does not mean that its various components may not identify conflicting purposes. In fact, it is quite common for an organization to have various conflicting goals, a condition that often leads to logrolling within the organization.[7] But even if its various constituents identify different purposes, the organization itself will ultimately choose one of these goals over others.

The problem for most organizations is that their primary purpose is a default setting: a defense of the status quo—perpetuation of the organization in its current state. And that status quo default tends to lead to bad outcomes.

Take, for example, the failed AOL–Time Warner merger of the early 2000s. For those with hindsight, the AOL–Time Warner merger was doomed from the beginning. It required blending an access provider (which needed to secure as many content providers as possible to attain its primary purpose of serving as many customers as possible) with a content provider (which needed to secure as many access providers as possible to attain *its* primary purpose of serving as many customers as possible). Indeed, at the time, the merger created issues among various media outlets owned by Time Warner, which jealously guarded their editorial independence.[8] The result was supposed to be a conglomerate that, because it married a major content provider with a major access provider, would dominate media markets. But that dominance never occurred; instead the company split up again, this time into four separate firms. Steve Case, the chairman

7. *See* chapter 3.

8. *Who's Afraid of AOL Time Warner?*, THE ECONOMIST, Jan. 24, 2002 ("parts of the empire are prickly about the very idea that they might favour in-house content"), *available at* http://www.economist.com/node/954013/print (last viewed Jan. 20, 2012).

of AOL and one of the architects of the deal, later explained where it all went wrong:

> Unfortunately, that "one company" strategy never got off the ground. Instead, each division "did its own thing." While that staved off turf wars, it did nothing to drive innovation. . . . having concluded that integration would never happen, I proposed to the company's board that it was time to "liberate" and split the conglomerate into four freestanding companies—Time Warner Cable, Time Warner Entertainment, Time Inc. and AOL—each with its own strategy, stock, balance sheet, management team and board.[9]

Without a guiding primary purpose, AOL–Time Warner not only did not dominate as a single firm, its stagnation revealed fault lines that already existed at Time Warner.

While identifying one's own primary purpose provides a competitive advantage, identifying the other side's primary purpose unlocks a number of options. It can, among other things, allow one to determine which actions or statements in a negotiation are trustworthy and which may be less so. (We use the word "trustworthy" here to mean predictable and reliable. One could make a statement that is not trustworthy, even though it may be truthful at the time it is made. It may just be that the party making the statement does not know that she will be overturned by her board of directors, or that some other unpredictable event will intervene.)

A clearly articulated primary purpose is also a good valuation tool. It allows members of the organization to make decisions during a negotiation to evaluate the options in front of them. Business professors Dan and Chip Heath write about this in their bestseller *Made to Stick*. In one of their examples, Southwest Airlines CEO Herb Kelleher made his company's primary purpose clear to employees: Southwest

9. Steve Case, *It's Time to Take It All Apart*, THE WASHINGTON POST, Dec. 11, 2005.

was *the* low-fare airline. So all the employee needed to know when making a decision was, "Will this help Southwest become *the* low-fare airline?"[10] Viewed in this way, a clearly articulated primary purpose can help to overcome a number of the nonrational judgments that arise in complex negotiations. (For more on these, see chapter 2.) In particular, a clearly articulated primary purpose can help to combat both *herding behavior* and *authoritarian bias*. To the extent these nonrational judgments arise because members of the team lack specialized knowledge or confidence, a primary purpose can empower those team members or provide a check against bad decisions resulting from these biases. (For example, it should often be clear which decisions would help Southwest become *the* low-fare airline.)

A clearly defined primary purpose can also help in multiparty negotiations. By forcing a debate on the point of the agreement *before* negotiation with another party begins, a primary purpose helps to build consensus among various organizational constituents. Shareholders and board members, for example, should already be behind the agreement. Therefore, they will not require much coaxing to consent to the final negotiated agreement. (This is the "internal campaign" we discussed back in chapter 3.) And corporate agents like lawyers or bankers should have a clear idea of what the organization is trying to accomplish, which should reduce the danger of having strategic decisions reversed mid-deal.

A clearly articulated primary purpose does have one large drawback, however. Arriving at one can expose latent conflicts within the organization. As Cass Sunstein has discussed, groups frequently paper over internal conflicts by reaching what he calls "incompletely theorized agreements," or agreements that leave open conflicting goals for each party.[11] In polite company, for example, people might refrain

10. Chip Heath & Dan Heath, Made to Stick: Why Some Ideas Survive & Others Die, Kindle location 483 (2007).

11. Cass R. Sunstein, *Incompletely Theorized Agreements*, 108 Harv. L. Rev. 1733 (1995).

from discussing religion or politics in order to avoid areas of potentially deep disagreement. In a business setting, different departments may not identify issues with a given deal in order to preserve the peace among various executives. Time Inc. and Warner Brothers, for example, kept to their own core businesses even after they merged, in part because Time's executives were determined to protect their corporate culture; melding the companies further would have required uncomfortable conversations neither side was willing to endure.[12]

And so we reach one irony about complex negotiation: to do it effectively, it may be necessary to have a frank, even heated, negotiation *within* the organization first. Of course, as the Time Warner executives learned, if that kind of conflict is inevitable, it is better to thrash it out with one's colleagues before engaging in a complicated negotiation with another organization.

8.2 Scorecard

"Life is a game. Money is how we keep score."

—TED TURNER

Once an organization has identified its primary purpose, it is important for it to perform an inventory of both its assets and its needs. This inventory is primarily to determine the organization's competitive advantages. But also, since any negotiation is about *exchange*, it is also important to know both what the organization needs and what it has to offer.

Failing to perform this inventory can lead to disastrous results in a negotiation. For example, in mass tort litigation, the settlements that meet with the most opposition from objectors are those that deviated from the stated goal of the litigation. If the litigation sought

12. Nina Munk, Fools Rush In: Steve Case, Jerry Levin & the Unmaking of AOL Time Warner, Kindle location 680 (2007).

to "recover damages for people who bought a defective air purifier," and the settlement resulted only in coupons for additional defective air purifiers, then the negotiation was likely a failure.[13]

Avoiding this kind of failure can be as simple as maintaining a checklist. There are common issues that arise in every negotiation, both in complex acquisitions and mass litigation settlements. Among them:

- *Immediate goal*. While we have discussed the organization's primary purpose, it is also important to determine its primary goal for the negotiation in front of it. What is the organization trying to achieve with this deal? How will that advance its primary purpose? For a business, it may be access to a particular market. For a class action defendant, it may be a global release from liability for a specific problem. Some have referred to this as the "target point" of the negotiation.[14] Terminology aside, this is the one part of the deal that the party absolutely cannot consummate without. Properly defined, it can help the firm decide what the negotiation is worth, and when to walk away.
- *Value of the deal*. What is the overall size of the opportunity? What is achieving this goal worth—in dollars—to the organization? Determining the value of the deal is more important than just filling in the right number on a balance sheet. It can help determine when it is worth abandoning a negotiation to pursue better opportunities that may arise, and when it may be worth staying the course through a troublesome period.

13. *See, e.g.*, Figueroa v. Sharper Image Corp., 517 F. Supp. 2d 1292 (S.D. Fla. 2007) (upholding objection to class action settlement involving coupons for allegedly defective products).

14. *See* Robert S. Adler & Elliot M. Silverstein, *When David Meets Goliath: Dealing with Power Differentials in Negotiations*, 5 HARV. NEGOTIATION L. REV. 1, 64–66 (2000).

- *Assets.*[15] What is the firm's existing set of capabilities? Does it have the capacity to take on the business this deal generates? Can it afford to pay the settlement and still operate as a business? Any number of things can be assets to a firm. Money is the most obvious, but even apparent liabilities can be assets in the right context. An unused factory, for example, may be a drag on a balance sheet but also the extra capacity needed for a new product.
- *Terrain.* Terrain can be thought of as a context. What does the market look like? Who are the major players? What are the governing legal rules? Which of these is currently changing?
- *Necessary changes.* No complex deal leaves a firm unchanged. Settlements may require large payments or corporate reforms. Mergers or major acquisitions will change the very structure of the company. Is the company prepared for these changes? Has it mobilized the resources to take advantage of them?
- *Best alternatives.* What alternatives are there to this negotiation that will help the firm meet this major goal?
- *Primary stumbling blocks.* Most organizations are aware of the issues that they will face in a given deal. The law may be unfavorable, or a key member of the other team may dislike the deal. Spoilers may be waiting in the wings. The more of these the firm faces in black and white before the negotiation commences, the better equipped it will be to take on unexpected problems.

This scorecard can also help with several of the nonrational judgments discussed in chapter 2. For example, many negotiations fall prey to *anchoring*, where the first number mentioned in a negotiation

15. *See* Simon, *supra* note 4, at 131, 138 (1993).

"anchors" the remaining discussion.[16] An organization that has a clear scorecard for a transaction—specifically one that has already identified the value of the deal—is less likely to succumb to anchoring. Why? Because it already has its anchoring number: the value of the deal. As a result, it is either equipped to throw out its own number first (in which case anchoring will work to its advantage), or it has the ability to judge whether the counterparty's proposed number is within its own acceptable range.

A good scorecard can also help counter *loss aversion*, the condition where the loss of $10 hurts us more than the gain of $10 pleases us.[17] A party with a good scorecard has the ability to judge how much a loss (in this case, the loss of the deal) will actually hurt. And if there is a clearly defined walkaway point, so much the better. At that point, there is little difficulty with losing the deal. Similarly, a good scorecard can also help with the *sunk-cost* fallacy, for the same reason: the negotiators will know when they may walk away without worrying about having "wasted" resources on the deal.

A scorecard also helps the organization when third parties enter the negotiation. When government agencies demand information about the value and the projected effects of a given deal, a well-prepared scorecard will help the organization locate the proper defenses and the necessary supporting information.[18] Similarly, if spoilers[19] enter the picture, either by demanding payment to go away or by turning what was a bilateral negotiation into an auction, the scorecard can help a party determine when it's time to walk away from the deal. (It is easy for individuals to "fall in love with the deal" for various reasons. And it is also disturbingly easy to get competitive and want to "beat" a spoiler.) If the firm is committed to an actual scorecard with clearly defined goals and acceptable costs, it can minimize the

16. *See* § 2.1.1.

17. *See* § 2.1.3.

18. *See* § 3.1.1.

19. *See* § 3.1.2.

risk of losing direction or entering an unwanted auction once a negotiation becomes more complex.

To the extent that a scorecard also requires some preliminary debate among organizational factions, it can smooth the ratification process for any deal.[20] If the negotiators can go back and show that the deal meets all of the conditions it was set up to address, there should be little reason not to approve it. And to the extent the scorecard reflects an internal consensus about the deal on one side, it should have resolved any major debates before the negotiation commences.

8.3 Internal Capacity Assessment

"We're putting the band back together!"

—JAKE BLUES,
The Blues Brothers

Before undertaking a complex negotiation, it is important to engage the right team members. Without the right team, completing a deal (or settling a lawsuit) can become significantly harder. There are a collection of roles—each of which requires a specific skill set—that need to be filled. The roles and people do not have to match one-to-one, but it is important to make sure that the team represents as many skill sets as possible. These roles include:

- *Master Strategist*. It is easy in any negotiation to lose sight of why you are pursuing it in the first place. There must be a leader who understands the macro issues and how this specific effort fits in the strategic initiatives of the business. The leader provides guidance to the team on the materiality of the various issues. She decides which issues are material.

20. *See* chapter 3.

In certain cases, it may be someone with less authority but who has been designated as the "last word" on the goals of the negotiation.

- *Lead Negotiator*. One of the fastest ways to get a negotiation going in the wrong direction is to have multiple people negotiating different aspects of the deal.[21] The 2011 debt-ceiling negotiations, for example, foundered once they began to proceed on three different tracks: one involving the president and speaker of the house, one involving the house majority leader and vice president, and one involving the Senate's so-called "Gang of Six."[22] As a result, it is critical to have a single "official" line of communication with the other side. This does not mean that there can be only one line of communication. As we discuss later in this chapter, having additional channels can be very useful. But having a single "official" voice that can speak on behalf of the team will cut down on the confusion that comes when multiple individuals are negotiating with each other across multiple issues. Without one person owning the communications back and forth of the critical issues, the negotiation can quickly get bogged down, dangerous misunderstandings can develop, or the opposite side can exploit the lack of prioritization.
- *Relationship Manager*. Because a complex negotiation happens over an extended period of time, it is important to have someone who has gotten to know the opposite side and the key decisionmakers or influencers. This individual ideally will also have particularly advanced "people skills." When issues arise that cannot be handled in the normal course of daily interaction, the relationship manager knows who on the opposite side to contact to find an alternate route to get to a conclusion.

21. *See* chapter 3.

22. Bob Woodward, The Price of Politics, Kindle location 4439 (2012).

- *Program Manager*. Complex negotiations have many moving parts. As a result, the team requires someone to manage timelines, pull in new resources, and book the conference rooms. While these are not the most glamorous tasks, if these activities are left to everyone to manage themselves, negotiations tend to drift. Just as armies rely on quartermasters, a negotiating team will rely heavily on its logistical manager.
- *Financial Analyst*. Understanding the overall financial materiality of issues is critical. Nonetheless, most teams rely on guesses or back-of-the-envelope calculations to judge the size of an issue. A capable financial analyst will understand how to model various scenarios and bring clarity to evaluating different options. They can tie these models to the overall strategy and business operation.
- *Legal Expert*. Ideally, this is a lawyer. Similar to the financial analyst, the legal expert understands the overall points of the legal and regulatory environment related to the issues being negotiated. While this person is likely to be supplemented by experts on specific issues (such as taxation), he can lay out the overall process that needs to be executed and the required documents and agreements to get there.
- *Analyst/Associate*. There is always more work than the team can do, which is why teams usually need someone to deal with the random tasks that come up during the course of negotiations. These can include tracking down specific pieces of information, writing rough drafts of agreements, and even physical delivery of critical documents.
- *Communications/Public Relations Expert*. As discussed in greater detail in chapter 3, the public is often an important additional party to negotiations. As a result, there are often significant issues that need to be publicized either during the negotiation or after it concludes. Understanding the

key audiences, communication outlets, and targeting of messages is essential if the results of the negotiation will be implemented successfully.

Each of these roles can scale to the size of the negotiation. In a small group, for example, one person may wear two or more hats; in a large firm, each role may have its own team. However, in the early stages of the project, it is important to identify who is filling each role, where there are gaps, and where the team has concerns about the resources assigned. If not, at some point during the process, you will find the need to add or swap out resources, which will take significant time and effort.

A proper team evaluation is as much an inventory of personalities as it is of skills. As described in greater detail in chapter 2, even the simplest of negotiations engages people on both a rational and an emotional level. We humans cannot help this mixing: as hunter-gatherer savannah apes, we are simply wired to have emotional responses,[23] and those responses will come into play in the course of a negotiation. Negotiators who are aware of the personalities at play in a given engagement—and who can rise above their own immediate reactions to effectively address others' blind spots—are critically important to a negotiation team.[24]

Properly done, the internal capacity assessment helps create more effective negotiating teams.[25] Indeed, that is the entire point of the exercise: it is designed to make sure that the team functions well as a whole and has the range of skills necessary for a complex negotiation.

23. *See* chapter 2.

24. *See* Adler & Silverstein, *supra* note 14, at 1, 60 (stressing importance of emotional awareness and self-control in negotiation).

25. *See* chapter 3.

8.4 Best Alternatives

"Would you rather get one shot in the head or five in the chest and bleed to death?"
"Are those my only two options?"

—MONEYBALL

Much negotiation literature stresses the "BATNA," an inelegant acronym for "Best Alternative To Negotiated Agreement." For our purposes, BATNA is too narrow a concept because it tends to be focused on only the immediate goal related to the negotiation. By contrast, a successful negotiation or deal is not an end in itself, it serves the firm's primary purpose. Therefore, when approaching the negotiation, it is important to look at what benefits a successful result will unlock, even if they are unrelated to the immediate goal.

Many experienced dealmakers will counsel negotiators not to "fall in love with the deal." And many leaders can feel trapped by the "best option": they see a particular acquisition or settlement as the answer to many of their business issues and can become so convinced of the benefits that it is difficult for them to see any alternatives that are nearly as good. This near-obsession can cause them not to take action on other fronts because they believe that a particular deal will "solve so many problems."

In fact, there are usually multiple options that will accomplish the same goals. However, they may require more creativity and investment than the perceived one-shot benefit of an acquisition or comprehensive class action settlement. For most of us, accomplishing one big thing is more satisfying than having to work to piece together many smaller things to achieve the same result.

For an acquisition, alternative paths include:

- *DIY*. The firm devotes the funds it would have used for acquisition to recruiting new talent, creating the product, or servicing it without involving another party. While this provides the clearest ownership, it is also challenging to pull together all of the right pieces quickly enough to stay competitive with other firms.

- *Partnership*. The firm establishes a set of commercial cooperation agreements with providers already occupying the market. This is usually one of the fastest and most flexible routes to deliver on your primary purpose. However, a business partnership is not a marriage. There is rarely much in the commercial agreement that prevents one side from doing something that undermines the other party's interest.
- *Joint venture*. A joint venture formally pools a firm's resources with another company to achieve the same goal. This is another, fast way to accomplish an immediate goal in a cost-effective manner. The challenge is that a joint venture typically requires more resources to negotiate than an acquisition. Joint ventures also have a high failure rate: almost 50 percent of joint ventures fail to deliver on their goals.[26]
- *Acquire an alternative option and build on top of it*. When an ideal acquisition candidate is not available, one alternative is to acquire a company with lesser or smaller capabilities and build on top of it. Though this option may require less up-front capital, the firm will often have to allocate additional funds to accomplish the immediate goal.
- *Wait, do nothing, and invest elsewhere (for now)*. Once work is started on a prospective deal, there is motivation to "get something done." Leaders and teams want to be able to show something for their efforts. If they are not able to get their top choice, then they may pursue the next best alternative, even if it is significantly less valuable. It may make sense to

26. *Strategic Partnering: Managing Joint Ventures and Alliances*, Center for Digital Strategies at the Tuck School of Business, Feb. 28, 2006.

stop work on this route and pursue other areas for growth for now. Customers, markets, and technology continue to change: so focusing elsewhere may be wise until a new opportunity presents itself.

A complex lawsuit offers a different set of paths, in part because the firm perceives its default not as a status quo, but as "suffering a loss" (for the plaintiff) or "defending a lawsuit" (for the defendant). Under these circumstances, since both sides will experience loss aversion, the status quo will be vigorous litigation. Nonetheless, there are a set of alternative paths for a given settlement that include:

- *Pretrial victory*. One of the parties convinces a court to either dismiss the case or grant summary judgment. Settlement may not be necessary under these conditions. The primary drawback to pursuing this path is that it may force an appellate fight that is just as costly as the litigation would have been.
- *Settlement with another party*. Under certain circumstances, the defendant can settle with a third party, like a government agency or alternative plaintiff, for more favorable terms. Pursuing this path often risks engaging in collateral litigation, since the original plaintiff will be unlikely to allow its potential recovery to disappear without a fight.
- *Arbitration*. Arbitration is becoming an increasingly desirable option because it is cheaper than litigation, offers more predictability, and yet offers the kind of finality that comes from a trial verdict.
- *Litigating to a trial verdict*. The rarest path is an actual trial verdict. (Very few lawsuits result in a trial verdict.) Trial verdicts tend to scare both sides in litigation because they are not predictable. Juries (or judges) can focus on odd issues.

8.5 Materiality/Leverage

"Two out of three ain't bad."

—MEAT LOAF,
"Two Out of Three Ain't Bad"

One of the largest challenges in long-term strategy is keeping one's eye on the firm's primary purpose. Things will come up, either as a result of the negotiation, or as outside events, that will derail the original plan. As Field Marshall von Moltke once said, "no plan survives contact with the enemy."[27] As a result, it is critical to understand both the importance in the course of negotiation and the value of the issue to your side.

It is all too common that both business people and lawyers will spend time and resources negotiating a specific issue that has no real importance to the overall goal. In the process of doing so, they will:

- *Create confusion.* "Why are they arguing this small issue? Did we miss something?"
- *Divert resources from strategically important efforts.* "We spent six hours on this point and I have to leave tonight. That leaves two hours to get to the critical issues or we will be delayed again."
- *Lose credibility.* "They just spent all of this time and energy on this irrelevant issue. I think they are idiots."

Understanding which key points drive the long-term value is critical in communication and prioritization of deal discussions. Not understanding these points will sow doubt, distrust and waste of

27. DANIEL J. HUGHES (ED.), MOLTKE ON THE ART OF WAR: SELECTED WRITINGS (1993).

resources. The motivation for diving into specific details can sometimes be borne out of relatively pure motives:

- *Perfection*. "I just want to deliver the highest value for my client and be thorough."
- *Risk aversion*. "We need to make sure that we don't miss anything that will come back to bite us later."
- *Fairness*. "They shouldn't get anything that they didn't pay for."

Unfortunately, as philosophers have long noted, the perfect is the enemy of good.[28] A negotiation is a compromise, a willingness to agree. There are no perfect compromises. Therefore, take the time to understand what are the critical elements that deliver on your primary purpose. Once you understand those, be prepared to negotiate away the other elements if necessary. Some of the most common critical elements are:

- *Products/Technology*. As part of a transaction, the products or technology usually form the framework. While it is possible that you would like to get representations and warranties on every single piece and skew, it is more common that 80 percent of the value is driven by 20 percent of the products. Knowing which ones those are and performing a thorough due diligence and tight agreements around them should be the focus of your efforts.
- *Customers*. Similar to products and technology, it is typically a small set of customers who account for the most sales and profitability of a company. The 80–20 rule typically applies here as well. First confirm the concentration of customers. Then assure that there is proper detail and care for them during a transaction.

28. Voltaire, La Bégueule: Conte Morale . . . , 15 (Nabu Press 2011).

- *Employees*. There is a great deal of personal uncertainty around an acquisition. The acquirer may want to get employment agreements from every single employee of the target company to ensure that they will be there after the transaction closes. However, this is neither practical nor necessarily wise. Understanding who are the key general managers, sales people, and technical experts should be the primary focus for retention efforts and agreements. It is not that the other employees aren't important. However, there are a handful that, if they were to leave, would have a significant detriment to the primary purpose.
- *Leadership/Operational control*. Who is going to be in charge? This is always a mix of both overall business goals and personal perception. The leadership of an organization sets the tone and focus for the rest of the team to achieve the desired goals. Making sure that the right team is put in place post transaction has a great effect on the likelihood of success. "[D]ifferences in top management styles have a negative impact on performance... Ensuing conflicts tend to reduce the probability that the two management groups will effectively work together towards achieving the goals of the acquisition."[29] In a recent case, this came to be a central issue in the hostile bid for Vulcan Materials by Martin Marietta. "The primary reason why this combination doesn't seem to be getting going is because the managers on the boards don't agree on who should run it," commented Leo E. Strine Jr., chancellor of Delaware's Court of Chancery.[30] The concept of combining the two businesses had been discussed for more

29. Strategic Management Journal, Vol. 12, 281–97 (1991) Organizational Fit and Acquisition Performance: Effects of Post-Acquisition Integration; Deepak K. Datta School of Business, University of Kansas.

30. *Who Would Run a Combined Martin Marietta and Vulcan?*, THE DEAL MAGAZINE, Mar. 9, 2012.

than ten years. However, the root disagreement between who would be CEO and the resulting integration plan led to a hostile bid by Martin Marietta and hearing in court regarding confidentiality and standstill provisions. Glencore-Xstrata face a similar challenge, but for different root issues: "The issue of Glencore-Xstrata's management is about more than corporate pride and the egos of its chief executives. It is also about business expertise. Xstrata is a powerhouse in mining, with large positions in copper, coal and zinc production. While Glencore has some mining operations, its main focus is trading. Glencore has unrivaled intelligence on the global supply and demand of materials like wheat, oil and copper...Those are fundamentally different businesses. Mining investments are long term, often taking a decade or more to generate a return. Trading relies on quick returns based on rapid, sometimes minute-by-minute decisions."[31]

- *Regulatory compliance*. While there are a wide range of regulations and approvals tied to an acquisition, it is critical to understand what are the critical few that will stop a deal and how those regulations are going to be decided. During its 2011 proposed acquisition of T-Mobile, AT&T learned that the hard way: "DOJ antitrust chief Sharis Pozen had reached her decision months sooner than anyone outside the agency had expected, short-circuiting what Stephenson and AT&T's government relations team had expected would be a lengthy opportunity to negotiate divestitures and other conditions that would address the DOJ's competition concerns.... But the company's well-connected representatives failed to persuade the agency to rethink its opposition. Four months later, the Federal Communications Commission indicated

31. William Macnamara, *As Time Wanes, Glencore-Xstrata Deal Hinges on Leadership*, N.Y. TIMES—DEALBOOK, Sept. 26, 2012.

> it would follow the DOJ's lead, and a federal district judge issued rulings negative to the deal, sealing its fate."[32] Even though it was clear to the AT&T team that they faced significant antitrust issues, they believed that they could get congressional officials to help drive approval, rather than wait for the technical analysis done by the legal and economic experts within the Department of Justice. Regardless if it is concerning antitrust, environmental, employment, tax, or other regulations, it is critical to map out not only what approvals are required but how those approvals will be granted. Otherwise, a significant amount of company resources will be spent for naught on a potential deal that may never be possible.

As noted at the beginning of this chapter, it is not only important to pull together the right resources needed to approach and execute a complex negotiation, it is equally important to map out how to use those resources throughout the process. Many teams assemble their A-players and show up for the game, but they don't necessarily think through how best to use those players over the course of the negotiation as they learn more about the overall situation and the opposite side.

8.6 Conclusion

The biggest challenge overall in negotiations comes when a company does not really know what it wants. A company that merely reacts to a class action being filed or a potential partner coming up for sale is already in trouble. That is why it is so important to understand what

32. Bill McConnell, *Lobbying AT&T–T-Mobile, Express Scripts-Medco*, THE DEAL MAGAZINE, Mar. 30, 2012.

the company's primary purpose is. It provides the overall guide to what the company needs to be successful.

It is also important to take a larger view of the company's purpose because making a choice based only on the options presented at a given time is dangerous. Companies that have a sense of larger strategy, that know what the settlement or the next deal is *for*, what it sets up, tend to accomplish more than those that simply try to grab the next available goal for the sake of doing something.

However, in order to deliver on a larger strategy, a company needs to have certain fundamentals already in place. It needs an identifiable team that, even if it is not exclusively dedicated to complex negotiations, has the capacity to take on these opportunities when they arise. It also needs a solid sense of its own capabilities and limitations, to prevent its pursuing deals that will bring it no long-term advantage, or that may even diminish its core strengths. And it needs leadership that is capable of discerning important issues from merely urgent ones.

In order for a company to put these fundamentals in place, it needs lots of information about the strategic landscape surrounding it. In other words, it needs good *intelligence* and good intelligence-gathering capabilities. In chapter 9, we will discuss the kinds of information that are necessary to keep a complex negotiation team adequately briefed about all of its options, as well as the best means of gathering that information.

9

Intelligence

The *Art of War* by Sun Tzu has the unfortunate distinction of being one of the most read and least understood "business books" on the shelves. Since the movie *Wall Street* first premiered, where Gordon Gekko recommended the book to his callow protégé Bud Fox, aspiring businessmen have mined it for aphorisms to justify just about any behavior one can imagine.

The overuse of the *Art of War* is particularly unfortunate because there is real strategic insight in the book. But rather than stemming from the various quotable lines, most of that insight comes from the author's overall approach to conflict. To take one particularly relevant (yet not often quoted) example, Sun Tzu devotes an entire chapter to analyzing terrain. He discusses various kinds of ground, including "accessible, entrapping, indecisive, constricted, precipitous, and distant." And in several other chapters (particularly on Marches and Maneuvers) he draws heavily on this analysis.[1]

1. *See generally* SUN TZU, THE ART OF WAR (Samuel B. Griffith trans., 1963).

How does the Chinese landscape relate to an activity usually performed across a long table in a conference room? Terrain matters because it is a central element of any strategy. For soldiers, that means terrain is the actual ground on which they fight. As Sun Tzu points out, it matters what kind of ground one occupies: certain ground offers tactical advantages, and different ground requires different tactics.

For modern businesspeople and lawyers, terrain is not physical. Instead, it is the economic conditions and governing law that surround the negotiation. But the effects are the same. Some of that terrain can be modified to help the negotiator, much as one might conform physical terrain into a defensible position. But some remains immovable. Or, as Sun Tzu himself put it:

> Conformation of the ground is of the greatest assistance in battle. Therefore, to estimate the enemy situation and to calculate distances and the degree of difficulty of the terrain so as to control victory are virtues of the superior general. He who fights with knowledge of these factors is certain to win; he who does not will surely be defeated.[2]

No negotiation happens in a vacuum, especially one that takes place across multiple parties. It must take into account the landscape where the negotiation is happening. However, this landscape is not static. The size and position of the key elements at the start is critical as they provide the basis for the primary purpose of the negotiation. However, changes in the landscape are like the shifts in a desert. Some of the changes just smooth out rough edges while leaving much of the navigation untouched. Others are more dramatic, requiring a rapid reevaluation of direction.

Negotiation needs to adapt to changes in these factors as they materially arise. What follows is a summary of the most common

2. *See generally id.* at 127.

factors and how they may impact a complex negotiation. A negotiator need not perform a detailed analysis on each factor when entering a negotiation. However, knowing what variables may come into play can be useful in understanding where the negotiation will likely be most sensitive.

In this chapter, we discuss two different aspects of intelligence in complex negotiations. First, we talk about what to look for: that is, what information will be of most use in either a business negotiation or settlement negotiations in a complex lawsuit. (Despite what one may think, there are some surprising overlaps between the two.) Second, we discuss the ways in which organizations have gathered this information.

9.1 What to Look For

Few negotiators would advocate walking into a discussion without any information. The real difficulty comes in determining what information is most relevant to the negotiation at hand. While it is almost impossible to identify every fact that could prove useful, there are broad categories of knowledge that it makes sense to master before engaging with another party in a negotiation. Roughly speaking, these would be called general market conditions.

9.1.1 Market Conditions

"It's the economy, stupid."

—JAMES CARVILLE

All negotiations—whether for the acquisition of a company or the settlement of a mass tort lawsuit—always come back to money. The value and volume for the products and services in scope create the earnings that will set the bounds for the monetary portion of the negotiation. That value and volume can be affected on two different levels—macroeconomic factors and market-specific performance.

Macroeconomic intelligence is easy to find, but more difficult to understand. Many news outlets regularly highlight changes in various economic indicators, spending a great deal of time (or column inches, or pixels) discussing the meaning of each change and its possible impact on the larger economy. These macroeconomic indicators are the aggregate of hundreds or thousands of different measurements that are systematically combined to give an indication of overall direction. This aggregation is what makes these indicators so useful to understanding overall trends.

Most business executives and lawyers have at least a passing understanding of these trends. However, until they hear news of some shift, many of them also tend to assume that the current trends will continue unchanged. Macroeconomic factors are rarely tied directly to the focus of the negotiation. Instead, they serve as important background to complex negotiations. If we continue the terrain metaphor, these indicators provide our 30,000-foot view. They are the sources of parties' confidence or concern over the longer-term direction of a given agreement. Many business executives are well trained to look at these indicators in the process of making a deal; lawyers less so. The following are a few common indicators and their potential meaning to a negotiation.

Gross domestic product (GDP). The grand summary of all indicators in a given country's economy, GDP is the sum of everything consumers purchase, businesses invest, governments buy, and the net of what the country exports to the rest of the world. It is the shorthand for talking about the overall attractiveness of a country and its direction. Two key elements to this indicator are its *absolute level* and its *growth rate*.

The *absolute level* of a country's GDP (basically, its size) provides an indication of the total amount it can buy relative to other countries. For example, while the average citizen of Luxembourg is wealthy relative to the rest of the world, the absolute size of the country's GDP (less than $60 billion in 2011) illustrates that it is a small overall market. In the course of a negotiation, a party may be willing to forgo an opportunity in a series of much smaller countries if it is willing to access one much larger one (or vice versa).

The *growth rate* of GDP shows the trend of a country's economic performance. The percent growth or decline illustrates where the country is headed. For a negotiation, a long-term trend or a dramatic change (up or down) will create urgency or cause significant delay to reaching an agreement. This indicator matters to legal negotiations as well as business deals. While litigation tends to be countercyclical, both a corporate defendant's ability to pay an award and a plaintiff's ability to finance litigation depend on overall trends in the economy. Moreover, popular attitudes toward corporate defendants tend to fluctuate with changes in economic direction.

While the *unemployment rate* holds the focus for many political leaders, it is the opposite measure—the *overall employment rate*—that holds more meaning for business leaders. The overall employment rate is a key indicator of how many people have jobs and so can afford to buy a range of products and services. As employment increases, so does the long-term market opportunity for a company's sales.

Similarly, the cost of adding additional workers may affect the attractiveness of a deal or of pursuing a lawsuit. (Complex lawsuits often involve hiring a large number of temporary lawyers and paralegal personnel to review documents or conduct other time-intensive but repetitive tasks.) For lawyers, unemployment rates may matter when choosing a venue for litigation. Areas with high unemployment may produce jurisdictions that rule more consistently against corporate defendants, or juries that favor hometown plaintiffs.

The *inflation rate* measures the change in the price level for a collection (often called a "basket") of goods and services across an economy. If the prices of products in general rise faster than the average consumer's wages, then the consumer will buy fewer products. (The reverse can also be true.) Dramatic changes in the price level will affect how each side perceives its long-term ability to make money in a specific market. Inflation also may affect the timing of any negotiation. In some cases the inflation rate may significantly affect the real cost of a deal.

Interest rates. The rate that banks charge companies or individuals to borrow money is a key driver of investment or consumption. Since many deals are financed at least in part with borrowed money, a rise in the interest rate typically slows down a company's willingness to make an acquisition. It cuts into the overall value of the transaction. Similarly, if a company must borrow money to fund litigation (or a settlement), interest rates will play a large role in the negotiation. The same holds true for complex litigation.

Exchange rates. Exchange rates are the "official" prices at which one can buy foreign currency. Given how interdependent the global economy has become, it is difficult to identify a company that is not affected in some way by changes in the value of different currencies. For example, a key source of supply may be located in another country, or the growing group of buyers may be across a national border. Similarly, a foreign defendant may be able to afford a larger award based on differences in currency prices. Because exchange rates change every day based on other economic indicators like GDP, inflation, and unemployment, the parties need to understand the sensitivity of their negotiations to each of these indicators.

Energy and commodity prices. These two inputs directly affect how much it costs a company to make and deliver its products and services. The supply of both energy and commodities tends to be concentrated and limited. It can take years to develop alternate sources, so a relatively small change in overall demand can have significant impact on a company's profitability. As with exchange rates, it is critical to understand a company's sensitivity to changes in energy and commodity prices.

Sovereign debt. Sovereign debt is the debt owed by a government, as opposed to a private company. If a government is struggling to repay loans borrowed to fund its operations or public investments, it may have to raise taxes (for revenue), lay off public sector workers (reducing total overall employment), or reduce spending (which can reduce overall demand). The wide influence of sovereign debt makes it particularly important to know one's counterparty's dependence on a specific country's support or on government contracts. For example, a negotiation around a company with a significant amount of business with a Greek government agency will differ significantly from one with a Chinese government entity. If nothing else, one will likely offer more perceived value than the other.

9.1.2 Market-Specific Drivers

Market-specific drivers typically have greater impact on a given firm than macroeconomic factors. While they will be affected by macroeconomic factors, they will not necessarily move in the same direction or to the same degree. As we discussed, GDP is an aggregation of summary of thousands of elements. Some of these markets may perform significantly better and some significantly worse. During a recession, certain stores or products (such as Walmart, McDonald's, and "generic" products) can actually sell more than they would during periods of economic expansion. Understanding these specific variables and how they relate to macroeconomic factors can help parties negotiate better by understanding the market terrain. The most common include the following.

Consumer/business demand. The actual purchases for products or services are what generate the value for the negotiation. (This is true even in the settlement of complex negotiation. The value of a mass tort action, for example, may depend on the number of allegedly defective products present in a given market.) Like with GDP, smart negotiators should understand both the absolute level and growth path. A new product category that has grown at 50 percent annually for the past five years may sound exciting. If its total sales are only $2 million in a $24 *billion* market, it will have less meaning or impact for any negotiation. In other words, context matters—a lot.

Saturated vs. developing market. A company or product may be experiencing fast sales growth today because they have come up with a significantly better solution than what previously was on the market. However, if the product they are selling has a ten-year useful life and 90 percent of the potential buyers already own one, then it is likely that future sales will be much slower. Unless they have other product extensions or services in development, there is likely little additional value to expect from sales growth. This is also true in complex litigation. Suing over older products leaving a market (or services no longer being performed) is unlikely to yield much demonstrable damage.

Margin/profitability levels. While revenue from selling products or services is exciting and is what typically makes headlines, converting that into profitability is what creates value. Even though Apple controlled only 5 percent of the mobile phone market revenues in 2010, they earned 25 percent of its profitability. That is why Apple's stock price is significantly higher than Nokia's, which actually sells more phones. A product related to much smaller sales or intellectual property can command much higher value if it allows a company to get higher profit or return from its investment.

It is important to look at the different players in this market and whether they all have similar capabilities, including profitability levels. One company *may* be making notably more or less money than the other players. Understanding differences in how they run their operations today versus what is possible in the rest of the market can affect your negotiating position.

Market production capacity/scale benefits. Tied to profitability, an overall market may be constrained by the amount of products that can be produced if all the market players operated at peak capacity. In that case, since supply has a built-in limit, the producers can afford to charge higher prices. However, if someone were to bring a large new factory online (which would increase supply), it could drive overall market prices down. The automobile and airline industries are well known for their low profitability levels. One reason is the significant amount of excess capacity in each industry.

When you combine the market-specific drivers with their associated macroeconomic factors, you can have a clear picture of the overall terrain for the negotiations and what impact they will have on each side's position and goals.

9.1.3 Legal/Regulatory Regime

"The worst thing in this world, next to anarchy, is government."

—HENRY WARD BEECHER,
Proverbs from Plymouth Pulpit (1887)

The market conditions described above are, for the most part, about opportunities for companies. They identify where the money is made. By contrast, the legal and regulatory regimes are about constraints: they describe the rules that serve as background for any negotiation and the ways in which those rules are applied. The following are a few of the most common areas that are important to understand.

Competition law/regulation. Perhaps the most important thing to know is the overall level of regulation in a given jurisdiction. Some jurisdictions (national and local) have many rules; others may be closer to the Wild West. The most important level of regulation to most business deals is antitrust regulation. Most countries have rules in place to limit the possibility of any one company gaining monopoly-like power in a specific market. These cases are regularly reviewed by competition authorities when there is an acquisition. While the parties involved in the transaction may define the market one way, another player with significant sales or profitability at risk may choose to testify to authorities that the market should be defined more narrowly to cause a change in the deal. The AT&T deal with T-Mobile in the United States fell apart based on the rival definitions of the market and the impact that any targeted divestments would have on the overall value of the deal.

Regulatory authorities may also on occasion step in based on class action results. For example, the Department of Justice's recent investigation of collusion among Apple and various New York book publishers came on the heels of a class action filed by the law firm Hagens Berman.[3]

Ease of doing business. On a more everyday level, the local permitting, licensing requirements, or employment law requirements can have a meaningful impact on the *ability* of a company to grow or access new markets. For example, even though a foreign company may acquire a Chinese company's assets or capital, the Chinese entity may have an operating license for a particular industry that is not transferrable to a non-Chinese parent.[4]

Transparency/corruption. The level of corruption in a given jurisdiction has a direct effect on the costs of doing business there. Corrupt regulatory agencies can impose significant obstacles to getting things done, either by holding up time-sensitive tasks or by adding significant costs in "fees." Corrupt judiciaries can significantly increase an organization's legal exposure.

As a result, some countries, like the United States and the United Kingdom have increasingly extended the reach of their anticorruption laws: the Foreign Corrupt Practices Act (FCPA) in the United States or the Bribery Act in the United Kingdom.[5] The penalties for noncompliance have been massive for some companies. Siemens had to pay over $2 billion in penalties related to settlements with both the U.S. and European governments related to findings against

3. Alison Frankel, *Why Isn't DOJ Seeking Money Damages in E-books Price-Fixing Case?*, REUTERS, Apr. 12, 2012, *available at* http://blogs.reuters.com/alison-frankel/2012/04/12/why-isnt-doj-seeking-money-damages-in-e-books-price-fixing-case/ (last viewed Oct. 18, 2012).

4. James Ahn, Thomas Luedi, & Isiah Zhang, *How to Make M&A Work in China*, 18 McKINSEY Q. 5 (Winter 2006).

5. For a fuller description of these laws, *see* chapter 6.

them and institute a rigorous company-wide compliance program.[6] Because government prosecutors are continuing to test the bounds of the law, understanding the conduct of a business's interaction with government officials is increasingly important. Knowing the level of corruption in a given area can help one determine whether a strategy really is worth its true costs: a company may abandon an otherwise lucrative deal or settle a frivolous lawsuit simply to avoid the costs of working in a notoriously corrupt arena.

Politics/enforcement. Though regulations may be on the books that require government agencies to regulate companies a certain way, the executive branch may exert pressure to relax regulation in order to attract jobs or investment.

Ease of bringing lawsuits. Another important factor to consider is the degree to which private parties can bring lawsuits. Since most agreements will be enforceable primarily by civil suit, knowing how local jurisdictions react to filing complaints (are they more or less likely to dismiss them?) and treat discovery (do they favor expansive discovery?) can influence the ways in which attorneys structure a deal.

Moreover, the ease of bringing lawsuits may also influence the degree to which local laws are enforced. Even when a regulatory agency might overlook certain activity, class actions may occur that pressure it to enforce preexisting regulations. For a buyer, acquiring a company that has benefited from lax enforcement may depend on how the value changes if one assumes full regulatory compliance.

Judiciary. At least in the United States, most regulation or enforcement must eventually come into contact with the judiciary. Judges either rule on the application of laws or on the propriety of their enforcement. Different judges, however, may rule differently on the same issue.

Safety/insurance certification. Regulation does not have to be public. It can also come in the form of requirements from insurance carriers,

6. *Business View: Siemens and Its Demons*, THE ECONOMIST, May 22, 2007, *available at* http://www.economist.com/node/9214367/ (last viewed Oct. 18, 2012).

who will increase their premiums because of a significant change in the risk profile. For example, new production locations, methods, or services that are entered into based on a negotiation may change risk. Insurance is particularly important to lawyers, who may see insurance companies as an available source for funding any settlements that they may negotiate.

Sanctions. Because of its structure and lack of a combined military, the European Union has deployed much of its strength on imposing sanctions as a means of showing its displeasure with another county's action. From 2010 to 2012, the European Union has imposed economic sanctions in various forms against Iran, Belarus, Myanmar, Zimbabwe, Côte d'Ivoire, Egypt, Tunisia, and Libya (some have since been relaxed, as regimes fall or change behavior).[7] Being unable to buy materials from or sell products and services to a certain country can have a material impact on the value of specific negotiation. Also, one country may have a permissive stance, while another country may have sanctions. Understanding these and their scope is critical.

Unlike other factors, the legal and regulatory rely on regulator's perceptions of what is significant rather than supply and demand conditions in the market. Though a given regulatory response may be specific to a small set of issues, those issues can significantly affect the value of the overall negotiation.

9.1.4 Competitive Dynamics

"You never open your mouth until you know what the shot is."

—DAVID MAMET,
Glengarry Glen Ross

The interaction among competitors, both before and after any negotiation, tends to be the major focus of interested parties and with good reason. Most other players involved with the negotiation

7. *Charlemagne—Tough talk, No Strategy*, THE ECONOMIST, Mar. 3, 2012.

(other than customers) will move on to other matters—judges and lawyers will take on other cases, regulators will move to the next issue. But the competitors must live with the consequences of any deal. The competitors' reaction to the negotiation will determine how their value is impacted. (This is true for complex litigation as well. Settlements can signal either opportunities or threats to competing plaintiffs' lawyers.)[8]

To understand how the competitive dynamics interact with a complex negotiation, there are several factors that you will need to assess for their importance.

The other side's best alternatives. Negotiations are only successful when they are better than the alternative for both sides. Therefore, it is just as important to know what the best alternatives are for one's counterparty. Sometimes, the counterparty will reveal its best alternative up front, as a means of focusing the negotiation. But just as often, a counterparty will seek to mask its best alternatives, either to preserve leverage at the early stages of a negotiation, or to allow it to present "alternatives" that claim more value.

As a result, negotiators often have to infer these best alternatives from other indicators, such as the opportunities they know are available in a given market, or a sense of the other side's ability to compete in costly litigation.

Definition of the market. The scope of offering in question is a fundamental element to any negotiation. Markets can be defined very broadly or very narrowly, depending on who is defining them and why. The more broadly a market is defined, the greater number of substitutes are likely available and the lower the market share of any individual player. There are a few keys to defining the market, and they point back to how the end customer actually uses their offering:

One piece vs. Total system. Does the product or service offer some independent value, or does it only work as part of a larger system?

8. Ben Depoorter, *Law in the Shadow of Bargaining: The Feedback Effect of Civil Settlements*, 95 CORNELL L. REV. 957, 960 (2010).

(For example, the European antitrust case of Microsoft's Internet Explorer having stand-alone capability versus being part of the entire Windows operating system.) Does the removal of one element deprive the system of its usefulness? There is usually no single answer to this question. However, talking to different types of customers and seeing how they actually use the offering generally provides the best context and understanding here.

Integrated package vs. one-stop shop. One common concern for regulators is that a market becomes so concentrated that it removes choice for consumers. The obvious example is a case where there are only one two suppliers of a given good, and one is trying to acquire the other. The various attempted or completed acquisitions throughout the 1990s and 2000s of the aluminum producers Alcoa, Alcan, and Reynolds are cases in point.[9] Most cases, however, are subtler. As a result, negotiators must watch out for certain red flags, among them whether the agreement proposes the technical integration of multiple elements versus the distribution and sale of those products.

Integrated package. An integrated package is one that fulfills all of a customer's needs in a single product. For example, Apple has been successful, in part, because it focuses on selling a complete consumer experience rather than the technical components for that experience like Samsung does. Apple's hardware, software, and services are all thoughtfully designed to operate together with little to no effort from the user. That technical integration makes it difficult to define what market Apple actually plays in because its reach overlaps to deliver on that end-user experience. When Apple released the iPod, for example, it was difficult to tell whether it was in the music player business (because the iPod was a music player) or the music business (because the iTunes Store offered a huge catalog of songs for $0.99 each). This was not an academic distinction; Apple faced litigation from Apple

9. Robert Guy Matthews, *Alcoa Acquires Reynolds Metals in a Deal Worth $4.5 Billion*, WALL ST. J., May 4, 2000.

Music for violating an earlier agreement not to compete in the music business.[10]

One-stop shop. This is a weaker form of integration. Customers may find it simple to come to one location or vendor to get the majority of elements that they need. This tends to be more powerful in products that have little technical specifications such as music, food, or clothing. This is one reason why Walmart, Target, and Amazon have each proven so popular. For industrial products, Grainger (which offers everything from office supplies to welding equipment) is a good example of a company that provides access to a broad range of products with low technical specification. The main benefit of a one-stop shop is that it simplifies the procurement and transaction process. The danger for a manufacturer pursuing this goal is that they can be easily picked apart if another manufacturer has built a better product and the technical integration from multiple manufacturers is relatively straightforward.

Current market share. Whether physical or virtual, the concept of "shelf space" carries through most industries. Market leaders tend to have their offering in prime view of most customers. Their brand is the one that end users identify with little or no additional aid. When approaching a negotiation, it is critical to understand how those shelves are currently arranged and how the negotiation might reconfigure them. (This is true for litigation-related negotiation as well. A finding of patent infringement may remove products from shelves; an injunction from a class action may force sales of particular accessories.) There are several angles to assess:

Relative current position. Analysts will often describe a market as either "fragmented" or "concentrated." For example, there is a difference between a market with one major player and four smaller ones, and a market where each of five companies possesses an equal 20 percent share. It is key to understand this baseline as it is a very clear

10. Dan Sabbagh & Charles Arthur, *The Beatles and Apple Finally Come Together, Right Now... on iTunes*, The Guardian, Nov. 16, 2010, *available at* http://www.guardian.co.uk/music/2010/nov/16/beatles-apple-itunes-emi (last viewed Oct. 18, 2012).

indicator to what each of the stakeholders have to gain or lose and their associated motivations.

Antitrust. The Herfindahl-Hirschman Index (HHI) is a measure of the size of firms in relation to the industry and an indicator of the amount of competition among them. The U.S. Department of Justice and many other regulators around the globe use this as one of the preliminary tests in determining if a transaction will limit choice to the detriment of consumers. While regulators evaluate mergers on a case-by-case basis, negotiators should understand how a proposed deal will affect market concentration. The need to satisfy regulators prior to closing a transaction can significantly affect its value if not properly addressed. To take a recent example, in early 2011, American telecom AT&T announced its intention to buy cellular phone company T-Mobile. The U.S. Department of Justice objected to the takeover and sued to block it. As a result, AT&T abandoned its bid in December 2011.[11]

Resulting final position/ability to hold share. A common assumption of businesses justifying a transaction is that market share will at least be the same, if not grow, after a transaction. The common justification for a merger is that the combined technology or team will be a market leader and be able to build on the combined strength. That result is rare, however. Seventy percent of mergers failed to achieve expected revenue synergies, according to the 2002 McKinsey Post-Merger Management Survey.[12] One of the major factors contributing to that fact is that the strategic intent was wrong or missed the mark. Acquisitions that focus on creating more value for the customer (and have a solid understanding of what the customer values) do tend to increase share. With the exception of natural monopolies like utilities, acquisitions that focus on cost cutting

11. *America's Mobile Merger: Tripped at the Altar*, THE ECONOMIST, Sept. 3, 2011, *available at* http://www.economist.com/node/21528282/ (last viewed Oct. 18, 2012).

12. Scott A. Christofferson et al., *Where Mergers Go Wrong*, 2004(2) MCKINSEY Q. 95.

or limiting choice for customers tend to lose market share over time. Integrating these assessments into a negotiation sets clear bounds on the value to each party.

Importance of "incumbency" (switching costs). Some industries are prone to dramatic shifts in market share over the course of a few short years. In other industries, market shares change at a glacial pace. One of the main factors behind this is perceived cost of change. Once a product or service has proved effective and a good value, an organization or an individual tends to build processes and/or other investments around it. Specific factors that highlight this include:

- *Familiarity with product/use and perceived risk of changing.* Products and services are used by people, and, as should be clear by now, people tend to exhibit similar reproducible habits. Once they find something that works, they tend to follow the same pattern. Ability to change that pattern is based on the ability to overcome the root risk/reward trade-off that establishes the pattern in the first place. Any class action settlement or acquisition needs to evaluate what are the needs to change that pattern or reinforce the pattern based on the agreement.
- *Switching costs.* Changing from one supplier to another imposes real costs. This leads directly to how a customer calculates value—what more will they get from the new supplier and will that benefit compensate for the changes they will have to make to use it? These switching costs can include:
    - *Physical changes.* Does the customer need to buy other new components or *change* the existing layout to take advantage of this new offering? This can range from changing a factory floor layout to buying a new entertainment center to accommodate the new big screen TV. All of these have quantifiable costs that must be overcome.

- *Process changes*. If a customer is used to buying an offering a certain way and the negotiation forces her to go to a new location to purchase or adjust code within a computer application, this will significantly affect any change. Adding steps or time is the same as adding costs.
- *People changes*. One of the most overlooked elements of the outcome of any negotiation is on the people who directly come into contact with the customer. Depending on the type of product or service, customers develop relationships with their "guy" at the company. This person knows the customer's needs and preferences specifically. He is able to react quickly when there is an issue. He is a guide when there is something new or different. Especially for industries with a high customer service component, if that employee leaves for a competitor, the customers will tend to follow. Though law firms are particularly strong examples of this, it carries through to many other service industries as well as products that require help with their technical application. Any successful negotiation needs to ensure that it strengthens these customer bonds or has a strong set of capabilities to mitigate any loss of key people.

9.1.5 Social Factors/End Customers

"As a paying customer, I expect to get what I want."

—ROSE,
Titanic (20th Century Fox, 1997)

In any complex negotiation, public opinion matters. For complex business deals, getting customers to buy in to the new business reality is vital. For complex litigation settlements, avoiding alienating customers is equally so. As a result, in any complex negotiation, the various sides will want to stay ahead of public opinion, including presenting a consistent, coherent story to the public about the nature of the deal. Otherwise, what happens in the media can quickly begin to obscure and convolute what is happening in the negotiation. Several cases highlight how the public perception can derail or reinforce a negotiator's position.

- In 2005, China's CNOOC Ltd. abandoned its effort to acquire U.S. oil producer Unocal Corp. CNOOC had made an $18.5 billion all-cash offer that was $700 million greater than its closest competitor Chevron's. However, Chevron lobbyists were able to exploit public concern over a Chinese firm's having "control" of U.S. energy supplies and convinced Congress to insert a provision into an energy bill that would have delayed completion of any CNOOC takeover for months.[13] CNOOC followed the proper process by filing a valid bid for review with the Committee on Foreign Investment in the United States (CFIUS). But because of this public pressure, CNOOC's bid never even made it to the CFIUS hearing.
- When Ross Johnson attempted his leveraged buyout of RJR Nabisco, he tried to keep the focus on the money the shareholders would make. Nonetheless, he found his bid derailed by press coverage of his proposed management contract, which included $50 million worth of preferred stock and more than $50 million in severance agreements. Instead of making his best case to the board about good value for shareholders, he had to reassure directors who were feeling public pressure that they would not be crucified for rubber-stamping his pillaging of the firm.[14]

13. Matt Pottinger et al, *CNOOC Drops Offer for Unocal, Exposing U.S.-Chinese Tensions*, Wall St. J., Aug. 3, 2005.

14. Bryan Burrough & John Helyar, Barbarians at the Gate: The Fall of RJR Nabisco 348 (2003).

Different customers will display different levels of concern for corporate social responsibility based on their familiarity with the issue and direct contact in their daily lives. Consumer product and service companies tend to have the highest level of scrutiny. According to Amy Hebard and Wendy Cobrda of Earthsense LLC, a consumer research firm:

> In the corporate world, perception is reality. And consumer perception—assuming you are on their radar—drives both boycotting and "buycotting" and, in these days of modern activism, positive and negative commentary on the web.[15]

The more indirectly a company's offerings relate to what a consumer actually uses, the less likely that the mainstream media will care enough to cover the deal. However, this does not mean that these agreements will escape scrutiny. Organizations like Institutional Shareholder Services have assumed the status of independent watchdogs that police corporate activities on behalf of shareholders. Similarly, nonprofits like Public Justice and the Center for Class Action Fairness do the same for class action and derivative lawsuit settlements.

Because all parties need to be mindful to varying degrees of the potential outcomes of their negotiation, there are several considerations that teams should take into account.

- *Major/target customer segments*. Customers are consistently among the most impacted groups when it comes to any complex negotiation.[16] Ideally, any business negotiation would already understand the customer base and

15. Amy Hebard & Wendy Cobrda, *The Corporate Reality of Consumer Protections*, GreenBiz Reports—GreenBiz.com, 2009 (last viewed Oct. 14, 2012).

16. *See, e.g.*, Darren S. Tucker, et al., *The Customer Is Sometimes Right: The Role of Customer Views in Merger Investigations*, 3 J. Competition L. & Econ. 551 (2007).

customers' preferences. Nonetheless, communications about the deal should be phrased in terms they find important. Because there are likely different segments of customers, it also makes sense for negotiating teams to keep in touch with their respective sales and marketing departments.

- *Employee concerns*. When an employee hears of a new transaction involving his company, his first question will be: "what does this mean to me?" There are often specific procedures for informing unionized employees of a given deal. Regardless, teams from all sides of the negotiation should be able to explain to employees in clear terms what the deal means to them, and specifically how it will affect their employment.
- *Public opinion*. Companies, like individuals, have reputations, and those reputations have real effects on how customers react to announcements of deals or allegations in litigation. Most large companies periodically run corporate or brand perception studies. Knowing what these perceptions are is critical when a negotiation will produce a significant change in company practice.
- *Social media*. The ability for just one person to bring significant attention to a single event or topic has exponentially increased through the rise of various social media outlets like Twitter and Facebook. Social media have made megahits out of insignificant South Korean pop songs, focused world attention on obscure African warlords, and caused companies to change ingredients in their products. Any issue in any negotiation has the capacity to go "viral." Social media's impact, though, is judged more by how the parties respond to the issue than the exposure itself. A thoughtful engagement of issues over social media can be an incredibly valuable method of creating popular support.

Because public opinion is difficult to control, public relations scares many lawyers and business executives. Nonetheless, engaging the public is unavoidable in a large merger or a class action settlement. To the extent the parties can monitor public reaction, they can thoughtfully engage customers. At the very least, they can minimize the risk of unpleasant surprises.

9.1.6 Technology Changes

"Shift happens."

—KARL FISCH AND SCOTT MCLEOD, *Globalization and the Information Age*

So far, we have assumed that the way a product or service is bought or used has remained constant over time. Any agreement, settlement, or transaction needs to be thoughtful of the changes in how the product is purchased, utilized, and serviced or supported. While the changes that sustain over time are the ones that provide better value for the customer, they can also have profound effects on the competitive environment.

Change in the offering itself. All products change over time, and understanding how they change is important for any forward-looking deal. A new merger may challenge long-held assumptions on how a particular industry operates. And, in doing so, it will likely change which areas of a given industry are profitable. Telecommunications continues to undergo significant changes for its third decade: what started out as a way to route phone calls has grown into an industry concerned with delivering bandwidth for digital entertainment and business computing. Similarly, utilities used to engage in the one-way street of delivering power to an end user; now users from industrial plants all the way to individual homeowners can generate their own power from various technologies, and some of them can even sell their excess back to the utilities. In the law, technology has led to increasing segregation of legal analysis from nonlegal work.

Nonlawyers (or part-time lawyers) increasingly handle issues like document review or discovery productions that used to be the province of young lawyers. These changing dynamics create opportunity for some players and new costs and challenges for others.

Change in the purchase process. We are living through a period of great change in purchasing: many of us are old enough to remember going into a bookstore or record store to buy entertainment, instead of downloading our books or music from Amazon or iTunes. There have been revolutions like these in the purchase process for hundreds of years. In 1896, the Sears catalog debuted to take advantage of a combination of population shifts, improvements in transportation, and changes in mail delivery. This had profound effects on local general store owners who could not match the range of inventory that Sears could offer. Though the products may have been sold in a series of stores in any given geography, now jewelry, watches, bicycles, clothes, and more were all available between the pages of an enticing new catalog to be delivered to your front door.[17] The root products did not change, but the party with the primary connection to the customer did and, with it, their market power.

Change in after-sale service and support. When the technology in a product changes, the service procedures usually do as well. For example, as cars have increasingly relied on onboard computers, the training and equipment needed to service the range of cars has largely outpaced the ability of an independent mechanic to repair them. The various changes—such as diagnostic computers—that bring customers back to authorized dealerships can represent a new revenue stream for mechanics. At the same time, they change the customer relationship for the automobile company—coming back to an authorized dealer becomes a better option than visiting an independent mechanic. When changes like this occur, any proposed transaction (or

17. History of the Sears Catalog, Sears Archives, http://www.searsarchives.com/catalogs/history.htm.

proposed remedy in a lawsuit) will need to take account of the new relationships it might disrupt.

This information can be equally important in settling bet-the-company lawsuits. In class action litigation, for example, the parties must provide notice of any classwide settlement to all of the absent members of the proposed class. Often, that notice consists of direct mail where possible, publication notice (in appropriate newspapers) if mailings are not possible, and supplemental publication on the Internet. Notice of this kind can be extremely expensive. If, however, the defendant company has a sophisticated after-sale support system, one that includes some method of identifying and communicating with customers, then using that infrastructure may reduce notice costs.[18]

These areas of inquiry are not comprehensive; nor is each of them required for a given negotiation. Each will have different meaning, depending on the situation. Instead, they are meant to provide a rough checklist of the most common and highest-impact issues dotting the landscape in which a complex negotiation happens.

9.2 How to Find It

9.2.1 Public Sources

"Satan delights equally in statistics and in quoting scripture . . ."

—H. G. WELLS,
The Undying Fire

There is a surprising amount of information available publicly, if one knows where to look. Most governments track and report macroeconomic indicators like GDP, inflation, and unemployment. Similarly, many companies announce significant personnel changes.

18. *See* BRIAN ANDERSON & ANDREW TRASK, THE CLASS ACTION PLAYBOOK § 6.2 (2d ed. 2012).

If they are publicly traded, they may be required by law to disclose certain information, like their earnings and profits. Given the ease with which information moves over the Internet, public information is easier to find than ever.

The mere fact that public information is *available*, however, does not mean that it is necessarily *useful*. Journalist Malcolm Gladwell has famously written about the great paradox of the Enron scandal: despite some of its executives' best efforts, they were unable to hide what they were doing. Jonathan Weil, the *Wall Street Journal* reporter who originally unearthed the financial wrongdoing at Enron, did not have to engage any private sources at the company. Instead, he received a tip from one of his sources in the investment community to check Enron's earnings, all of which were publicly available. There he found all of the information he needed to report that Enron was seriously short of any actual income, although he needed some assistance in making sense of all of it. Gladwell contrasts Weil's efforts to Bob Woodward and Carl Bernstein's reporting on the equally infamous Watergate scandal:

> Did Jonathan Weil have a Deep Throat? Not really. He had a friend in the investment-management business with some suspicions about energy- trading companies like Enron, but the friend wasn't an insider. Nor did Weil's source direct him to files detailing the clandestine activities of the company. He just told Weil to read a series of public documents that had been prepared and distributed by Enron itself. Woodward met with his secret source in an underground parking garage in the hours before dawn. Weil called up an accounting expert at Michigan State.[19]

Public information is like raw, unprocessed ore. It's right there for anyone to pick up (providing they know what they're looking for),

19. *See* Malcolm Gladwell, *Open Secrets*, NEW YORKER, Jan. 8, 2007, at 44, 48.

but it must be processed for it to be worth anything. This is often why consultants and other knowledge workers are so valuable. They can actually turn raw, unprocessed, but still public information into something digestible, and therefore usable, by people.

9.2.2 Private Information

"Every man is surrounded by a neighborhood of voluntary spies."

—JANE AUSTEN,
Northanger Abbey

Private information is not necessarily available just through the expenditure of more effort. It is information that parties have chosen not to make available. Private information tends to be valuable in no small part because it is private. A firm's strategic plan, for example, or its lawyers' litigation strategy, may be private information. While this information may partially reveal itself through the act of negotiating, that information is usually less valuable at that point.

There are several ways of gaining private information.

Espionage. It is useless to deny that espionage exists. Corporations use it every time they conduct a price check. So do law firms, every time they hire a private investigator. And firms can engage in more sophisticated espionage techniques. When Chrysler was fending off a leveraged-buyout attempt from major shareholder Kirk Kerkorian and former CEO Lee Iacocca, it hired investigators to document all contacts between the two men; it also hired security firm Kroll Associates to track down any potential leaks within the company.[20]

Nonetheless, there are several significant risks to industrial espionage. The most obvious is that it is often illegal. In particular, information that comes from breaking and entering or wiretapping is not admissible in court, and could expose the company that uses

20. Bill Vlasic & Bradley A. Stertz, Taken for a Ride: How Daimler-Benz Drove Off with Chrysler 84–90 (2009).

it to criminal sanctions. This is not a made-up concern: companies like Hewlett-Packard—which, in an effort to determine the source of several media leaks, authorized one of its investigators to deceive a phone company into providing call data about some of HP's employees—and News Corp—which, in pursuit of exclusive stories bugged private individuals' cellular phones—have found themselves the subject of government investigations.[21]

Back-channel communications. Back-channel communications refer to information that comes from sources other than the officially appointed negotiator for each party. Back-channel communications are usually covert.[22]

Often, back-channel communications are possible through the development of personal relationships among various other members of the negotiating teams. In their account of the RJR Nabisco leveraged buyout deal *Barbarians at the Gate*, authors Burrough and Helyar noted that these kinds of communications are frequent, even when they're not supposed to be. In fact, in the 1980s, the "merger bar" (those lawyers who worked on mergers and acquisitions for banks and large companies) was small and close-knit enough that attorneys would regularly share information with each other: "Even when on opposing sides in a billion-dollar takeover contest, [the merger bar's] members are constantly talking to one another; these 'back-channel' communications have become a staple of their deals."[23] Similarly, Vice

21. *See* Ellen Nakashima, *Between the Lines of HP's Spy Scandal*, WASHINGTON POST, Sept. 28, 2006, *available at* http://www.washingtonpost.com/wp-dyn/content/article/2006/09/27/AR2006092701304_pf.html (last viewed Sept. 8, 2012); Katharine Rushton, *News Corp Posts Loss on Restructuring Charge*, THE TELEGRAPH, Aug. 8, 2012, *available at* http://www.telegraph.co.uk/finance/newsbysector/mediatechnologyandtelecoms/9463284/News-Corp-posts-loss-on-restructuring-charge.html (last viewed Sept. 8, 2012) (News Corp. paid out $242 million in costs related to *News of the World* phone hacking scandal).

22. Niali Ó Dochtaraigh, *Together in the Middle: Back-Channel Negotiation in the Irish Peace Process*, 48 J. PEACE RESEARCH 767 (2011).

23. BURROUGH & HELYAR, *supra* note 14, at 189; *see also* Ó Dochtaraigh, *supra* note 22, at 768.

President Joe Biden made attempts at back-channel negotiation with both Senate Majority Leader Mitch McConnell and House Majority Leader Eric Cantor during the 2011 debt-ceiling negotiations, although neither was able to break the very public deadlock between the two parties.[24]

Back-channel negotiations can be particularly useful when the primary negotiation faces serious problems. One popular reason cited for using back-channel communications in international diplomacy, for example, is that it allows representatives from each side to reach agreements in principle before constituents who may take harder lines can interfere with the process.[25] Many negotiating teams view a back channel as a safety net. Formal meetings between both sides serve clear purposes with set agendas. But the constraints on formal meetings mean that sometimes statements or actions can be misperceived. Finding a good "translator" who can interpret moves by the other side can help in quickly and discreetly sorting out the true status of negotiations.

Some negotiating teams go so far as to openly encourage the use of back-channel communications. The Japanese practice of setting up a "meeting before the meeting" where junior executives can mingle and trade information is discussed more extensively in chapter 7. The "meeting before the meeting" helps the senior executives to appear knowledgeable once negotiations officially begin, but it also creates the kind of informal back channels that can facilitate negotiations through trickier points later.

Backbearings. Backbearings are the inferences about private information one can draw from public (or semipublic) actions. The term comes from John le Carré's novel *The Honourable Schoolboy*, which features George Smiley, the rotund, perpetually cuckolded, but brilliant spymaster at the heart of many of le Carré's books. At

24. Bob Woodward, The Price of Politics, Kindle location 1316, 2260 (2012).

25. Ó Dochtaraigh, *supra* note 22, at 768.

the beginning of the novel, the Circus (the British Secret Service) is in disarray. The mole that George Smiley uncovered in a previous novel, who was run by the Soviet mastermind Karla, had stopped critical missions and fed various misinformation to the government. None of the Circus's information is trustworthy, because they do not know who or what has been tainted by the mole. So Smiley decides to take some backbearings.

> [Smiley's] premise was, that in briefing [the mole], Karla was exposing the gaps in Moscow Centre's knowledge; that in ordering [the mole] to suppress certain intelligence which came the Circus's way, in ordering him to downgrade or distort it, to deride it, or even to deny it circulation altogether, Karla was indicating the secrets he did not want revealed.
>
> "So we can take the backbearings, can't we darling?" murmured Connie Sachs, whose speed of uptake put her as usual a good length ahead of the rest of the field.
>
> "That's right, Con. That's exactly what we can do," said Smiley gravely. "We can take the backbearings." . . .
>
> By minutely charting [the mole's] path of destruction—his pugmarks as he called them—by exhaustively recording his selection of files; by reassembling, after aching weeks of research if necessary, the intelligence culled in good faith by Circus outstations, and balancing it, in every detail, against the intelligence distributed by [the mole] to the Circus's customers in the Whitehall marketplace, it would be possible to take backbearings—as Connie so rightly called them—and establish [the mole]'s, and therefore Karla's, point of departure . . . [26]

26. John le Carré, The Honourable Schoolboy 70–71 (1973) (identity of mole redacted).

Backbearings are not a fictional invention. During World War II, American and British analysts would listen to German propaganda broadcasts, trying to tease out hints about German war strategy; the program (named Operation Screwball in the United States) correctly predicted the development and eventual deployment of the V-1 rocket.[27] Nor are spies the only ones who can take backbearings. This is something many lawyers do intuitively: carefully reading subpoenas, document requests, interrogatories, and deposition questions can help a lawyer learn where his opponent thinks her case may be the strongest, and where she may think she needs more evidence. Similarly, looking at where a plaintiff chooses to spend her resources (when that spending is visible) helps to give an idea of both the resources a plaintiff has available and her priorities in the case. And there is no reason the practice need be confined to litigation: as we discussed in chapter 1, Drexel Burnham banker Jeff Beck and KKR buyout specialist Henry Kravits deduced RJR Nabisco was up for sale from the fact that its CEO, Ross Johnson, had stopped taking calls. In short, reverse-engineering a counterparty's priorities from its publicly visible actions is a viable strategy for discovering new information for businesses as well.

9.2.3 Experts

"Experience is the name everyone gives to his mistakes."

—OSCAR WILDE

Finally, some companies hire third parties to gain information that will be necessary to their negotiations. In both litigation and in business, companies may hire either private investigators or expert consultants to provide additional information.

27. *See* Gladwell, *supra* note 19, at 44, 50–51.

Private investigators can unearth information relevant to a case. While the name conjures up images of Humphrey Bogart playing Sam Spade or Philip Marlowe, the reality is more prosaic. (In fact, many modern private investigators eschew the term, preferring to say that they are in "risk mitigation," or even just "management consulting.")[28] These modern private investigators—like "management consultants" Kroll Inc.—may be owned by insurance conglomerates, work for institutions like Goldman Sachs and Skadden Arps, and conduct background checks, FCPA compliance reviews, and "competitor analysis."[29]

Expert consultants can provide analysis about specific issues, such as the damages likely to result from allegations in a class action, or the possible areas of antitrust concern in a proposed merger. They can range from small solo shops to large multinational consulting firms like Compass Lexecon or Navigant. Smaller shops may include experts with long years of experience working for companies in a given industry. The larger firms tend to employ professionals with postgraduate degrees in areas like economics and political science, who study industries from the outside rather than working their way up from the equivalent of the mailroom.

Experts are also crucial to helping the parties make sense of the information they receive. As discussed in greater detail above, much of the information necessary to a successful negotiation may be publicly available, but that does not mean that anyone knows how to make sense of it.

To return to the exposure of the Enron scandal, reporter Jonathan Weil was no financial slouch himself (he was, after all, writing for the premier financial newspaper in the United States); he could make sense of some of what he was seeing in Enron's public filings. But he still wound up consulting, among others, an accounting professor at Michigan State, an official at the Financial Accounting

28. William Finnegan, *The Secret Keeper*, New Yorker, Oct. 19, 2009, at 42, 43.

29. *Id.*, at 43–44.

Standards Board, and an analyst at the credit rating agency Moody's before he really understood the implications of the information he had collected.[30] Why? Because these individuals had the knowledge to walk him through the portions he did not understand.

In this sense, negotiators of complex deals are no different from a *Wall Street Journal* reporter. They are likely to be very intelligent, and they will often have a great deal of industry-specific knowledge. But if the deal itself involves any new markets or industries, or new financial tools, or any number of other new issues, expert help can prove invaluable. No one knows everything; trusting an expert to guide the team through uncharted territory allows team members to focus on what they each do best.

Experts may also be valuable as trusted third parties in a negotiation. Providing one's own estimation of damages from infringement of intellectual property, or one's own valuation of the start-up one has built, will often appear self-serving. But providing an expert—even one who has been paid—will often add an extra layer of legitimacy to a specific position.

9.3 Conclusion

As we talked about in chapter 8, assembling as much intelligence as possible allows the negotiators to see the entire board. Good intelligence offers an understanding of the primary elements for each side's negotiating position, as well as identifying the pressures, internal and external, that may further shape that position. The intelligence allows negotiators to assess, quantifiably in some cases, which issues are material and which are not. And it helps both sides guard against foreseeable risks from an agreement.

Proper intelligence allows parties not only to understand who is with them at the negotiating table but which key players are absent.

30. *See* Gladwell, *supra* note 19, at 44, 46–47.

Knowing how the public is likely to receive news of an acquisition, which regulators might take interest in investigation developments in an industry, which public-interest groups might wish to object to a global settlement, or which competitors are angry about being left out of a deal can allow the negotiators to design the best agreement they can, one that—while it may not forestall outside assaults—will at least withstand them.

Finally, doing your homework will allow you to see how these positions and pressures may change over time. Watching the evolution of technology, the adoption of different consumer tastes, or the use of new litigation tactics over time allows the negotiator to come up with better intuitive judgments about the relative value of a lawsuit or a deal, and allows her to conduct more focused inquiries about the deal itself.

Of course, intelligence on its own means nothing. At some point, the negotiation must begin. In chapter 10, we will examine the various tactics that work best in complex negotiations, and the processes that allow negotiators of "bet the company" deals to navigate whatever terrain they encounter.

10

Tactical Moves

Throughout this book, we have described various ways in which complex negotiations differ from simple, person-to-person negotiations. And throughout, we have posed a number of problems and identified—in general terms—solutions that help to address those specific problems. In this chapter, we will tie these various approaches together and show how these solutions actually work in practice.

We will walk through the entire process of a complex negotiation, from start to finish. We will be descriptive rather than prescriptive; in other words, given the vast range of possible tactics one can employ in various negotiations, we will not be so foolish as to recommend a "one-size-fits-all" strategy that works in every complex negotiation. But while we cannot offer a "one-size-fits-all" strategy, we can offer insights into the *processes* that successful negotiators have used. These processes are often far more valuable in the long run than a specific strategy, because they identify the issues worth focusing on and allow the negotiators to spend the majority of their brainpower on solving those issues rather than trying to guess the unguessable.

10.1 Deploying Resources

"Smithers, it's time to deploy those kangaroos we've been training."

—MONTGOMERY BURNS,
The Simpsons, "Them, Robot"

Most complex negotiations are not routine events, and most firms do not have infinite resources, which means that most firms do not have people dedicated to consummating complex deals. Instead, the people who conduct complex negotiations usually have "day jobs" that involve managing the company, seeing to customer needs, or litigating other cases. Firms that engage in more than one complex negotiation over time (as many do) do not necessarily fare much better: often their people may be tied up negotiating other deals. As a result, finding the "right" resources to conduct a complex negotiation while still managing the day-to-day business of a company (or a law firm) can be challenging.

Assuming that the negotiator has engaged in the grand strategic exercises we outline in chapter 8, she should be well equipped to make tactical decisions about how best to deploy the people at her disposal. Of course, as strategists have long pointed out, there are large differences between planning something in the safety of a conference room and actually getting it done in the heat of the moment. Deploying one's resources well is difficult in part because, by its very nature, a complex negotiation often does not start at a definable point in time. More routine tasks often have an organizational trigger that allows the firm to specifically deploy its people, such as a manufacturing plant's receiving an order that allows the firm to specifically deploy its people. By contrast, the need for a complex agreement like a comprehensive class action settlement may arise long before a lawsuit is filed, in a risk management discussion spurred by a particular pattern in warranty claims. It can come up as part of a corporate development review during a management meeting. Or it may be the suggestion of the lawyers litigating the case, because they sense that the pressures on a plaintiff's firm may provide an opportunity for a deal on favorable terms. Indeed, even a brief review of judicial opinions approving class action settlements shows that they can arise at any point in litigation.[1] Similarly, a complex business deal often begins as the result of informal conversations, so identifying the precise moment when idle chatter turns into firm commitment can be difficult. As a result, we will begin by describing some of the strategic choices that a negotiator faces in setting up her team.

Right resources vs. available resources. In more complex negotiations, as an issue or opportunity develops, the organization must assign additional resources to address it. (For example, if a question arises about the size of an unknown market, or the effect of a particular statute, someone will have to research the answer.) Because complex negotiations often involve issues that will have a significant impact on the company, managers will frequently react by pulling in whoever is immediately available to address the issue rather than taking the time to assemble those people who would make the best fit.[2] Managers justify this practice by telling themselves they will adjust the team to get the "right" resources when it is clear the negotiation is "real." Unfortunately, the people most "available" at a given point in time are usually those who are least busy; they may not be the best suited for the job.

Two problems further complicate this balancing act between the "right" and the "available" resources. First, the "available" personnel may not set up the right conclusion. Putting in a placeholder set of resources to get by until the negotiation turns "real" runs the risk that the "available" team may lack the expertise in either the issues or the process to make the negotiation work. As a result, the "right" team may never get called into action because the negotiation falls apart

1. *See* Brian Anderson & Andrew Trask, The Class Action Playbook § 8.3 at 246–47 (2d ed. 2012) (discussing timing of various class action settlements).

2. For more on finding the "right" people, *see* § 8.3.

before the opportunity arises. This is a problem that has happened to both authors, repeatedly.

Second, because they will enter the negotiation after it has already commenced, the "right" team may not be able to create trust with the other side. Assuming that the process gets off to a good start, members of the "available" team will likely build a working relationship with their counterparties.[3] However, if the "available" people do not have the skills to take the process to conclusion, then the project will have to deal with either redundant staffing or with challenging relationship hand-offs once the "right" team members are assigned.

These are the reasons the internal capacity assessment we discussed in chapter 8 is so important: knowing what skills are required for a given negotiation task, and which people in the organization have those skills, allows the negotiator to properly balance assigning the right resources and the available resources in a deal.

Uneven requirements over time. As we discussed in chapter 5, because of the need to reconcile many conflicting factions and issues, complex negotiations rarely happen quickly. But just because they take longer does not mean that they progress smoothly and steadily. Instead, progress tends to occur in fits and starts as the parties engage in periods of discovery, analysis, discussion, and negotiation. As a result, the workload for any given team member will vary significantly over the course of the negotiation. Moreover, because typically the most experienced team members are needed for other pressing issues for the firm, it is expensive and impractical to dedicate them to a single effort for an extended period of time. And, of course, even the less experienced team members will retain their "day jobs." Proper project management (discussed in the next section) can help to alleviate some of the more dire choices, but a negotiator may still find herself making constant adjustments to

3. *See* chapter 2.

her team based on the workload a given member can handle at a given time.

Cultural/process match with other parties. Assuming the negotiator has the right team in place and has tasked the members properly to make sure no one is overwhelmed, the team still must work with its counterparties in the negotiation. Since no negotiation operates perfectly smoothly, the negotiator will often face the question of how to handle miscommunications and personality conflicts. There are often minor incidents that happen early in interactions between the teams. The 1919 Paris peace talks, for example, famously began with friction among all three principals on the Allied side: American President Woodrow Wilson, British Prime Minister David Lloyd George, and French Prime Minister Georges Clemenceau all had difficulty getting along with each other.[4] Similarly, at the start of the 2011 debt-ceiling negotiations in Washington, D.C., Republican negotiators had difficulty working with Jack Lew, whom they viewed as condescending and disrespectful.[5]

The primary question the negotiator must answer, then, is when to replace members of the team and when to allow them to work through their issues. Barring a major incident of inappropriate behavior, it can be difficult to remove a team member once a negotiation has commenced because of the learning curve (real or perceived) the new team member will face. More prosaically, sometimes people can work out their differences. By the end of the Paris peace talks, for example, Wilson, Lloyd George, and Clemenceau had developed a decent working relationship that at times bordered on intimate friendship.[6] Sometimes, however, team members cannot work out their differences. The 2011 debt-ceiling negotiations really

4. *See* MARGARET MACMILLAN, PARIS 1919: SIX MONTHS THAT CHANGED THE WORLD, Kindle location 864 (2007).

5. *See* BOB WOODWARD, THE PRICE OF POLITICS, Kindle locations 2881, 4012, 4163 (2012).

6. *See* MACMILLAN, *supra* note 4, Kindle location 5249.

did not progress until the White House replaced Jack Lew with Bill Daley, whom the Republican House members found more agreeable to work with.[7]

10.2 Process—The Importance of Project Management

"I love it when a plan comes together."

—HANNIBAL,
The A-Team

None of the challenges described above is unique to complex negotiations. But they can prove particularly difficult in that context because many lawyers and executives are not skilled in traditional project management. As a result, there is a strong tendency to treat each negotiation as a new event, reinventing the process from the ground up. There is an easier way, however. While it is hardly the sexiest topic we will address, sound project management can save valuable time and allow the negotiator to draw on relevant information when necessary.[8] At a high level of generalization, most complex negotiations look the same. Each party must make sure its negotiation strategy is *aligned with its primary purpose*. It must *identify the constraints* on the negotiation. Once it understands these, it must *decide the strategic options* that will best address those constraints. Then it must *model the negotiation*. Finally, it must make sure it has proper *maintenance procedures* in place to keep the negotiation running smoothly, even when key team members' attention may be elsewhere. And each of these steps allows firms to place roughly similar processes in place to keep the negotiation proceeding without major incident.

7. Matt Bai, *Obama vs. Boehner: Who Killed the Debt Deal?*, N.Y. TIMES MAGAZINE, Mar. 28, 2012.

8. The Project Management Institute, http://www.pmi.org, http://marketplace.pmi.org/Pages/ProductDetail.aspx?GMProduct=00100348100&iss=1.

Aligning on primary purpose. Most organizations heading into a large and complex negotiation would say that they are already aligned on their primary purpose; it is, after all, to get the deal done. But this nominal alignment is often not enough. Many firms, before embarking on a new negotiation, will ask specific questions about the primary purpose to make sure everyone is actually one the same page. Among those questions are:

- What is the immediate goal of the deal?
- What is the deal worth to us? At what point does it become too expensive?
- Are there any major developments (such as a change in the law or the emergence of a new competitor) that would make us change our minds about this deal?
- What is our best alternative should this deal fall through?
- What are the most predictable obstacles we face?

Careful readers (or those just foolhardy enough to read this book straight through) should recognize many of these questions. They are versions of the scorecard we discussed in chapter 8. Identifying a specific moment to walk the team through these questions (and any others a negotiator finds useful) is an excellent way to ensure that all team members have the same understanding of their goals in the negotiation. It can help to identify areas where team members have papered over their disagreements and can also help negotiators envision which tactics might work best during the negotiation itself.

This process applies to lawyers as well as business executives. For lawyers representing a company in a high-stakes transaction or lawsuit, aligning themselves with their client's grand strategy is particularly important. It is entirely possible to advance a legal argument that may win a particular case but undermine the company's longer-term goals. Similarly, offering questionable strategic options that create short-term gains but increase "compliance risk" (that is, the risk of being investigated or sued for violating the law) usually run counter to a company's grand strategy.

Identifying constraints. Every negotiator faces limits: no one has unlimited time, an unlimited budget, or an omnicompetent team. While there are many potential limits, most of the constraints tend to relate to money: will the negotiation produce enough value to offset the cost of engaging in it in the first place? Among the most common constraints one might face are the following.

- *Available capital*. Very few companies—save perhaps Apple or Berkshire Hathaway—have enough cash to fund any conceivable effort without outside help. As a result, most companies have to play within a defined set of financial limits. These include maintaining a credit rating that allows them to borrow money to fund operations, legal restrictions on how much stock the company may issue, or debt covenants with creditors that limit what risks the company may take.
- *Earnings expectations*. Public companies must report their financial results on a regular basis. Those reports must include any significant gain or loss, and some companies must report any significant risk exposure (such as the possibility of a large verdict against them) as well. Complex negotiations may have "nonoperating" impacts, meaning that the company deems them as one-time events that will not have material long-term effects on the underlying performance of the business. However, companies strive to report consistent, predictable earnings for their investors. As a result, a given company may need to move risk (like the legal exposure from a class action or an antitrust investigation) off its books, or report a significant gain (from a consummated agreement) within a specified time period. These needs may create pressure to complete negotiations within a specific time period. So, for example, while a

company may need to settle a class action suit, it may be more tolerable to investors if that is offset by a similar nonoperating gain in the same quarter.

- *Future ability to compete.* Despite what some critics might have argued, most companies do think further ahead than just the next financial quarter. In keeping with longer-term thinking, access to where a company can sell its products and services have a real effect on its long-term growth rate, and that long-term growth rate is a major driver in determining a company's value. As a result, deals that open up new markets or provide new opportunities will be very attractive. Conversely, settlements (with private plaintiffs or with the government) that limit the areas in which a company can operate are likely to encounter heavy resistance and must require skillful negotiating to overcome.

All of these conditions set boundaries around a given negotiating position; an effective team will recognize and manage them from the start.

Deciding strategic options. Once a team has established the boundary conditions it faces, it must lay out options available for achieving its goal. Too often, a negotiating team will go with an intuitive choice but justify it by arguing that "we have looked at all of the options and this is really our only choice." While that statement may end up being true, it often represents a shortcut by a team with limited resources that still wants to do "something," and do it fast. Evaluating all of the available options does not need to be an all-consuming months-long process. It does, however, need to be thoughtful and thorough, covering at least the following questions.

- *Negotiate or litigate?* Many business decisions come down to this fundamental choice: do we make a deal with our adversaries, or do we confront them in some way? In many instances, organizations will view "litigate" and "negotiate" as two sides of the same coin; they will consider a lawsuit just the conduct of business by other means. Starting from an adversarial position, however, creates a negotiation very different in character than starting from a more cooperative footing. (IBM and Fujitsu, for example, spent years engaged in litigation, inefficient shuttle diplomacy, and mediation before reaching a mutually beneficial deal for licensing IBM's operating system software, one they might have arrived at much quicker had they begun by negotiating.)[9] In some cases, however, litigation really is the stronger starting point. Beginning with litigation makes sense when a company wishes to signal that it has a strong legal or factual basis for its demands.[10] Similarly, in class action litigation, a defendant may have to demonstrate a certain degree of confrontation to establish that a settlement was conducted at "arm's length" in order to satisfy the court it was not collusive.[11] Finally, of course, a company may choose to litigate a dispute when it believes that it simply has nothing to gain by negotiating.

- *DIY, rent, or buy?* This question allows the negotiator to frame an additional series of choices. Sometimes (albeit rarely) a company can make what it needs in-house. If the value of adding another capability exceeds the costs of in-house production, there may be no need for a deal at all, or the company can negotiate on extremely favorable terms. More often, a company must consider some form of outsourcing its needs, either by negotiating a supply agreement with a vendor or by pooling resources with another firm. Vendor negotiations tend to be simpler, but might prove

9. *See* Robert Mnookin, Bargaining with the Devil: When to Negotiate, When to Fight 139–76 (2010).

10. *See generally* Robert Powell, *Bargaining & Learning While Fighting*, 48 Am. J. Pol. Sci. 344 (2004).

11. *See* Anderson & Trask, *supra* note 1, § 8 at 228–30, § 8.3.1 at 248–49.

expensive. Joint ventures or strategic alliances can save immediate costs, but often require some degree of merging organizational cultures (at least among the joint team) and may not prove stable over the long term. Finally, a company may consider just buying another firm that does what it needs. Acquisitions work well at aligning goals but face the same cultural challenges as a joint venture and add the risk that the acquisition will not prove profitable.

Once the negotiator has decided what kind of deal to pursue, she must identify her partner—in other words, the specific target with whom she can deal that will fulfill her primary purpose. There are four general criteria to picking a partner.

First, on the criteria, there are four critical elements:

- *Alignment with primary purpose*. There is no such thing as a perfect match, but different potential targets may offer distinct advantages for achieving a firm's primary purpose. For example, one firm may have access to a given market, while another offers better technology with which to develop new products. These choices apply to litigation as well. For a given lawsuit, there are often a range of potential defendants, some of whom may pose specific obstacles to achieving the primary purpose of the suit. Particular defendants may lack the funds to pay a substantial judgment, may have already cut deals with government agencies that undermine private litigation, or may not have engaged in the kind of conduct the litigator wishes to fight.[12]
- *Match with financial constraints*. Because complex negotiations rely so heavily on private information held by each side, it is usually not possible for the negotiator to

12. For more on this process from the perspective of a class action litigator, *see* ANDERSON & TRASK, *supra* note 1, § 3.4.

know the specific value of an option until she is well into the negotiation. However, as discussed in greater detail in chapter 9, it is often possible for the negotiator to estimate a range of values based on different financial metrics, such as the publicly declared share price or the local market conditions. Doing so will help narrow the choices. This analysis also works for litigators: if a firm lacks the money to pay a substantial judgment, it may not be the best choice to be a primary defendant in a lawsuit.

- *Willingness to partner/will to fight*. For dealmakers, it is possible to determine ahead of time whether a given firm will be open to negotiation. Based on observable facts, one can usually make educated guesses about whether a firm wishes to enter new markets or whether a start-up founder is looking to cash out and move to the Caribbean. One can also determine whether a company wishes to partner specifically with the negotiator's firm. (For example, if a direct competitor owns a stake in the firm or is a primary business partner, a deal is unlikely.) Finally, one can also usually make a rough estimate about a firm's ability to make deals in general, by looking at whether the target has a history of working with other companies through supply agreements or manufacturing private-label products. For litigators, similar questions apply, although they are aimed more at what military strategist Carl von Clausewitz called "strength of will."[13] Does the potential defendant have a history of settling cases? Is it currently fighting bad press? Who has it traditionally retained as counsel? Has it established a reputation for scorched-earth litigation?
- *Observable benefits*. Every deal comes with certain benefits, from "expands our product line" to "buys peace for our patent licenses." Before engaging with a counterpart, many

13. Carl von Clausewitz, On War 77 (Peter Paret trans., 1989).

> negotiators will solicit input from specific teams at their firm to ensure they have a complete inventory of specific, concrete benefits that could result from an agreement. Doing so allows the negotiator to focus her discussion on observable facts rather than perceptions or other nonrational judgments.

Most negotiators will look at a wide range of potential partners. While the first search for a partner does not have to be lengthy or exhaustive, it should be thorough enough to unearth a variety of options, so that the negotiator understands the actual alternatives and trade-offs rather than dealing in loose hypotheticals. How do negotiators find this information? There is usually a range of market research covering most industries. Popular sources like the *Wall Street Journal* are also surprisingly effective. (Plaintiff's lawyer William Lerach, for example, used to peruse various newspapers to decide which companies should serve as defendants in new class actions.)[14] The negotiator might also ask her customers, particularly if her firm tabulates their opinions in some way. Since different information will be useful for evaluating each of these four criteria, the key is to find a broad range of sources, both internal and external.

Depending on the deal the negotiator wishes to pursue, some of these criteria (such as the match with financial constraints) may matter more than others. What these criteria do is provide the negotiator with a method of screening out the many less suitable options available. (As discussed in greater detail in chapter 4, screens are a very effective way of dealing with multiple options.) By walking through each of these criteria (not just the most material), the negotiator should have sufficient facts available to evaluate alternative partners should her first choice not work out for some reason.

14. PATRICK DILLON & CARL M. CANNON, CIRCLE OF GREED: THE SPECTACULAR RISE AND FALL OF THE LAWYER WHO BROUGHT CORPORATE AMERICA TO ITS KNEES 383 (2010).

Modeling the negotiation. Once the negotiator knows who her partner is, she creates a model of the proposed deal. This model does not have to be a complex computer simulation; it can be as simple as a decision tree or set of calculations on a sheet of paper showing the value of different outcomes. The only necessary elements are the facts the negotiator has gathered about each option and each potential player, a determination of what one option is worth (that is, the benefits it will bring minus the costs the firm will incur) versus another. Even in this simplified state, this modeling can flush out important issues, such as what effect a minor change in personnel may have on the value of a deal, or the effect a dispositive motion may have on a settlement position. Identifying these effects will help the negotiator separate true dealbreakers from mere bumps in the road.

The most effective models are not single-use. Instead, the negotiator will return to them many times over the course of the negotiation, either to test new tactics or to determine the effect of unforeseen developments or exogenous events.[15]

Maintenance procedures. The maintenance procedures used to move the deal forward are what many people think of as "project management." Most teams will identify a specific project manager, who is responsible for (or "owns," in current jargon) the day-to-day management of the deal. The project manager maps out the key events in the process and the key decisions that will be required, and ensures that the appropriate resources are available at the right times. In the business context, this person may actually hold the title of "project manager." On a legal team, the project manager will likely be either a senior associate or junior partner at the firm. In either case, it is common to use someone with enough experience to recognize recurring issues and enough authority to delegate work when it arises and to set others' schedules.

In addition to designating a project manager, most negotiators will establish a core project team, which can be as small as a single full-

15. For more on the effect of exogenous events, *see* chapter 5.

time person. The core team allows other team members to work their "day jobs" while remaining known resources the project manager can draw on as needed. Meanwhile, the negotiator should also make sure the various "day job" teams understand that the team members may be called into action at any time and are prepared to cover them while they work on the negotiation.

Sound project management also takes advantage of periodic reviews, which can help the team identify new decisions it must make or actions it must take. These reviews can last as long as several hours or as little as ten minutes, depending on the progress of the negotiation. What is important is that these reviews exist to prod actual decisions, as opposed to just keeping the team updated on progress. In addition to these periodic reviews, many negotiators will also conduct private discussions with individual team members. Individual team members may censor themselves in a meeting by, for example, refraining from contradicting a more influential colleague. While team meetings are important to move the overall process forward, gathering the right information from the team sometimes requires moving behind closed doors. In addition to one-on-one check-ins with team members, small, regularly scheduled meetings between the team leader and the project manager can be extremely helpful in resolving issues among team members or making mid-course corrections to a negotiation. It is also helpful to periodically check in with any back channels to ensure that there are no problems developing between parties in a negotiation. Making each of these meetings a regular occurrence can also take the pressure off of any one communication, allowing the team leader or project manager to catch issues while they are still small and more easily resolved.

Without the right team and a good process to manage the flow of the negotiation, small issues that should be resolved quickly can become unmanageable. It is well worth making more difficult choices up front to get the right people and process in place to give the negotiation the best likelihood of success.

10.3 Approaching the Other Side

"What's your name?"
"What do you want it to be?"

—EDWARD AND VIVIAN,
Pretty Woman (Touchstone Pictures, 1990)

Regardless of whether one begins negotiations at some venue designed to facilitate deals (plaintiffs' lawyers in complex litigation often prefer conferences about mass torts; CEOs may take advantage of "mover and shaker" meetings like Davos or Sun Valley have), or by just sitting in one's office in front of the phone, there comes a time when one must approach the other side.

To an outsider, the beginning of any complex negotiation can appear similar to middle-school students negotiating a date: a series of moves and countermoves designed to gauge the other party's interest. ("Do you like me?" "That depends: do *you* like *me*?") Each side must determine how much interest it can afford to show in the other side and how much leverage that expressed interest confers. (The more interest one side shows, the more confident the other side will be in demanding concessions.) But while the middle-school students are balancing puppy love against the risk of semipublic humiliation, participants in complex negotiations are balancing the value of the deal with the amount they must ultimately pay to close.

As a result, many negotiators consider the approach to be one of the hardest steps in a complex negotiation. Like the start of any relationship, the primary obstacle is the fear of the unknown. And among the many unknowns negotiators face are the following questions.

- Who exactly am I supposed to contact?
- What method do I use to make contact? Phone, e-mail, letter, etc.?
- What do I say is the premise for making contact?

- What am I asking them for?
- What do I do if they say no?

These are not small concerns. We have seen many negotiations fail to launch because both sides were constrained by their lack of familiarity with the other party. Consequently, we provide the following "typical" flow of events as a guide to dealing with unfamiliar parties.

First contact. Most people spend their time looking for the "right" person to approach, usually the person they believe can make "the decision." In most complex negotiations, however, there is no one "right" person who can make a final decision by herself. (Even chief executives must report to their board of directors.) Instead, the negotiator simply needs to find someone who understands why she is being contacted and who can motivate action on her side. This may be a general manager of some kind, the general counsel, or the head of corporate development. For a legal negotiation, this is often the lead counsel in the lawsuit or the general counsel at the company. (This does not always mean the top-ranked counsel on the team. If a junior member has assumed much of the day-to-day responsibility for running a case, she may well be the best first approach.) Titles will vary widely, but the key is to find the person with the set of responsibilities that best corresponds to the deal. LinkedIn, Google searches, and public company filings are often excellent resources for a cold approach.

Even that level of precision, however, may prove unnecessary. In most organizations, almost any point of contact will at least know how to refer one to the appropriate people. Assuming the proposed agreement will offer mutual benefits, the other side has little incentive to ignore any overture. (This is not the same as a salesman cold-calling an office manager, where there will be many reasons why one might not choose to respond.)

Making contact. Actually making contact is usually as easy as picking up the phone, although face-to-face meetings are excellent, too.

(The advantages of face-to-face contact explain why many deals begin at industry conferences.) Effective negotiations rarely start with written correspondence. Text is terrible at transmitting social cues, and, as a result, too much information can be taken out of context and misunderstood. (Despite this difficulty, lawyers often begin their negotiations with written demand letters.)[16]

The premise for contact. Explaining why one side is making contact often derails people. This is no surprise: cold-calling is scary. To compensate, many negotiators believe that, at first contact, they must have an elaborate proposal ready. While a solid outline of how to proceed is always helpful, the justification for the initial exchange is very simple: the negotiator is just calling to set up a meeting to get to know the other side better and explore areas of mutual interest. In the case of a potential acquisition, the meeting can be to discuss possible initiatives that will help both companies grow faster. The situation is not much different in complex litigation. While proposals are certainly useful, just having a common interest in resolving major differences may be enough. (And, since both parties are operating from at least a written complaint and possibly extensive legal briefing, it will be clearer what any potential issues or proposals may be.) In any of these cases, the premise for discussion is most effective if it is simple, allowing the parties to return to it when discussion of various issues goes awry.

The initial ask. At first contact, the negotiator is asking for a meeting. An in-person meeting is best, if possible, since it humanizes each side quickly. The agenda for this meeting is also fairly simple: only a brief overview of each organization (or each side's case) is necessary. This baseline step is important because it ensures that

16. Carrie Sperling, *Priming Legal Negotiations through Written Demands*, 60 CATH. U. L. REV. 107, 117–18 (2010) (discussing prevalence of demand letters at beginning of legal negotiations). One reason many lawyers prefer written correspondence is that they have been trained to document communications. In adversarial settings, should the negotiation fall apart, a written record is better evidence than "he said/she said" testimony.

each side understands the other party. From that starting point, both sides can discuss the major issues related to the potential negotiation, filling each other in on differences in perspective. At the end of the first meeting, the parties should identify the specific next steps each side will take. These "next steps" do not need to be all-encompassing but should be both tangible and achievable so that accomplishing them shows progress in the negotiation and builds trust with the other side.

Dealing with rejection. Much like dating in middle school, rejection is rarely the end of the world. If an overture does not work, the negotiator might try a different part of the organization to find a more receptive audience. Similarly, she might try a common friend or other intermediary. Or she can just move on to other deals (or the prosecution of the lawsuit) and come back when conditions are more favorable to an agreement. For litigants, parties will often agree to mediation, if only to create a record that the issues facing each side are intractable without litigation.

Regardless of whether the initial approach works out, the downsides of trying to start a conversation are small. Starting the conversation transmits some minor information to the other side. In cooperative business transactions, it can simply signal that part of the company's business plan is to grow in some specified ways. This information is unlikely to reach the level of "proprietary," however. As discussed in chapter 9, it is possible to infer most companies' business plans at the same level of generality by looking at publicly available information, such as public filings.

In litigation, starting a conversation may create greater vulnerability. Offering to talk about settlement may signal that a party's costs have risen to the point where it can be persuaded to accept comparatively unfavorable deal. Alternatively, offering to talk settlement may signal that a party believes that the case has more merit than it actually does. However, if a party is truly ready to talk, that sacrifice in leverage is likely to be outweighed by any gains to be made from the negotiation itself.

10.4 Putting Things in Motion

"It's 106 miles to Chicago, we got a full tank of gas, half a pack of cigarettes, it's dark . . . and we're wearing sunglasses."
"Hit it."

—ELWOOD AND JAKE BLUES,
The Blues Brothers (Universal Pictures, 1980)

Once the preparatory work has been completed and the other side has agreed to talk, it is time to put all of the work that has been done into action. While each negotiation will take a unique path, there are some common steps that tend to recur in most complex negotiations.

Draft framework for discussions. Assuming that both sides wish to continue the discussions because they see potential gain, a small group with members from each side—no more than six total—will need to create a map for the negotiation. (In keeping with the issues discussed in chapter 3, capping the group at six minimizes the problems that might arise from competing agendas or personality conflicts.) This group's main goal is to lay out what each side hopes to accomplish, the priority areas for negotiation, and a rough timeline in which the negotiation will proceed.

The most effective frameworks create a work plan that includes specific plans, deliverables, and milestone reviews. It is important not to overengineer the negotiation: organic discussions will usually focus on the major, critical issues, while the framework just ensures a logical flow to the negotiation. Issues that depend on others being resolved (in other words, contingent issues) occur later in the talks. Issues that are interlocked (in other words, linked issues) are best discussed at the same time.

A good discussion framework is more than just an agenda, however. It also establishes the ground rules for the discussion. For example, based on the type of negotiation, it may be necessary to put in place ground rules on how to treat proprietary information. It may be worthwhile, for example, to have the internal business team sign a confidentiality agreement specific to the discussions. While most companies have a code of conduct regarding confidentiality overall, having a specific reminder to reinforce the need to keep things in confidence is helpful. (Attorneys, both inside and outside the firms, are already required by their legal obligations to confidentiality.)

As discussed in chapter 6, acquisitions may require a stricter confidentiality agreement because even public acknowledgment that discussions are happening may be enough to jeopardize the deal by, for example, causing the price of the target's stock to move significantly. For example, in April 2011, the stock market reacted to rumors of acquisition talks between Schneider Electric and Tyco International, causing Tyco's stock to jump 18 percent in only a few trading days. That jump, which significantly increased the price Schneider Electric would have to pay for Tyco, killed any chance of a deal between the two succeeding.[17]

Leadership meeting. For a potential acquisition or partnership, it is valuable to get the executives from both teams together (especially if they have not met already) to jointly review the scope of negotiations. This serves two main purposes. First, it aids in the alignment process. Once the smaller team has mapped out the process for the negotiation, and before both sides commit significant resources, both sets of leaders can look each other in the eye and agree to proceed. While this meeting may be more symbolic than substantial (because the joint working team has largely framed the issues), hearing, seeing, and agreeing to the plan in the presence of each other cements the progress made. Second, this kind of meeting can build trust and establish a direct channel that may be necessary when pointed issues with clear winners and losers arise later in the process. In addition, some matters—like deciding who will lead a merged entity—may just require direct, high-level communications. Once the leaders have met

17. *See* Joann S. Lubin & Gina Chon, *Schneider Backs Away from Tyco Deal*, WALL ST. J. EUROPE ED., Apr. 13, 2011, *available at* http://online.wsj.com/article/SB10001424052748703730104576260381974324692.html (last viewed Dec. 30, 2012).

face to face, it may be easier for them to resolve some issues with just a phone call.

Deal design. Once both sides have agreed to proceed, the work begins on getting to the major terms of the agreement. With most business agreements, the devil is in the details. So both sides exchange data, proposals, and issues related to the framework's major issues. (This may include due diligence for mergers and acquisitions, or confirmatory discovery for class action settlements.) Given the need to preserve as much money as possible for the deal itself, most negotiators will strive to ensure that this early structure includes only material terms. These usually include:

- *Business operations*: customer access, technology assets and development plans, operations resources, and financial performance.
- *Legal structure*: type of agreement (asset vs. stock), governing jurisdiction.

The joint team's job at this stage is not to hammer out the final agreement but to get move each side's position into a range of potentially acceptable agreements.

If these initial agreements are not possible, and direct discussion between the leaders cannot break the impasse, then both sides should part ways. Leaving on good terms is usually smart strategy; many agreements have stopped and restarted over time as a company's position or market conditions shift, bringing teams back to the table under more favorable circumstances.

Initial agreement. Assuming that discussions proceed well, the next step is to document the agreement to the overall terms. This documentation can take many forms. Some negotiators may choose a memorandum of understanding, others may write a letter of intent or simply a term sheet. While legal scholars may debate whether the proverbial "back of a napkin" agreement is enough to constitute a complex contract, this document will serve as an important reference for the negotiators as they go forward.[18]

Align working team with everyone in the room. Once the initial agreement is in place, the negotiations change focus to fill in the specific terms that will govern the larger agreement. This less glamorous work is often left to the attorneys and working team. To begin this process, many organizations will distribute a copy of the initial agreement to a wider team from each side. The wider teams then set up meetings to work on their specific sections of the agreement. This stage of the negotiation can pose a number of challenges. For example, while these team members are knowledgeable and well-meaning, they often lack the context for the overall negotiation. As a result, they may create dozens of additional issues within the overall negotiation, many of which may not be of material value to either side and eat up significant resources and time.

To address that process shortcoming, it is worthwhile for the lead negotiators from each side to hold a joint meeting with all of the people who will be involved in the next steps (due diligence in the case of an acquisition) and contract drafting. This can be only a sixty-minute meeting and can even be done by conference call. However, the purpose is for the executives from both sides to provide the overall context and goals for the negotiation, as well as jointly set the agenda and tone for the rest of the team from each side for the next steps.

Now, once the individual teams begin their specific work, they have an indication of what they are trying to accomplish, what is material to the negotiation, and—just as important—what is not. While this meeting will not solve all challenges, it helps to streamline the number of participants and ensure they work from the same information.

Final agreement. All of the work of the negotiations has to be memorialized in a final agreement. For an acquisition, this essentially amounts to a "bill of sale," accounting for all of the different elements

18. For more on the specifics of contract law, *see* chapter 6.

of the business being sold, potentially including dozens of schedules outlining the specific transfers of specific elements such as customer lists, physical assets, intellectual property, and employees. It will also include representations and warranties that cover detailed elements of the target business that either could not be assessed effectively during due diligence or—like accounts receivable—would only become apparent after time had passed. A final settlement document will be similar, beginning with a recitation of the reasons for the settlement, then laying out specific terms, and ending with any necessary representations and warranties, such as a mandated percentage of participation in a mass tort or class action settlement.

Popular media often depicts the final signing of big agreements as a ceremony: the senior executives from each side sit in a wood-paneled room at an elaborate conference table with special pens, like President Reagan and Chairman Gorbachev signing a nuclear missile treaty. In fact, most of these negotiations conclude at unpredictable times of the day or night with the principals from each side in different cities or countries. There are separate signature pages for each side that are prepared and signed in advance and are held until all points of the final agreement are reached. Once the final documents are set, the pages are exchanged via fax or email, and the deal is complete. It tends to be an anticlimactic ending to months of work. Hopefully, one of the team members has thought ahead either to have champagne on hand or to identify the local bar where a celebration can begin.

10.5 In the Room

Once the preparation is done, it is finally time to sit in the room with the other side. This process also has a certain set of tactics associated with it, most of which involve exchanging information with the other side in the hope of persuading it to acquiesce to one's own offers. As we have described in earlier chapters, this process can occur over long periods of time.

In general, like negotiations themselves, the "in the room" tactics fall into two basic categories. *Cooperative tactics* try to find a true agreement between the parties. While they may seek to elide some differences, the general thrust is to allow both parties to walk away from the negotiation roughly satisfied with the outcome. *Coercive tactics*, by contrast, are aimed at securing a particular result, regardless of whether the parties are mutually satisfied at the end of the process.

10.5.1 Cooperative Tactics

"Negotiation is an art. Back and forth. Give and take. And today, both Darryl and I took something: higher salaries. Win, win, win."

—MICHAEL SCOTT,
The Office, "The Negotiation"

Many negotiation tactics focus on cooperation among the parties. In fact, many negotiation scholars simply focus on "cooperation" as a tactic and discuss various ways to either justify cooperation for oneself or induce cooperation in one's counterparty. Certain tactics, however, can help to build cooperation by signaling to the other side that a mutually beneficial negotiation is possible.

Moving between specifics and generalities. The level of specificity in the negotiation can often mean the difference between agreement and impasse. Roger Fisher and William Ury recognized this in their groundbreaking book *Getting to Yes*, although they recommended using this tactic in only one direction: taking negotiations from specific disagreements to more abstract principles that might allow consensus.[19] But sometimes the tactic works in reverse. Sometimes, it is possible to move from fundamental disagreements over abstract principle to agreement on specifics that both

19. Roger Fisher & William Ury, Getting to Yes: Negotiating Agreement Without Giving In, Kindle location 176 (1991).

sides want for different reasons. These are what law professor Cass Sunstein refers to as "incompletely theorized agreements."[20]

Show of good faith. Committing a little to the success of the negotiation from the beginning can often go a long way toward building some goodwill from one's counterparty. A show of good faith does not have to be a grand gesture. This is one reason why many cultures place importance on gifts or informal discussions over food and drink.

In complex negotiations, certain shows of good faith may be out of bounds. Class action lawyers, who must avoid the appearance of collusion with the other side, may have to do without taking their adversaries to dinner. Similarly, companies doing business with foreign officials would be well advised to ensure they understand the anticorruption laws of both their own country and their host's.

Reduce demand. A party can also voluntarily reduce its demands on a particular issue. This is a frequent cooperative tactic in negotiation. Reducing the price (or the damages sought) or reducing other requirements signals movement toward some "zone of agreement" where a deal can be made. Reducing demands works best as a cooperative tactic when it is a genuine movement toward agreement, as opposed to part of a pre-scripted "dance" that only offers the appearance of movement.

Offer new benefits. This is the classic version of "creating value" or "integrative bargaining" that works like *Getting to Yes* focus on.[21] If a party is unable to move on price, for example (say, because it absolutely must record a certain amount of revenue in a given quarter), it may instead offer more for that price.

Forgiveness. This can be forgiveness of some perceived transgression (like breaking a previous contract) or of some obligation (like a loan). In either case, forgiveness—for our purposes here, the formal

20. Cass R. Sunstein, *Incompletely Theorized Agreements*, 108 HARV. L. REV. 1733 (1995). For more on how incompletely theorized agreements may work in a negotiation, *see* chapter 4.

21. FISHER & URY, *supra* note 19, at Kindle location 915.

discharging of a grudge or obligation—works much the same as reducing a demand. But it carries with it an extra emotional benefit that may help two adversarial sides find common ground. (This is one reason why some legal reformers have focused on making it safe for tort defendants to apologize as a means of reducing unnecessary litigation.)[22]

Trimming. As defined by law professor (and former chief regulator) Cass Sunstein, "trimming" "steer[s] between the polar positions and . . . preserve[s] what is deepest and most sensible in competing positions."[23] Trimming is slightly more nuanced than a mere "meet in the middle" compromise, because it tries to respect (and preserve) the more deeply felt commitments that underlie a given position.[24] So where a simple compromise might offer a midpoint price for a corporate acquisition or a damages demand, a trimming offer might allow a target's CEO an active role in the new company or injunctive relief that will prevent a bad customer experience from recurring. The advantage of trimming, where used properly, is that it can build consensus, making it a particularly important tactic in multiparty and multi-issue negotiations.[25] Moreover, to the extent that trimming shows overt respect for a counterparty's position, it can build goodwill, which is particularly important where there may be nonrational or nonmonetary reasons for the negotiation.[26]

Inviting. A negotiator may start out by stating, "We want to build something better together," or "Let's come to a conclusion that is fair

22. *See, e.g.*, Peter H. Rehm & Denise R. Beatty, *Legal Consequences of Apologizing*, 1996 J. DISPUTE RESOLUTION 115; Jonathan R. Cohen, *Advising Clients to Apologize*, 72 CAL. L. REV. 1009 (1999).

23. Cass R. Sunstein, *Trimming*, 122 HARV. L. REV. 1049, 1053 (2009).

24. *Id.* at 1055.

25. *Id.* at 1067.

26. *Id.* at 1069; *see also* Richard Birke & Craig R. Fox, *Psychological Principles in Negotiating Civil Settlements*, 4 HARV. NEGOTIATION L. REV. 1 (1999).

for all sides." Cynical observers might dismiss those statements as vague and therefore meaningless. But the vagueness is deliberate: by using either of those statements, the negotiator is signaling that she is willing to explore a range of options to see which are most agreeable to both sides. From this point, the negotiation can follow one of three paths.

- *Genuine exploration*. This path works best for parties that do not know each other very well but see possibilities in an agreement, because it allows them to learn more both about the other side as well as how the pieces might work together. As a result, both sides commit to extensive fact-finding and frequent review points during the process to make sure they each understand what information they have collected and that they are interpreting it the same way. This mutual search for knowledge allows for open exploration of options, which provides a number of possibilities for a final agreement.
- *Attempt to educate*. This path is more appropriate when one side has more data, experience, or knowledge of a desired outcome than the other. Instead of mutual fact-finding, in this case, one side ends up educating the other about the most desirable outcome and the best way to get there. In the wrong hands, this approach can look—or actually be—more self-serving than cooperative. However, when properly executed, it means that one side is making a substantial investment to bring the other side up to speed so that they can reach the same logical conclusion of a settlement or transaction. (Indeed, in some cases—such as class action settlements—the side doing the educating may be taking a calculated risk by providing so much information to its potential adversary.)
- *Probing*. Probing works best when both parties are fairly well educated about the other side and the overall market.

> A probing strategy allows each side to share information, but for the purpose of testing which option appeals most to the other side and determining how close the other side's preferred option is to one's own. As both sides share data and discuss options, each side's preferences (in particular, their most and least preferred options) become clearer. Probing by exploring options prepares each side for a very specific negotiation at the end, in which the effective choices for the settlement or transaction have been narrowed substantially. (In fact, this is often how mediators operate when dealing with adversarial parties.)

In all of these cases, this cooperative approach requires each side to commit significant resources and time: sharing data with the other side takes time, human effort (much of the data must be reviewed first), and resources; so does reviewing the other side's data once it is received. As a result, cooperative discussions involving extensive information sharing run the risk of running on for months or years, eating resources and possibly reducing the value of a final agreement. Worse, in adversarial (or even just potentially adversarial) negotiations, one side may take advantage of this issue and use supposedly cooperative negotiations as a stalling tactic, dragging out talks until circumstances have changed in its favor. As a result, successful negotiations rely heavily on good process management and effective scheduling to reach a satisfactory conclusion.

This does not mean that cooperative tactics are only for suckers. Cooperative tactics have the significant benefit of aligning both sides' goals and making them more committed to implementing whatever agreement they reach. The process of discussing the various options for a deal will likely allow them to vet the implications of various decisions and determine what their next steps are at each stage. As a result, the negotiation has a higher likelihood of success in achieving the primary purpose.

10.5.2 Coercive Tactics

"My father made him an offer he couldn't refuse. . . . Luca Brasi held a gun to his head, and my father assured him that either his brains or his signature would be on the contract."

—MICHAEL CORLEONE,
The Godfather

Some tactics are more coercive in nature. Parties often employ these when persuasion seems to be ineffective but consummation of the deal is still important. Coercive tactics do not rely on one's counterpart agreeing to certain points or principles. Instead, they are designed to manipulate or otherwise force a result even in the face of disagreement.

Coercive tactics also carry a high cost. The parties might arrive at an immediate deal but be unwilling to negotiate with each other again. Or the level of trust necessary to work through difficult issues may be compromised. In certain instances (one-off litigation, hostile takeovers), these may be costs a party is willing to pay. However, in any situation where the parties are likely to encounter each other again, the use of coercive tactics tends to unacceptably endanger future negotiations.[27]

Threats. In any negotiation, there is always an element of threat. For cooperative negotiations, the threat may simply be the loss of a mutually beneficial deal. (This is the reverse of the "best alternative." The best alternative tells a party when to walk away. The counterparty's fear is that the party's best alternative will be reached before the negotiation has become profitable.) In adversarial negotiations, the threat looms larger. In fact, the threat is often the impetus of the negotiation. In legal negotiations, for example, the best alternative to the negotiation is often litigation, which can cost each side a great deal of time and resources.

27. For more on this phenomenon, *see* chapter 5.

Ultimatums. An ultimatum is a threat to cease negotiations unless the other side makes specific concessions. Did you ever wonder how, when Daimler-Benz and Chrysler merged, Daimler got its name first? So did the executives at Chrysler. According to one account, the name was an issue all the way through the negotiations, but Daimler CEO Jürgen Schrempp and Chrysler CEO Bob Eaton—while each advocating for their company to come first—kept agreeing to put off a final resolution. Finally, after the Daimler board had met and approved the merger, and literally as the Chrysler board was sitting down in its investment banker's conference to do the same, Schrempp insisted on Daimler going first. As Bill Vlasic and Bradley Stertz report the exchange:

> "You tell your board that Daimler has to be first in the name," Schrempp said.
>
> "Jürgen, that's not possible," Eaton said.
>
> "Then," Schrempp said, "we have to cancel the whole deal. It is the showstopper for me."[28]

Identifying the "showstopper," and doing so at a time when the other side could no longer afford to back out of the deal, was enough to secure the preferential placement of the Daimler name. Of course, the tactic created resentment among the Americans.

Ultimatums do work under specific circumstances. Daimler's ultimatum came at a time when Chrysler believed it had committed too much to the negotiation to walk away without significant cost. But these tactics are unlikely to work in the long term unless the party making them has significant leverage that it is unlikely to sacrifice in the course of the negotiations.

Deadlines. Deadlines are not inherently coercive. However, imposing a deadline simply to get the negotiation moving, or to reduce the

28. BILL VLASIC & BRADLEY A. STERTZ, TAKEN FOR A RIDE: HOW DAIMLER-BENZ DROVE OFF WITH CHRYSLER 238 (2009).

amount of time that one party has to think about proposals they might object to, does contain a coercive element.

Moreover, it takes a great amount of skill to negotiate under a deadline.[29] Among other issues, many negotiations face a perpetual issue with last-minute changes and revisions. Both the Paris peace accords and the RJR Nabisco leveraged buyout involved dramatic last-minute changes to the agreements. In Paris, there had been so many last-minute changes that a final version of the treaty was not available for the plenary session participants to review before voting; instead the entire treaty had to be read out in French.[30] When bids were due on the RJR Nabisco buyout, lawyers from Davis Polk were making last-minute changes in a taxi stuck in midtown Manhattan traffic; they finally shoved a twenty-six-year-old associate out of the cab to sprint the last few blocks to deliver the bid.[31]

While the dreaded deadline doom may make for entertaining war stories afterward, it is a recipe for malpractice (or breach of the duty of care) in the moment. Courts have not hesitated to unwind deals reached in the heat of the moment. The Supreme Court once overturned one of the largest asbestos settlements in history because of the legal errors it contained. The settlement had been hashed out in a coffee shop across from the trial court in the last hours before a midnight deadline. While the court recognized in that case that "speed was important," it pointed out it could not ignore the parties' legal errors just because the "clock is about to strike midnight."[32] Similarly,

29. *See* Robert S. Adler & Elliot M. Silverstein, *When David Meets Goliath: Dealing with Power Differentials in Negotiations*, 5 HARV. NEGOTIATION L. REV. 1, 101 (2000) ("Negotiating under a deadline requires skill, persistence, patience, and brinkmanship to be successful. Because deadlines can help as well as hurt weaker negotiators, we cannot offer a 'one remedy fits all' suggestion. When facing deadlines, one needs constantly to weigh the benefits of agreeing versus not agreeing.").

30. MACMILLAN, *supra* note 4, Kindle location 9119.

31. BRYAN BURROUGH & JOHN HELYAR, BARBARIANS AT THE GATE: THE FALL OF RJR NABISCO, Kindle location 8001.

32. Ortiz v. Fibreboard Corp., 527 U.S. 815, 863 (1999).

the Delaware Supreme Court, when reviewing the transaction at the heart of the *Van Gorkom* case, found that the board's rushed decision (it approved the merger in a matter of days after a few brief meetings) was a sign it had not met its duty of care.[33]

In other words, deadlines work because they can force a decision before one's counterpart has the information or resources to make a better offer. But deadlines often force bad deals into existence for exactly the same reason. Ironically, the negotiators may feel better about these bad deals in the moment, because they conflate the relief they feel at having reached *some* agreement with the positive feelings from reaching a good agreement.[34]

Arguments. At one level, arguments are simply how everyone communicates. Some arguments in negotiations are designed to persuade the other side. These often appeal to the other side's enlightened self-interest. In fact, any time a negotiator talks about a "win-win" situation, she is appealing to her counterpart's self-interest: who doesn't want a win? Alternatively, one can make persuasive arguments to the principles one's counterpart proclaims. During the course of the 1919 Paris peace talks, Hungarian delegate Count Albert Apponyi, knowing he was negotiating from a weak position, made an impassioned appeal to the Council of Four's stated goal of encouraging national self-determination. He was so persuasive that British Prime Minister David Lloyd George immediately approached him to say, "You were very eloquent," and even the irascible Georges Clemenceau, sensing the mood of the room, was conspicuously polite to him.[35]

The problem with persuasive argument like this is that it does not reliably yield results. For all his eloquence, Apponyi did not obtain the concessions he sought. Arguments tend to work better when they

33. Smith v. Van Gorkom, 488 A.2d 858, 877 (Del. 1985).

34. *See* Özüm Saygi et al., *Too Little Too Late: How Out-Group Negotiation Strategy Drives Intergroup Relations*, presented at 24th Annual Int'l Ass'n of Conflict Mgmt., July 3–6, 2011, *available at* http://ssrn.com/abstract=1872559 (last viewed Oct. 5, 2012).

35. MacMillan, *supra* note 4, Kindle location 5358.

are employed at a more coercive level, as a preview of how the threatened alternative will play out. Legal negotiations, for example, often involve a relatively shallow and stylized exchange of arguments.[36] Some scholars have concluded that argument has little place in negotiation. But a negotiator may employ argument not to persuade her counterparty but to explain how she will persuade a *third* party to compel the result she wants. Lawyers often do this by pointing out the issues they would like to try out in court and the costs of losing (or even just litigating) those issues.[37]

Creeping attack. The main value in this approach is to remove options for the other party in advance of any offer or case filing, significantly limiting the party's ability to negotiate. For a transaction, this can be winning a key customer contract or filing a specific patent. It could involve capturing critical distributors through new terms. For a class action, this may involve filing in a jurisdiction that does not accept certain defense-oriented arguments.

Executing this tactic requires careful planning and sometimes superhuman patience. In some cases—such as patent filings—the party may need to have the overall game plan mapped out well in advance and be prepared for efforts expended over several years. And this is the downside of this approach: it takes a long time to execute and therefore, as we discussed in chapter 5, will likely need to deal with a wide range of contingencies. On the positive side, it means that

36. *See* Robert J. Condlin, *"Cases on Both Sides": Patterns of Argument in Legal Dispute-Negotiation*, 44 Md. L. Rev. 65, 66 (1985) ("Negotiation argument is more simplistic, chaotic, predictable, and illogical than is generally believed to be the case, partaking more of stylized dance or game-playing than of political discourse or analytic investigation. These qualities suggest that it is discounted in negotiation because it ought to be.").

37. *See id.* at 113 (in simulated negotiation, law student asks: "How much is it worth to you to litigate this question[?]...I think that [my client] would like nothing better than to have a case as egregious as that to test this regulation."), 126 n.95 (lawyer in simulated negotiation: "This is the type of case, Mr. Harris, that I like to try and I want to try.").

the transaction has a higher likelihood of success, likely at a lower price.

Lying. As we have said throughout this book, negotiations are about the exchange of information. And, as most people are aware, one way to control the other side's actions is just to give them the wrong information.[38]

It is difficult to say how common lying is in negotiation, because lying can be difficult to detect in certain contexts. (In fact, in some contexts, like international politics, it may be that lying is actually less common than most believe.)[39] That said, most negotiators seem to agree that *some* level of misdirection is acceptable—or even necessary—in a successful negotiation.

Lying carries serious risks. First, if one is found out, or even just suspected, trust gets destroyed. Even worse, being caught lying may invite reprisals from one's counterpart, whether or not those reprisals are rational. Second, if one gets a reputation as a liar, future parties are less likely to negotiate. (In fact, they may be more likely to engage in retributive action.) Third, lying often has legal consequences. If the lie was central to the deal, the lying party may be liable for fraud. (Lawyers must also be careful about lying during negotiations because of their professional duty as officers of the court not to lie. This duty has proven controversial since it may conflict with the lawyer's professional duty to zealously represent his client.)

Lying also carries a personal cost. Most individuals like to think of themselves as honest people; as a result, lying produces psychic distress in most negotiators.[40] It may also—even when the

38. *See, e.g.*, Peter Reilly, *Was Machiavelli Right? Lying in Negotiation & the Art of Defensive Self-Help*, 24 OHIO ST. J. DISPUTE RESOLUTION 481, 496 (2009).

39. *See generally* JOHN J. MEARSHEIMER, WHY LEADERS LIE: THE TRUTH ABOUT LYING IN INTERNATIONAL POLITICS viii (2011).

40. Karl Aquino & Thomas E. Becker, *Lying in Negotiations: How Individual & Situational Factors Influence the Use of Neutralization Strategies*, 26 J. ORG. BEHAVIOR 661, 662 (2005).

lie is minor—lead an individual to overcorrect by offering larger concessions than she might otherwise.[41]

Madman's advantage. Sometimes, a negotiating team can make a virtue out of seeming irrational. By not hewing to rational offers, and by reacting irrationally to the other side's proposals (either through anger or some other nonrational display), a party may raise the cost of not reaching an agreement to levels that will compel an agreement on more favorable terms to it.[42] (This is hardly a new insight. Thomas Schelling has long observed that the best way to win in adversarial bargaining is to precommit to a strategy that makes one appear irrational. The paradigmatic example he cites is, in a game of chicken, throwing the steering wheel out the window.)

Publicize negotiations. Publicizing negotiations may sometimes pressure one side to make concessions it might not otherwise consider. Parties will often feel more comfortable negotiating behind closed doors, in no small part because under those circumstances they can speak freely and consider concessions that their constituents might not approve of.[43] However, when both parties include multiple factions, one party may choose to reveal the existence of negotiations, or the substance of negotiations, in order to create public pressure for concessions on a specific point.

The primary drawback to coercive tactics is it immediately puts the parties in an adversarial position. Just like a conquering army leaves many casualties in its wake, this approach, if successful, means that there is a clear winner and clear loser. In the case of significant

41. *Id.*

42. *See* Adler & Silverstein, *supra* note 24, at 96 ("At the more extreme levels of fury lies what Professor Schoonmaker refers to as the 'Madman's Advantage.' That is, negotiators can sometimes achieve their goals by acting irrationally. This approach works, he notes, because irrational parties appear indifferent to the possibility of retaliation or revenge that might deter others, thus raising the cost of conflict to potentially unacceptable levels.") (internal footnotes omitted).

43. *See* FISHER & URY, *supra* note 19, Kindle location 624 ("A good case can be made for changing Woodrow Wilson's appealing slogan 'Open covenants openly arrived at' to 'Open covenants privately arrived at.'").

litigation like a class action, that may be exactly the point. But in the case of an acquisition, coercive tactics can undermine the value of the company being acquired. Unless the transaction is focused specifically on a piece of technology or something tangible, this will likely poison relations with the employees of the acquired company, making implementation of the final deal very challenging.

10.6 Putting the Agreement into Action

Once all of the haggling is done and the agreements are signed, most people believe that they are finished with the negotiation. In some cases, it is customary to pop a bottle of champagne at this point. However, as we pointed out at the beginning of this book, complex negotiations occur between two *organizations*. These organizations will still have to continue to operate, employ people, and serve customers well beyond when the agreement is reached. Long after the outside lawyers or investment bankers have closed their files and collected their fees, the teams within the businesses will still have to put the agreement into action. From that perspective, the signing of the agreement is not the end of the negotiation; it is really just the beginning.

As we laid out in chapter 8, the company needs to deliver on its primary purpose. This agreement is not an end in itself but a tool to allow the company to deliver on that purpose. Teams inside the business should begin planning for an eventual signing well before those signatures are dry. Their most important task is to develop formal action plans that map out the first ninety days after the agreement, providing clear direction to each organization about what it must do to meet the agreement's terms. There are dozens of books that get into the postagreement process. And, for both acquisitions and class actions, there are many examples of where agreements have been implemented well enough that they draw no remarks. However, there are many more times where follow-through has been less than expected, resulting in those acquisitions we discussed earlier that do not provide the value they promised. Similarly, in class actions, some settlements may require further monitoring from courts or government agencies.

The exact same principles apply for the implementation of any agreement as for the beginning of the negotiation. It is critical to assemble the right team for the process; having a leader in place supported by other key resources, a communications plan, and clearly identified milestones can ensure the agreement comes to life and deliver on its promise.

Throughout this book, we have focused on the various problems that arise when high-stakes negotiations become complex. Individual negotiators can—knowingly or unknowingly—distort information. Adding people to a deal exponentially increases its difficulty. Adding issues to a deal can create potential for logjams. Complex deals take longer, which creates opportunities for new misunderstandings to arise, new parties to intervene, and new issues to take shape. Governments regulate large, high-stakes negotiations, so that firms must retain legions of lawyers (who are themselves new parties to the negotiation). And firms have their own individual cultures, which may also be influenced by the region where they are located, all of which distort the ways in which their individual representatives understand issues. Each of these complications makes these negotiations more stressful, which itself is an emotional state that can distort the ways in which the negotiators understand their tasks.

Understood like this, negotiations appear more complex than any human (or group of humans) can handle. But complex negotiations are hardly hopeless. Companies merge and resolve significant lawsuits all the time. How do they do it? Carefully, and sometimes badly. But those organizations that succeed most often tend to have certain processes in place that help them over the various challenges. Companies with clearly articulated strategies, that understand the terrain in which they will be negotiating, and that have gamed out the various tactics likely to come into play, tend to succeed where others might fail spectacularly. Human beings are fallible. Even successful CEOs can fall victim to such basic personality flaws as hubris or a quick temper. But human beings aided by good organizational processes can complete deals that may seem impossible at first.

When we began, we discussed how the Dragon Systems acquisition and the *Figueroa* settlement were failures, not of human intelligence, but of *process*. The Dragon acquisition was marked by poor coordination that led to poor information gathering, which itself led to a cataclysmically bad deal. The *Figueroa* settlement was a rushed deal that tried to sidestep various processes in order to deliver an inexpensive resolution to a potentially costly case; those shortcuts wound up costing much more than slowing down at the beginning would have. Good process is not infallible, but it will save us from errors in judgment likely to arise in the heat of a complex deal. The processes we have outlined in the last three chapters are—in our experience—those best suited to help even fallible humans navigate the difficulties that arise when big firms make big deals. Using these processes cannot guarantee success, but it will make sure that when you are betting the company, the odds are in your favor.

Index

CPSIA information can be obtained
at www.ICGtesting.com
Printed in the USA
LVHW020300070821
694286LV00007B/105

9 780199 846252